Copyright, Fair Use, and the Challenge for Universities

©opyright, Fair Use, and the Challenge for Universities

Promoting the Progress of Higher Education

Kenneth D. Crews

The University of Chicago Press
Chicago and London

Kenneth D. Crews is associate professor of Business
Law in the College of Business at San Jose State Uni-
versity. He studied history as an undergraduate at
Northwestern University, received a law degree from
Washington University in St. Louis in 1980, and re-
ceived a Ph.D. from the University of California,
Los Angeles in 1990.

The University of Chicago Press, Chicago 60637
The University of Chicago Press, Ltd., London
© 1993 by The University of Chicago
All rights reserved. Published 1993
Printed in the United States of America

02 01 00 99 98 97 96 95 94 93   1 2 3 4 5

ISBN: 0–226–12055–4 (cloth)

The University of Chicago Press gratefully acknowledges the contribution of the Exxon Education Foundation toward the publication of this book.

Library of Congress Cataloging-in-Publication Data

Crews, Kenneth D. 1955
    Copyright, fair use, and the challenge for universi-
ties: Promoting the progress of higher education /
Kenneth D. Crews.
        p.   cm.
    Includes bibliographical references and index.
    1. Photocopying processes—Fair use (Copyright)—
United States.   2. Universities and colleges—United
States.   I. Title.
Z649.F35C74   1993
025.1′2—dc20   93-3839
                                                     CIP

The paper used in this publication meets the minimum
requirements of the American National Standard for
Information Sciences—Permanence of Paper for
Printed Library Materials, ANSI Z39.48–1984.

To Elizabeth

Contents

Preface

The need for a full reappraisal of copyright law, fair use, and their relationship to higher education could never be more clear. The 1991 decision in *Basic Books, Inc. v. Kinko's Graphics Corporation* has released a wave of new articles in the press and in the professional literature about limits on photocopying for classroom use. It is a rekindling of old concerns and obligations that burned for years as Congress prepared to pass the latest revision of the Copyright Act in 1976 and as New York University settled its infringement lawsuit in 1983. Thus, as universities struggle with the copyright implications of new technologies—especially the electronic storage and transmission of information—the *Kinko's* case makes clear that even the rules of older technologies are far from resolved. For college and university officials to properly address these current and future copyright challenges, they must develop a fresh understanding of the law and of their response to the law. They must also take a critical look at their pattern of experience in meeting legal pressures in the past.

Copyright and fair use at universities are worthy of extensive study because the law leaves ample room for diverse interpretations of user rights, and because the choice of interpretation directly affects the university's academic objectives. Differences of interpretation are legitimate, and they often result from diverging perspectives on, and interests in, copyright's role. Those perspectives and interests can appear in university policy statements. Some interpretations will better serve the university's objectives of teaching, research, and service. Other interpretations are aimed almost entirely at warding off potential legal liabilities. A principal objective of this study is to identify and define a role for universities in the copyright equation and to show that universities need to reevaluate the relationship between copyright and higher education. That relationship—and the educator's understanding of it—are often lost in a muddle of administrative expediency and simple fear.

Because I believe that one's perspective has a leading role in copyright interpretation, readers are entitled to know my perspective. My view of copyright is rooted in my education, career, and values. In law school I learned copyright as a set of legal rights that belong to the copyright owner and are to be aggressively enforced. Major cases on fair use received some attention, but the broader public or social purposes of copyright were secondary concerns. My doctoral work at UCLA enlightened me to the importance and practical necessity of limited user rights. While law school imbued me with a legalistic approach, my graduate studies gave me a broader understanding of copyright as a potential regulator on the flow of information—especially information vital to advancing education and social awareness. My investigations of copyright also underscored the central connection between the growth of knowledge and both owners' and users' rights. That perspective fits well with my appreciation for higher education.

My respect for the academic mission of advancing and disseminating knowledge compelled me to pursue an academic career. That same appreciation moves me to identify and support fair use rights for educational purposes. This book is not about carving out new rights or circumventing the commercial viability of copyrighted works. My objective is instead to highlight rights of use for educational purposes allowed under current copyright law. This book analyzes a limited and controversial right of fair use that Congress established, but that is constantly eroded by opposing interests and by universities that inadequately recognize and protect their own interests.

Some readers might conclude that I am antagonistic toward owners' rights. That conclusion would be completely wrong. My objective is not to attack or threaten the rights of copyright owners. In fact, I am one of the lingering believers in the premise that copyright protections do promote new creativity and its publication. In my legal career I also have represented many clients in securing their copyright privileges. I have actively protected their copyrights and my own. My goal here is to articulate the educator's perspective in order to regain the essential balance between owners' rights and public rights that copyright law is intended to embody. I bring to that task an acute appreciation of both sides of the debate.

Other readers will open this book looking for specific answers to their immediate copyright concerns. This study should provide important guidance for anyone working with copyright and fair use issues in higher education, but it is neither a "how-to" nor a pro forma answer book. Indeed, a central theme here is that policymakers must avoid easy solutions to complex issues. By readily accepting standard "definitions" of fair use, universities have failed to pursue the law's opportunities and to preserve rights allowed under existing law. Moreover, copyright is a dynamic force, demanding regular reevaluation as courts hand down new rulings and as technologies give rise to new possibilities. Any "answers" set forth today may not be valid in the years to come.

From its inception, this research has attracted wide attention within the academic community. The earliest research stages were supported by a grant from the Council on Library Resources. Significant portions of this work first appeared in my doctoral dissertation, which received the annual dissertation awards from the Association of College & Research Libraries and the Association for the Study of Higher Education. I also have tested many of my views by presenting related papers at conferences of educators, administrators, lawyers, and librarians. Not all listeners have welcomed my news and views, but I have been able to reaffirm the significance and sensitivity of copyright on campus and to identify ways to present the material in—I hope—a convincing and comprehensible manner.

Many readers, critics, and supporters contributed to this book in a multitude of ways. The influence of my UCLA dissertation committee remains with me. John S. Wiley, Jr., of the law school scrutinized my grasp of copyright law. Paul I. Rosenthal of Communications Studies assured that I addressed the duties and challenges of academic needs. Robert M. Hayes, former dean of the library and information science school was most influential in guiding me to the subject, underwriting the early surveys, and shaping my perspective—although he probably does not share all my sympathies. Donald O. Case watched the details of my methodology. My chair and long-time friend, John V. Richardson, Jr., grilled me on every detail and constantly challenged my writing, research, and presentation.

In the few years since completing the dissertation I have substantially reevaluated many of my thoughts, I have brought my study current with the latest developments, and I have fully revised my conclusions about the future of the copyright dilemma and the means for addressing it. Those reconsiderations appear in this book. I sent an intermediate draft of this work to three reviewers, and I have greatly benefited from their advice, insights, and support: Stuart Gullickson, Emeritus Habush-Bascom Professor of Law at the University of Wisconsin; James S. Heller, Director of the Law Library and associate professor of law at The College of William & Mary; and Todd L. C. Klipp, General Counsel at Boston University.

Lester F. Goodchild, associate professor of education at the University of Denver, advised me on specialized issues related to higher education. Randall E. Stross, my colleague here in the College of Business at San Jose State University, provided helpful comments on the computer software chapter. Peter Jaszi, professor of law at The American University, became a crucial supporter and an enthusiastic advisor after he refereed the manuscript on behalf of the publisher. He allowed his name to be disclosed, and he was always ready to field my questions and to read a few more pages. I also thank the two other referees who offered valuable comments: Douglas Baird, professor of law at The University of Chicago, and another reader who contributed useful insights, but who remains anonymous.

A special appreciation is reserved for John Tryneski, Kathryn Kraynik, and their colleagues at The University of Chicago Press. They recognized the viability of this book when it was in its earliest form; they worked with me through two years of revision; and they supported me when the finished product seemed so far way. I also thank Marshall J. Burak, Dean of the College of Business, for his generous provision of summer grants and assigned time during the academic year to keep this project on schedule. A grant from my Academic Senate enabled me to employ one of my best students, Lori Gollnick, as an assistant during the laborious process of final editing, reading page proofs, and writing the index.

This study depended on the participation of nearly two hundred university officials and other interested persons who shared their policies and insights. I have thanked them before, and I thank them again. EDUCOM and the American Library Association graciously permitted me to reprint their model copyright policies.

The decisive contribution to this work came from my wife, Elizabeth St. Clair Crews, who supported me when I entered the Ph.D. program years ago, who enthusiastically made the move to the San Jose area, and who has given strength and guidance to me and our children, even when the pressure on all of us seemed insufferable. I give her my endless thanks. I dedicate this book to Elizabeth.

Copyright at American Universities: Conflict and Perspective

Because intellectual property policy, and especially copyright policy, serve as a policy tool that structures the use and flow of information, it is likely to play a major role in an information age. How the intellectual property system is structured will determine not only which individuals and groups benefit from the new opportunities afforded by the new technologies, but also in what ways and the extent to which, as a society, we might take advantage of them.

U.S. Office of Technology Assessment (1986)[1]

In light of developments in copyright law, postsecondary institutions should thoroughly review their policies and practices on photocopying and other means of reproducing copyrighted works. An institution that does not have a written policy on reproduction of copyrighted works should develop one.

The Law of Higher Education (1985)[2]

Policies as a Balance of Competing Objectives

Copyright is among the most misunderstood and contentious rules of law to affect colleges and universities. It encourages the creation and dissemination of intellectual works, but it restricts their availability. It promotes creativity and publication, while inhibiting research and learning. Copyright secures the ability of some faculty and universities to receive an income from their efforts, but it also requires educators to pay a fee for the works of other authors. Zechariah Chafee

1

described copyright as the "Cinderella of the law"; its neglected beauty was revealed only with the technological advances of recent decades.[3] Copyright is indeed a powerful and important intellectual property tool that can foster the development and dissemination of valuable resources. But many academicians unfortunately see it more often as a hobgoblin interfering with teaching and research and imposing royalty fees for the benefit of relatively few authors and publishers. These perceptions lead to misunderstandings and conflicts.

Copyright law also leads to lawsuits. As detailed later in this book, a case brought against New York University in the early 1980s and a federal court ruling against Kinko's Graphics Corporation in 1991 have tightened the scope of fair use at universities and copy shops throughout the country. Heightened restrictions on making copies for teaching and research often lead to faculty outrage. Rightly or not, many educators perceive copyright as a barrier to significant classroom materials, with apparently little redeeming value. Yet the conflicts are far more complex than just debates between copyright owners and users. Within individual campuses, conflicts arise among faculty, administrators, librarians, and legal counsel, as constituents establish diverging responses to the rights, obligations, and liabilities that copyright law represents. Individual members of the university community may also feel torn between their roles as both copyright owners and users.

These conflicts arise because much of copyright, in its current form, is an inherently flexible doctrine. For much of the public, the law is shaped by perceptions and perspectives as well as by legal mandates. The law grants exclusive rights to copyright owners and secures such limited privileges as "fair use" for the public. Yet statutes and court rulings seldom define the exact scope of these privileges. Fair use determines the amount of photocopying, software duplicating, and television videotaping permissible at American universities, but the legal rights depend almost exclusively on imprecise factors, such as the extent of use and its educational utility. The absence of precise standards leaves individual users to evaluate circumstances and to conclude for themselves whether they are within the law or at risk of civil and criminal penalties. The lack of precision in the law means that many uses of copyrighted works may be construed either as coveted privileges for higher education or as blatant violations of federal law, depending on the copyright interpretation employed. The forces compelling one interpretation or the other are of growing importance as copyright-related activities proliferate on American campuses.

As technologies have become cheaper and more practical, faculty, students, and staff have discovered the usefulness of inexpensive and immediate copies. Professors duplicate book chapters for classes; librarians photocopy journal articles for faculty, staff, and interlibrary loans. Computer facilities make software available to dozens of users simultaneously; and faculty tape television broadcasts for instructional uses. While these uses may benefit teaching and research, they also motivate copyright owners to assert legal rights to their intellectual products. Copyright law is a balance of exactly those concerns: the rights of owners to control and exploit their works, and society's demand to use, to learn from, and to build upon the same materials.

Nearly every law that affects universities may have some inhibiting effects on academics. The uniqueness of copyright, however, is the law's openness to interpretation. Copyright law can be perceived as a barrier to knowledge or as a catalyst of innovation. The law can therefore comport with the academic mission or conflict with it. Ideally, the legal interpretation chosen will balance the law's diverging goals. In this respect, the analysis of copyright policies at universities is a microcosm of copyright law in general. Just as copyright law in general is a balance of owners' and users' rights, a local university copyright policy must balance private interests and academic pursuits and supply descriptions of permitted and nonpermitted uses of protected materials.[4]

NYU AND THE NATURE OF FAIR USE

The best known of all university copyright policies is at New York University. In April 1983, New York University settled a copyright infringement suit brought against the university and nine of its faculty members by a group of textbook publishers.[5] The settlement was not a payment of monetary damages, but rather the agreement by NYU to accept as its official policy a set of guidelines detailing the photocopying permitted for teaching and research. The guidelines did not originate just for NYU; they were developed by representatives of publishers, authors, and educators, and they appeared in a congressional report accompanying passage of the 1976 Copyright Act.[6] Under these so-called "Classroom Guidelines," NYU faculty may make single copies of articles or book chapters for personal research or for teaching, and they may distribute multiple copies to classrooms of students, but only within rigorous limits. Any additional copying requires permission from the copyright owner or approval from the university legal counsel. The settlement received widespread attention and fueled a growing awareness that copyright law can directly impede teaching and research—the fundamental pursuits of higher education. Universities were thrown into a quandary. They needed to avoid infringement liability, but they also had to minimize impediments on their very reasons for existing.

American copyright statutes themselves reflect that duality. The law gives authors exclusive rights to most reproduction, distribution, and other uses of their creative works—from journal articles and books to motion pictures and computer software.[7] Copyright law also allows the public to make limited use of protected works, particularly if the uses are for research, education, or scholarship.[8] "Fair use" is the most important of these public rights. This statutory blend of exclusive rights and limited fair use is intended to balance the encouragement of creativity and the public's need to build upon and to learn from existing works. But copyright is rarely a neat balance that satisfies opposing interests. Instead, copyright arguments sharply divide owners and users. Many owners, publishers, and their supporters argue that exclusive controls over protected works are essential to assure an economic return on investments in creating and publishing a new work.[9] Without the promise of income, many new works might never reach their readers. The clause of the United States Constitution authorizing copyright law arguably favors this view by empowering Congress "To promote the Progress of Science and useful Arts" by giving authors exclusive rights to their "Writings."[10]

By contrast, other observers contend that copyright is unnecessary for either inspiring creativity or for encouraging publication.[11] At the very least, critics argue that the exclusive rights claimed for copyright owners are simply too broad; "fair use" should allow users to quote, copy, and distribute copyrighted works, especially if the uses serve copyright's intended purpose—to "promote the Progress of Science and useful Arts." Promoting progress through teaching and research seems to fulfill that constitutional mandate well.[12] In reality, both arguments have merit simultaneously, because different works and different uses deserve different copyright treatment. Commercial products or expensive publications may indisputably require legal protection to be feasible, but the creation and dissemination of many scholarly or public-interest works is motivated by other factors, such as the drive to advance knowledge. Further copying may only enhance that purpose. The law is sufficiently flexible to meet diverse conditions, and it is sufficiently unclear to allow a multitude of interpretations.

Examples of diverging interpretations abound. A 1991 book by L. Ray Patterson and Stanley W. Lindberg is an extraordinary reevaluation of current fair use law and an argument for broader public rights.[13] They assert that copyright law is not a set of rights belonging to creators; instead, it is fundamentally a "law of users' rights." With an enlightening exposition on the history, purposes, and consequences of copyright law, they support the exclusive rights of authors, but they properly attack efforts to extend owners' rights through unilateral interpretations and rigid guidelines on fair use. In the end, Patterson and Lindberg propose that the law embodies sweeping grants of "personal use" and fair use that might create problems for implementation by university officials who seek to work within existing legal structures and who want assurance of basic protections. Patterson and Lindberg advocate a "liberal" interpretation that reaches far beyond the current state of the law as the courts have been willing to accept.

Broadsides from the more "conservative" view are equally fraught with hazards. The Association of American Publishers has circulated an analysis of a 1992 case in which the Federal District Court held that an employee of Texaco Inc. committed infringements when he photocopied journal articles for his individual research needs. The AAP analysis states prominently: "'research' (and, by implication, 'teaching') activities (even if not for profit, but market-impairing) are not entitled to special claims to free use of copyrighted material. . . . "[14] Read in isolation, that carefully crafted statement could severely retract fair use and might lead university administrators to believe their special opportunities have been repealed. The *Texaco* case itself, however, actually makes a significantly different point. The court's opinion states more placidly that uses for research or teaching are not automatically entitled to fair use.[15] That conclusion is little surprise, and an academic purpose remains a factor in support of fair use.

Assertions from either extreme in the copyright debate are often statements of desire. However powerful, and however well reasoned, they are commonly someone's argument for what the law should be. There lies a fundamental problem of copyright: it can be the object of hopes and dreams. Its flexibility is both an opportunity for serving complex and changing needs and an open invitation to argue that the "law" is what we believe it to be. Many of the strongest proponents of either owners' rights or users' rights have succumbed to the fallacy of projecting their desired outcome onto the supine and malleable body of copyright law. Their arguments may eventually influence the shape of the law. Until then, however, readers must judge critically almost all literature on copyright and must scrutinize all recommendations, whether they appear in a scholarly book or in an imposing announcement of current litigation.

Regardless of anyone's argument about what the law should be, Congress and the courts have established what the law is. Congress passed its first copyright statute in 1790, and it adopted the most recent full revision in 1976.[16] Despite hopes that the 1976 Copyright Act would respond to rapidly changing media and demands, copyright owners and users alike have struggled with the law's meaning and applications in a panoply of circumstances. Nearly all of these struggles lie on the frontier between the rights of owners and the rights of users. That "frontier" is actually a gulf of uncertainty about copyright's true scope and effect—current law is deliberately vague in many respects, and it answers few specific questions.[17] The law often leaves individuals to their own judgment about whether specific actions are permissible or unlawful.

REACHING FOR A BALANCED POLICY

Some of the most complex and bewildering copyright questions encompass exactly the types of activities frequently occurring at universities: photocopies for reserve rooms and classroom distribution, sharing or networking software, performances of plays or motion pictures, and a host of other pursuits. The ideal university policy will embrace a thoughtful and helpful discussion of these issues. At NYU, however, the policy was driven by a lawsuit. But at most universities, policies are developed voluntarily and ideally after considering institutional needs and applicable law. Implicit in such a process is the availability of various policy options. A policy could range from curtailing all uses to barring none. The task is seldom easy, but policymakers must consider the vague and imprecise factors underlying the law, such as the educational or research purpose of the use and the likely effects on potential markets for the original work. The educational purpose relates directly to the university's central function, while inroads on market potential may invite a lawsuit. As a result, university copyright policies may become a response to competing institutional obligations. That response demands a balance between the university's internal and external obligations.[18] The internal obligation is to meet the information needs of higher education. The external obligation is to respect the legal rights of copyright owners and to avoid copyright infringements and liabilities.[19]

As in any attempted balance, the resulting policy could be on either extreme or at any point between extremes, depending on the policymaker's awareness and priorities. A university's position may manifest whether it perceives both the internal and external demands and how it has chosen to balance them. For example, if policy development were motivated solely by internal demands, then the policy might logically leave all activities completely unhampered, but such a policy would be unrealistic and would most certainly invite challenges from copyright owners. If motivated solely by external demands, however, educational needs would disappear, and the interests of copyright owners would erase legitimate fair use rights. The NYU lawsuit revealed the strength of external demands; a lawsuit compelled adoption of a policy that leaned heavily toward the owners' position. Under better circumstances, universities might find some position between extremes, giving weight to all perceived demands and balancing them in a workable and lawful manner.

Despite the appeal of a thoughtful balance in copyright policy development, the process can be simplistic and highly mechanical, with policymakers merely transposing some relevant law into written directives. The 1991 court decision against Kinko's Copies has compelled exactly that superficial reaction by some universities. A Federal District Court ruled in *Basic Books, Inc. v. Kinko's Graphics Corporation* that a private, for-profit copy shop infringed several copyrights when it made "anthologies" of photocopied book chapters for university classroom use.[20] The publishers had argued that no photocopied anthology could be fair use, but the court rejected that position, choosing instead to apply the detailed rules of fair use to each photocopied work. The decision was ultimately a fierce indictment of Kinko's practices, but it left ample room for the survival of fair use for photocopies—especially if the copied excerpts are short and if they are made by a nonprofit educational institution. Nevertheless, the signal reaching universities has been the looming threat of a lawsuit. Faced with the specter of litigation and the confusing rules of copyright law, many viewers understand the *Kinko's* case exactly as it was not intended: as a broad prohibition of anthologies. The simplistic analysis prevails.

Adding to the confusion was the court's use of the narrow "Classroom Guidelines" that NYU had adopted in 1983 to settle its case. Although the court had already found no fair use, and even though the guidelines were intended to apply only to copying by nonprofit organizations, the educational function of the copying at question made use of the guidelines "compelling." That part of the case was both superfluous and deleterious. Nevertheless, it reasserted the guidelines as an easily available map for the fair use maze. Consequently, as universities now respond to the *Kinko's* case, they see the guidelines as the tangible device for evaluating legal compliance.

Like the NYU case, the single case is having widespread effects. Press reports and a new wave of legal challenges have private copy shops and on-campus copy facilities alike reviewing their activities. In general, the shops have not endorsed the remaining opportunities of fair use; instead, they typically have prohibited all anthologies, or they have allowed copies only in strict accord with the Classroom Guidelines.[21] These typical reactions might successfully avoid liabilities, and they might find some justification in fair use theory, but they also ignore the clear ruling in *Kinko's* that all anthologies are not prohibited; each item must be individually evaluated. Grasping for the expedient and easy response to a copyright issue can undermine privileges that the law allows. A central thesis of this study is that isolated events—such as either the NYU or *Kinko's* case—can derail a sophisticated exercise of legal rights at campuses everywhere.

DEVELOPING A NEW COPYRIGHT PERSPECTIVE

Critical to developing a new perspective on copyright is an understanding of copyright's relationship to the university mission. If the policymaker bears in mind that copyright policies are integral to furthering the university mission—and that permissible uses for academic purposes are relatively broad—legally sound interpretations that better serve higher education can shape university copyright standards. By viewing copyright as an external force that allows optional interpretations, university officials can assume the initiative in determining how to accept copyright's influence on the institution. Policymakers can decide whether they will view the law as a set of inflexible mandates regulating activities according to prescribed guidelines, or whether they will exert control over these environmental influences and moderate copyright's potential constraint. Organizations of all types are affected by their environment, but organizations can also influence the environment's effects.[22]

Given the "gulf of uncertainty" in copyright law and the need for balancing competing demands, copyright policy development is necessarily both complex and dynamic. Policymakers must comprehend the details of copyright law and be aware of the unanswered issues needing fresh analysis. They must recognize alternatives and the relationship of each approach to teaching and research. A policy emerging from such a process should be a deliberated balance of university goals. For all these good intentions, however, the complexities and subtleties of policy development are seldom apparent. Indeed, the purpose of copyright policies is usually stated simplistically as to set standards for complying with the law or for avoiding copyright infringements.[23] If users adhere to those policies, the expectation is that infringements will not occur and that the institution and its personnel will not face lawsuits from copyright owners.[24] Avoiding infringements is important, but if that concern fully controls the policy, the university's academic mission can be jeopardized.

OVERVIEW OF THIS BOOK

This book analyzes and ultimately criticizes the nature of university responses to copyright in light of the competing objectives that their policies serve. To accomplish that task, this book will examine university copyright issues as a multidisciplinary subject. Development of copyright policies requires an understanding not only of the law, but also of the nature of the university as an organization that comprises diverse constituents making decisions within a fluid environment. The university is also striving to achieve its academic mission, and in that regard, copyright policies must give practical guidance for the common needs of faculty, students, and librarians. This book is accordingly structured around these facets of the copyright dilemma.

This chapter sets the framework of university objectives, the diverse constituents on campus, their typical outlooks on copyright privileges and responsibilities, and their decision-making processes. It draws upon an understanding of the university as an organization of individuals seeking to reach a common pursuit, but pulled by differing forces. Chapter two examines the basic principles of copyright law and the legislative history of the 1976 Copyright Act. It also reveals the emergence of the Classroom Guidelines as a prominent measure of fair use. Chapter three examines the NYU case and the *Kinko's* decision, elucidating their legal frailties and their tremendous influence on universities nationwide. That chapter also traces the origins and influence of the American Library Association's model policy. Chapters two and three together show that Congress shaped the law in many respects to serve education needs, but once the law took effect, a combination of high-profile court rulings, restrictive fair use guidelines, and acquiescent and fearful universities effectively narrowed the special privileges that Congress intended.

The following four chapters—the heart of this book—are an empirical analysis of written copyright policies actually in force at ninety-eight research universities across the country. Those chapters detail how university policies have addressed the practical issues of copyright. Those chapters also identify patterns in existing university governance and policy-making. They demonstrate the overwhelming force of "model policies" on key copyright issues, and they reveal the principal constituents responsible for policy-making. Those chapters also show some surprising trends among constituent groups in their adoption of relatively "strict" or "lenient" standards. They further demonstrate the distinct lack of creativity among policymakers, who instead grasp for external guidance and easy solutions to difficult challenges.

The final chapter synthesizes and scrutinizes major findings. It makes specific proposals for improved university policies, and it sets forth a framework for "strategic management" of university copyright perspectives and positions. It further encourages, although with considerable caution, the emergence of "collective administration" for copyright issues. In the wake of *Kinko's,* the Copyright Clearance Center, in particular, has renewed its offer as a potential solution to the challenge of fair use limits on photocopying. Collective arrangements—from the massive CCC to local library resource-sharing—bring enormous promise, but they also bear their own baggage and cannot replace a meaningful right of fair use. That chapter finally turns attention back to the fountainhead of American copyright law: Congress. It contends that Congress is the linchpin either for shaping the law or for allowing others to shape it. Thus, Congress is the essential player with the most significant potential effect on restructuring university copyright perspectives and policies.

The Significance of Copyright at Research Universities

While this study focuses on prominent research universities, it should offer guidance for diverse institutions wherever copyrighted works are used. Indeed, copyright policies can be useful in private businesses, government agencies, and nonprofit organizations, as well as in all types, sizes, and levels of educational institutions.[25] In every instance, policy developers may balance liability avoidance against the need to use copyrighted works. Yet research universities provide a most insightful forum. Unlike junior colleges, four-year colleges, and other establishments of higher education, research universities are distinguished by their paramount commitment to original research in addition to teaching.[26] By virtue of both their combined teaching and research goals, as well as their sheer size, research universities are host to many different uses of copyrighted works: photocopying, software duplication, database downloading, and video displays, along with the traditional quoting in journals and anthologizing of other writers' works. Research universities also produce numerous copyrighted works. Faculty members have written articles and books for centuries, and in recent years software, video, motion pictures, and other developments have become the media of new copyrighted products. In addition, staff members create various campus publications—from printed catalogs to computer databases—that are copyrighted in the university's name.

A long-standing tradition at most universities has allowed faculty authors to own and control copyrights to their scholarly articles and books.[27] Universities expect professors to write scholarly works, and the institution's investment related to individual works is typically modest or is subsumed into general operating overhead. Furthermore, professors seldom receive substantial income from their projects. At a minimum, universities accept their financial investment as an appropriate cost of advancing and disseminating new knowledge. That university attitude toward copyrights—and their monetary value—has begun to change as the products of academic pursuit have shifted toward software and video—materials with a potentially large and immediate market value. Universities are understandably concerned when faculty derive enormous profits from the software market; and universities are particularly disturbed when the profit motive may replace scholarly drive, and when the valuable product is created with university resources.[28]

Copyrights at universities are no longer incidental niceties of scholarship; they are increasingly the result of massive investments in equipment and personnel, and they are the deed of rights to potentially lucrative creations.[29] Some institutions have begun to claim an ownership interest and a share of the profits, much as universities long have laid claim to patents from faculty research.[30] With their commitment to new research, and with the trend toward university ownership of intellectual property, research universities are on both sides of the copyright issue at once: they are home to widespread uses of copyrighted works, and they are owners of copyrights in the creations of their own faculty and staff. Many faculty members are also both copyright owners and users; they individually embody the conflicting perspectives on copyright.

Research universities—like most educational institutions—are preferred for this type of study because of the broad scope of "fair use" and other user rights that they exercise under the Copyright Act. Fair use is generally limited to teaching, research, scholarship, criticism, and other pursuits common to higher education. A special provision of the 1976 act for library uses is generally restricted to libraries open to the public—such as many university libraries.[31] Further, the copyright owner's exclusive privilege to display or perform motion pictures, plays, and other works is limited by the right of educators to use those works in classroom teaching.[32] User rights for educators greatly surpass the rights of noneducators.

Finally, research universities have an enormous influence on many institutions of higher education. The extent or merit of that influence may be debated, but research universities in fact set many research, curriculum, and governance standards that eventually shape other colleges and universities. Moreover, research universities—more often than other educational institutions—have been the targets of high-profile copyright lawsuits. NYU settled its lawsuit in 1983. UCLA was sued in 1987, and the University of Oregon was sued in 1991, both for allegedly reproducing software.[33] The 1991 *Kinko's* case was not brought against a university, but it involved photocopying for classes at Columbia and NYU. University policies must therefore respond not only to academic missions, legal obligations, and ethical duties, but also to the actual imposition of burdensome litigation.

The most important characteristic of copyright law at universities is the range of alternatives for policy terms. This study is not about skirting, avoiding, twisting, criticizing, or ignoring the law. It is not even about civil disobedience or changing the law. It is about comprehending the law as it now exists and identifying the crucial balance it embodies. Educational institutions have alternatives under current copyright law, and as long as the alternatives are soundly based on statutes and judicial decisions, they will meet the university's external obligation of avoiding infringements. The difference among alternatives, however, is that some options are better than others in meeting the university's internal obligations of teaching, research, and service.

Copyright as a Control on Institutional Objectives

To propose that copyright policies are a balance of competing university obligations is to suggest that the policy-making process adheres to some identifiable patterns. But behavioral patterns are seldom discernible within large and cumbersome entities, such as research universities. Organization theory can offer a framework for identifying such patterns, even when the institution is large, unfocused, or perhaps even divided within itself.[34] An understanding of university copyright policies must therefore begin not merely with the law, but with a comprehension of the university as a decision-making entity comprising groups of individuals that are responsive to environmental demands—such as threats of lawsuits—but that should ultimately serve one or more of the institution's objectives—particularly teaching, research, and service.

Universities have centuries of tradition surrounding a complex social structure of faculty, administrators, staff, and students. Universities also have the relatively specific objectives of teaching, research, and service, even though each member of that social structure may have a different understanding of—or responsibility for—fulfilling those objectives.[35] Yet these institutions are in no way monolithic. They are instead collections of individuals with often divergent interests, activities, and pursuits. Faculty engage in teaching, research, and service; students attend to their studies and projects; administrators are responsible for the effective functioning of the institution; and staff employees support the goals of their particular departments, agencies, or superiors. Exacerbating the complexity, universities are deeply affected by an environment comprising the general public, donors, lawmakers, materiel suppliers, and all others who provide or utilize the university's resources.[36]

To bring some structure to this disarray, a university may be perceived as a "system" that utilizes certain "inputs" in order to achieve particular "outputs" (see figure 1.1).[37] "Inputs" embrace all the essential ingredients of a functional university, including students, faculty, libraries, classrooms, and money. "Outputs" are the products of those processes. Ideal outputs include educated students and new research findings. Because of the central significance of information processing in higher education, universities may be understood as specialized "information systems." Thus, "inputs" include diverse information resources, such as books, journals, videos, and software. "Outputs" may include new publications and better

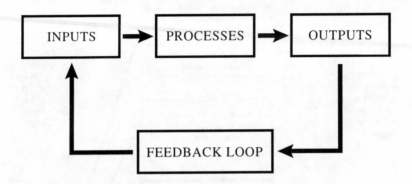

Figure 1.1 Basic System Structure

educated citizens through a fuller exposure to valuable information. Added to this system are "processes," which range from simply reading the input-materials to duplicating them for distribution. "Feedback" allows the outputs to be evaluated in light of objectives from other system elements. To best serve the academic mission, each component should bolster the advancement and dissemination of knowledge.

Two other aspects of a system are imperative here. First, processes are often regulated by a variety of controls, particularly by policies that direct or restrict certain activities.[38] These policies and other controls should ultimately serve the system's general objectives. Second, the effectiveness of a system and each component—including its policies—can be evaluated only in an environmental context (see figure 1.2).[39] The entire system is set within an immediate environment shaped by the university's social mission to advance and disseminate knowledge; the quality of a copyright policy must be measured by its response to that mission.[40] But universities are also surrounded by another environment comprising the rights of copyright owners to restrict some uses. The effectiveness of copyright policies must be judged in light of those demands as well.

These two basic environmental forces can be in direct conflict with one another. In specific, publishers and copyright owners exert pressure on universities, sometimes threatening liability. In addition, the public and academic community—including faculty, students, and university employees themselves—look to universities for education, research, and the advancement of knowledge.[41] Demands conflict when academic pursuits require uses of materials that overlap with copyright owners' rights. They also conflict when copyright owners and users diverge on their legal interpretations. Organizations must undertake a goal-setting process to resolve such conflicts, and policies can manifest that resolution and articulate a

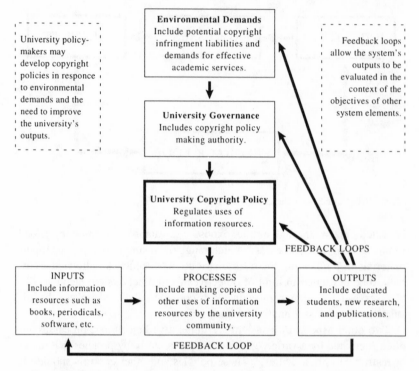

Figure 1.2 The University's "Information System" and the Role of Copyright Policies

relationship between environmental demands and organizational objectives.[42]

Diverse Constituents within the University

Environmental demands can influence policies only to the extent that policymakers perceive the demands and give them heed. Within universities, many different constituents are responsible for developing copyright policies, and they bring to the task their individual awareness of copyright and institutional obligations. The "interest groups" within the university may have diverse and even conflicting goals.[43] A differentiated view of the university is essential, because—as with many organizations—the individuals and not the entity itself ultimately make the decisions.[44]

Each group or individual within a university may be susceptible in differing ways to environmental forces. Thus, policymakers from different parts of the university are likely to make different policy statements. For example, faculty members and librarians are users of copyrighted materials. They make wide uses of information resources and consequently may advocate relatively lenient copyright policies.[45] Administrators often have a primary responsibility to assuage conflicts and to work with demands originating outside the institution.[46] They may therefore be most sensitive about keeping the university away from lawsuits and may accordingly create relatively strict policies.[47] According to one observer: "The ultimate difference between a professor and a trustee is a difference of opinion about whom the university serves—the public or the professors."[48] This chapter reviews common traits of constituents who have proved central in the policy-making process: administrators, faculty, librarians, and legal counsel.

ADMINISTRATORS

Whether deserved or not, some administrators are frequently accused of overlooking the university's academic pursuits. Administrators have been attacked for their attention on immediate concerns and mere survival, rather than on the institution's academic strength. "Standard business practices" or "shortcuts" tend to dominate short-run business decisions.[49] University administrators who are responsible for implementing the law, in particular, have been accused of self-preservation and resisting change.[50] If true, these attitudes among administrators could lead them to adopt standard policies that respond only to perceived legal mandates. Administrators are also aware of tight budgets, and they may be acutely sensitive to the financial burden and adverse publicity from a lawsuit. Given the intangible character of academic objectives, administrators may see immediate monetary implications as the most salient measure of a copyright policy's effect.[51]

Administrators are university employees responsible for the effective operation of the university as an institution. Where faculty may focus on their individual tasks, the perspective of administrators is broader: they are the connection between individual faculty and the university as a cohesive society, and they are the link between the university community and the public, the government, and most other external parties. Administrators must balance the rights of individuals against the interests of the university community. They must also balance internal interests against outside demands. This perspective often divides faculty from administrators.[52] For this study, "administrators" include all ranks and types of deans, provosts, vice presidents, and university presidents. Administrators who have been responsible for university copyright policies range from campus presidents to directors of claims and risk management.

FACULTY

Faculty members avoid many administrative pressures. They are also not common targets in lawsuits, and they can often shift liability back to the university through indemnification or some other legal theory.[53] Faculty are employed by the university with the primary duty of teaching, conducting research, and providing service to the institution and the public. Seldom are their duties outlined in any greater detail, and they are often left to their own judgments about teaching and scholarly inquiry. Indeed, strong principles of academic freedom help ensure their independence.[54] Faculty as authors of copyrighted materials may have an interest in securing maximum legal protection, but as users of copyrighted works they may seek maximum uses to further their research and teaching. Faculty usually espouse relatively lenient copyright standards, despite their conflicting interests in the copyright debate.

LIBRARIANS

Librarians are employed by the university library and are charged with its effective operation. They have a mission to acquire, store, and retrieve information resources in furtherance of the university's academic mission, giving them a unique perspective on the demands for information.[55] Librarians also serve the needs of diverse university constituents, while working with limited information resources and limited budgets. These pressures have moved librarians to campaign for expanded rights to use copyrighted materials.[56] From their perspective, copyright law limits the full exploitation of their resources and the ability of the library to fulfill its charge. A prominent librarian wrote in 1968: "Where his own official activities are concerned, a librarian must now increasingly view copyright as a form of exterior control which threatens serious limitations of his library's freedom to put its collections to work in the service of its users."[57]

Recognizing these tendencies, Irving Louis Horowitz of Rutgers University has attacked librarians as virtually reckless infringers of copyrights:

> Copyright holders have little control over social practice. Users and their agents such as libraries have tended to interpret the guidelines contained in the 1976 law very broadly. . . . Those who argued for maximum liberalization of the copyright law have simply behaved as if the new law gives them all that they had demanded. Librarian groups, for example, issued explanations and clarifications of the law to their membership that go far beyond the limited guidelines given in the law.[58]

But not everyone believes that librarians have been successful proponents of lenient copyright standards. At least one prominent historian has lamented that librarians tend to adopt strict copyright policies, exhibiting little willingness to take risks.[59]

LEGAL COUNSEL

A fourth constituent group important in university copyright policy formulation is the legal counsel, or attorneys, who may be employed by the university or retained through private law firms. Legal counsel are trained as practitioners of the law, and they primarily serve the interests of the university as an entity. As a result, their attention may be akin to that of administrators. Legal counsel must comprehend the university as a whole and particularly grasp its relation to the external forces of legal rights and duties. The role of legal counsel has increased greatly in recent decades with the rise of litigation, student activism, government regulation, innovative technology, and university entrepreneurship.[60] As attorneys for the institution, legal counsel often need to reconcile competing interests. Yet counsel also tend to be conservative, with a dominant objective of avoiding litigation.[61] One university attorney stated that his objective in addressing copyright problems was "to understand and apply the general principles of copyright law so as to avoid taking *unreasonable* risks."[62]

University constituents are identified in this study by their titles or positions, rather than by any individual's background. For example, a law professor at the University of Hawaii had a leading role in formulating a new draft policy.[63] He is trained as a lawyer, but his position within the institution is on the faculty. At the State University of New York at Albany, a vice president developed a policy in 1987.[64] Her education and former position were as a librarian, but at the time of developing the policy, her institutional responsibility was as an administrator. In a few other cases, a policymaker has held dual positions. Many administrators—especially deans, provosts, and presidents—are current or former faculty. They are treated here as "administrators." Some librarians also have faculty status or may principally have administrative duties. Nevertheless, within this study, "librarians" include all persons identified as members of the library staff, regardless of their rank, title, or professional training. These labels are assumed to comport with the primary duty that the person has within the institution. A provost may be a professor, but policy-making responsibilities stem from the administrative assignment. A librarian may administer, but those duties are usually confined to the library system.

PROFESSIONAL ASSOCIATIONS

These constituents are rarely isolated within their own universities. Numerous professional organizations share information and experiences and recommend means of addressing common concerns.[65] These associations are one more element of the university's environment, and some organizations advocate particular positions on copyright matters. For example, the American Library Association (ALA) has encouraged libraries and universities to adopt its model policy on photocopying. Nonacademic associations are also influential; the Association of American Publishers (AAP) has urged universities to adopt guidelines that originally appeared in the legislative history of the 1976 Copyright Act and that NYU accepted in its settlement.[66] The ALA policy follows the philosophy of librarians to encourage dissemination of information, while the AAP policy allows only limited copying, thereby furthering the objectives of publishers and copyright owners. The AAP also implies that it will not sue universities that follow its standards. Policymakers most concerned about external obligations will embrace the AAP's consolation.

Historical Perspective on University Control

These expectations about universities, their constituents, and their copyright policies also find credence in university history. In the nineteenth century, when teaching was the primary mission, university facilities were neither large nor complicated, and little central administration was necessary. Relatively few conflicts arose between faculty and administrators. The advent of research as a fundamental mission equal to teaching required new organizational structures and the growth of administrative oversight.[67] By the early 1900s, many universities were establishing a pattern of centralized authority, delegated in part to deans and department chairs. For most of the twentieth century, these officers and the faculty had primary responsibility for academic policies, often leaving more senior university administrators to focus on managerial tasks and nonacademic issues.[68] In the meantime, faculty became increasingly specialized or focused on their teaching and research, and academic policies were sometimes poorly planned and coordinated.[69]

Some universities have reverted to stricter central control in more recent years. University relations with the public have become more complex, and tightened budgets have compelled more efficient uses of resources.[70] These general trends suggest a split in policy development, depending on whether the issues are academic or managerial. For many years, academic policies have been the domain of faculty and department heads, while management policies have remained with central administrators. But copyright policies have both academic and managerial characteristics. They regulate information uses needed for academic purposes, and they respond to the university's need to reduce liability exposure. Thus, responsibility for copyright policies could appropriately reside with either faculty or administrators.

When copyright is treated strictly as a managerial problem, its important relationship to the university's academic mission may be lost. Any diversion from the university mission may have damaging consequences for the whole institution. The Carnegie Foundation has articulated the importance of the university mission in the balance of internal and external obligations:

> There are times, of course, when the essential core of the university collides, or appears to collide, with other values of equal or, perhaps, transcendent merit to society at large. These dilemmas must be candidly confronted and, we hope, resolved. A discussion of the governance of higher education must begin, however, with the recognition that the university is a unique institution with a unique mission. At the heart of the enterprise are those who teach and those who learn. Since human curiosity and potential cannot and should not be constrained, scholars and students must have the freedom required to carry on their essential work.[71]

While copyright is an incentive to write and publish, it is also one possible constraint on the freedom to advance knowledge. Limits on academic pursuits are more often described in terms of freedom of expression and academic freedom. These concepts embody the ideals and aspirations of scholarly inquiry, yet they face constant challenges from both inside and outside the university. This study will focus particularly on the interrelationship between copyright law and the university's mission.[72] Grasping that connection is the first step toward formulating lawful policies that better harmonize with academic pursuits.

Copyright and Universities:
The Law and the Foundation
of Policies

The fair use doctrine, recently revamped by the Supreme Court, is in bad shape. . . . The difficulty of predicting how courts will make such [fair use] judgments has left many producers and users of copyrighted materials uncertain as to their legal rights.

William W. Fisher III, Harvard Law School (1988)[1]

But it would be a mistake to conclude that simply because the statutory language and legislative history are difficult to interpret, they convey nothing about what the 1976 Act was intended to accomplish.

Jessica D. Litman, University of Michigan (1987)[2]

University copyright policies may be integrally related to the university's academic mission, but they are obviously rooted in the law. Without the system of legal rights and responsibilities, the policies would not exist. This chapter accordingly reviews copyright law and its application in the university context to reveal how Congress intended the law to affect higher education. The emphasis here is on Sections 107 and 108 of the Copyright Act for the simple reasons that they are the most prominent, the most utilized, and the most problematic provisions of the current law for universities today. This chapter will review basic principles of copyright and explore the legislative history of Sections 107 and 108 in detail. It will reveal not only the nature and objectives of copyright, but also the emergence of the Classroom Guidelines as a central force in shaping fair use, and the role of a single lawsuit in the development of the law affecting the entire country—a phenomenon that continues with recent litigation.

The Rights of Owners and Users

Copyright law is a regime of privileges established by federal law to define and allocate rights to duplicate, distribute, and make other uses of original works, whether those works are writings, music, art, photographs, sound recordings, or a host of other creative materials. Ownership of the copyright vests initially with the creator, who possesses exclusive control over most copyright privileges.[3] Those rights may be transferred to others. Authors of written works typically assign their copyrights to publishers by contract, enabling the assignee to exercise rights of reproduction and distribution and to combat infringements. The United States Constitution empowers Congress to enact American copyright law,[4] and Congress passed the first federal copyright statute in 1790.[5] It made the most recent complete revision in 1976, which took effect on 1 January 1978. The current law gives authors rights to their creative works generally for a term of the author's life plus fifty years. Special terms apply to works by pseudonymous, anonymous, and other authors.[6]

Copyright privileges apply only to works that are original with the author and "fixed in any tangible medium of expression, now known or later developed."[7] The originality requirement is fundamental to the law. The commonly stated purpose of copyright is to encourage original works by granting exclusive privileges to authors. Creators of nonoriginal works are denied the exclusive rights, and nonoriginality may itself amount to a copyright infringement. The level of required "originality" is low. So low, in fact, that many observers were surprised when the Supreme Court ruled in 1991 that copyright protections do not extend to routine "white pages" telephone books.[8] The "tangible medium" requirement is not even that clear. It traditionally meant that copyrighted material must be written. Indeed, early statutes itemized all allowable "tangible" media and had to be amended to keep pace with modern technologies, such as the invention of sound recordings.[9] The "tangible medium" language today is flexible for future developments, but it leaves unprotected such intangibles as ideas and story plots, despite arguments that they include valuable information worthy of copyright.[10]

Significant debate also stems from the constitutional provision on copyright. It provides for exclusive rights, but expressly for promoting "the Progress of Science." Courts have struggled to fulfill that constitutional objective by tailoring the extent of the author's exclusive rights in a way that best promotes progress and learning.[11] In 1984 the United States Supreme Court acknowledged that the law rewards copyright owners for their efforts, but that the law should also encourage "public access to the products of their genius." [12] According to the Supreme Court, the exact scope of rights is "a difficult balance between the interests of authors and inventors in the control and exploitation of their writings and discoveries on the one hand, and society's competing interest in the free flow of ideas, information, and commerce on the other hand. . . . " [13]

Universities and professors may benefit from access to copyrighted materials, but they also assert ownership claims to newly created works. In the late 1970s, Iowa State University sued the ABC television network for broadcasting portions of a film about a university athlete. [14] A student produced the original film and assigned the copyright to the university in exchange for financial support. The appellate court acknowledged the public interest in the life history of a public figure, but it ruled in favor of the university, condemning "corporate theft" in the form of copyright infringements. [15] In 1986 the University of Illinois argued before a U.S. Court of Appeals that it owned the copyright to an article written by a faculty member in connection with his directing a clinical program for pharmacists. The court ruled that writing articles was not one of his administrative duties, but rather part of his general academic responsibilities, thus leaving the copyright with the professor and his co-authors. [16] In another case, a medical professor sued a colleague who claimed co-authorship of an article that the plaintiff had written alone. The court found an infringement in the false authorship claim and in the distribution of copies of the article. [17]

Recent years have brought conflicts among faculty members and their universities surrounding the ownership of newly created computer software. These controversies have generated internal disputes, elaborate policy statements, and interesting articles. [18] As yet, however, they have not produced any reported judicial opinions. These controversies nevertheless are good reminders that universities are on both sides of the copyright debate. Universities and their faculty are simultaneously owners and users of protected works. They must balance their arguments carefully to avoid letting one set of interests undermine the other; and they can allow these diverging interests to expand their appreciation of owners' and users' privileges.

THE RIGHTS OF USERS: FAIR USE

Another basic element of American copyright law is the "fair use" doctrine. Fair use reduces the scope of exclusive rights granted to copyright owners by allowing the public to make limited uses of copyrighted materials, particularly if the uses have social benefits. [19] The doctrine helps ensure that owners' exclusive rights do not overwhelm the constitutional objective of promoting learning.[20] The public needs to make some uses in order to build on the efforts of others and to expand knowledge and creativity. Common examples of such uses include quoting from published material in reviews, books, and articles.[21] Fair use also sanctions limited photocopying of printed works and analogous uses of videotapes, software, databases, and other copyrighted materials.

Courts originally developed fair use to dismiss cases of minute or socially beneficial infringements, and the doctrine was largely a rule of reason; courts could excuse an infringement if it "reasonably" should have been allowed.[22] In the university context, however, fair use is intrinsically aligned with the notion that education deserves preferential treatment and should not be unduly inhibited. Fair use undoubtedly gives special deference to academic needs, although Congress and the courts have made clear that a nonprofit educational purpose is no free license to appropriate protected works. Nor should it be. Any open-ended claim would eradicate scores of creative works that depend on the copyright system for survival. Thus, fair use for education must be held to reasonable limits; within those limits a privilege for education is justified and indeed imperative for achieving copyright's goals. Many common uses of copyrighted works at American universities can serve the objective of "promoting progress" without jeopardizing the creator's incentive. The creator still retains exclusive rights, but fair use adjusts the balance to better serve the constitutional purpose.

Today the rules of fair use are codified in the 1976 Copyright Act, which elaborates the doctrine and expressly allows some copying for educational uses. The statute also retains many of the judicially developed fair use principles:

> Notwithstanding the provisions of sections 106 and 106A, the fair use of a copyrighted work, including such use by reproduction in copies or phonorecords or by any other means specified by that section, for purposes such as criticism, comment, news reporting, teaching (including multiple copies for classroom use), scholarship, or research, is not an infringement of copyright. In determining whether the use made of a work in any particular case is a fair use the factors to be considered shall include—
> (1) the purpose and character of the use, including whether such use is of a commercial nature or is for nonprofit educational purposes;
> (2) the nature of the copyrighted work;
> (3) the amount and substantiality of the portion used in relation to the copyrighted work as a whole; and
> (4) the effect of the use upon the potential market for or value of the copyrighted work.
> The fact that a work is unpublished shall not itself bar a finding of fair use if such finding is made upon consideration of all the above factors.[23]

As now cast in statutory language, fair use specifically supports teaching and research, but only within the four general criteria: *purpose, nature, amount,* and *effect.* These criteria evolved in judicial decisions before the 1976 act, but they remain only elusive guidelines.[24] What are the outer boundaries of fair use? How much copying or other use is allowed or not allowed under various conditions? The statute avoids specific answers. Courts have given occasional meaning to the four factors in fair use, but courts decide cases only on the particular facts presented; a slight change in facts could alter the outcome. A universal definition of fair use is indiscernible. For example, most courts have favored a public-interest purpose over a commercial purpose.[25] But a lack of profit alone does not lead to fair use, and a quest for profit does not preclude user rights.[26] An educational purpose also has moved courts toward finding fair use, but not without exception.[27] Thus, courts have recognized that instruction and scholarship necessitate the use of pre-existing works, such as reprinting quotations in works of biography[28] or history.[29] But a teacher may not draft new arrangements of copyrighted music and distribute copies to a school choir,[30] and an educational television station cannot broadcast a protected motion picture without permission.[31] Another court ruled that the recipient of unpublished letters could not read them to students without the copyright owner's permission.[32]

The statute directs that all four factors should be evaluated together, but courts have given greatest emphasis to the fourth factor—the effect on the potential value of or market for the original work.[33] The fundamental rule of fair use is often described as whether the use would reasonably substitute for a purchase of the original or impair its market.[34] The answer is often mere speculation. Quantity measurements alone cannot determine infringements,[35] and even small uses can potentially violate the law.[36] "Quantity" is also not just a counting of words. Courts have found infringements in borrowing the "organizational scheme" of a manual on guitar playing[37] or a book's "manner and style,"[38] or the "total concept and feel" of computer software.[39] One court ruled that scales to measure "love and liking" developed in a doctoral dissertation could not be copied in a magazine under a fair use claim.[40]

These cases reveal the difficulty of working with fair use, yet its transformation from a judicial doctrine to a statutory provision has stirred other, more subtle implications.[41] A statutory fair use assures that the right exists, but it also means some loss of flexibility. Basic changes must now pass congressional scrutiny, where action is slow. The 1976 revision, for example, required two decades of discussion, research, and lobbying, and some commentators objected vehemently to any codification of limited copying.[42] A recent commentary on fair use by members of the publishing industry alleged that a statutory fair use weakened the position of copyright owners and upset the purpose of copyright: "Because the notion of copyright itself balances the rights of creators and the needs of users, exemptions interfere with its internal workings."[43] Such views imply that authors' rights alone reflect an appropriate balance among competing interests and fulfill the constitutional mandate of promoting knowledge. Nevertheless, fair use assures universities that limited uses are lawful, but fair use requires careful monitoring, and it does not respond to all academic needs.

THE RIGHTS OF USERS: LIBRARY COPYING

Fair use may be the best known of all rights secured for the public under the 1976 act, but several other provisions grant more specific opportunities, especially for higher education. Section 108 is an extraordinary innovation that clearly enables libraries to reproduce protected works pursuant to detailed provisions.[44] Congress adopted Section 108 after years of hearings and debates, and it originally mandated that the Register of Copyrights report every five years on its effects.[45] Congress affirmed the social significance of Section 108: its privileges are reserved only for libraries open to the public or to outside researchers.[46] Most academic libraries allow public access, but corporate or private libraries often do not meet that standard. Indeed, Section 108 dictates that library copying rights must be exercised "without any purpose of direct or indirect commercial advantage. . . ."[47]

Section 108 sanctions activities that are central to basic library functions of acquisition, retention, and access. Libraries may copy unpublished works to preserve the original or to deposit the copy in another library.[48] They may also copy published works if the original is damaged, deteriorating, lost, or stolen, but only if "after a reasonable effort" the library cannot find an "unused replacement . . . at a fair price."[49] Section 108 allows libraries to duplicate part or all of a copyrighted work for a patron's "private study, scholarship, or research." Libraries, however, must post a warning notice about copyright infringements, and entire works may be copied only after searching for a copy at a "fair price."[50] "Fair price" is undefined.

Perhaps the most visible effect of Section 108 is the library's immunity from copyright infringements made at unsupervised "reproducing equipment."[51] The familiar warnings placed on photocopy machines at colleges and universities are the only special prerequisite to this immunity.[52] Also significant are the limits of Section 108. Many of its rights do not apply to musical or artistic works, to motion pictures, or to most other audiovisual works.[53] Section 108 expressly permits "isolated and unrelated reproduction or distribution of a single copy"; it prohibits making or distributing multiple copies and the "systematic" copying of individual works, other than limited copies for interlibrary lending.[54]

Interlibrary lending is a basic service of university libraries, and it is an essential means for obtaining materials available only from other depositories. Often an original book, periodical, or other work is loaned from one library to another by specific request. Sharing the original work is not a copyright infringement; owners of "a particular copy . . . lawfully made" are entitled to sell or otherwise dispose of it.[55] This provision underlies every sale of a book, magazine, sound recording, or videotape, whether at a retail store or in a secondhand shop. It also enables libraries to acquire and circulate their collections. But much interlibrary "lending" is actually the transmittal of photocopies. Sharing an original publication risks loss or damage, and it removes the work from the home library. Sending a photocopy is safer, but it may constitute a copyright infringement.

Section 108 attempts to resolve this dilemma by allowing libraries to make limited copies from their collections for patrons—and for interlibrary lending—so long as each request for copying is an isolated event, and not part of a "concerted" plan to generate multiple copies. While prohibiting "systematic" copying, the statute offers this reassurance:

> nothing in this clause prevents a library or archives from participating in interlibrary arrangements that do not have, as their purpose or effect, that the library or archives receiving such copies or phonorecords for distribution does so in such aggregate quantities as to substitute for a subscription to or purchase of such work.[56]

Once again, an underlying test is whether the user reasonably should have purchased the work, rather than make the copies. That standard remains imprecise and subject to some dispute.[57]

Several other provisions of the 1976 Copyright Act limit the exclusive rights that copyright owners enjoy. Many of those provisions specifically serve education and research. Section 110 allows teachers to perform works and to display motion pictures and videotapes in classrooms, and educational institutions may transmit, through television or other broadcast systems, certain musical works or readings of nondramatic literary works in classrooms or other places of instruction.[58] Congress revised Section 117 in 1980 to permit the owner of a computer software copy to adapt it for use on a particular computer or to make an "archival" or backup disk for use in the event of damage to the original.[59] Many software producers even encourage customers to make "backup" copies, recognizing that their expensive products are easily damaged or destroyed. University policies sometimes focus on such familiar activities. Several other provisions of the 1976 act limit the rights of copyright owners. For example, Section 111 deals with "secondary transmissions" of broadcasts by cable television systems,[60] but these technical delineations of rights do not directly affect many individuals at universities, and they are seldom the subject of university policies.

Consequences of Infringements: Liabilities

Copyright owners who bring lawsuits and successfully prove infringements are entitled to various remedies from many potential defendants. Lawsuits involving universities may be filed against the individuals accused of committing infringements, their supervisors who direct activities, the university itself, and its officers, regents, or trustees.[61] Available remedies include a recovery of damages suffered by the owner and profits obtained by the infringer.[62] Plaintiffs may seek injunctions against future infringements and the impoundment and destruction of the infringing copies and of the equipment used in the transgressions.[63] These remedies may be appropriate for bootlegged records, pirated videotapes, and other large-scale commercial infringements, but they may not be so meaningful against isolated copying on campus. Actual damages or lost profits may be small or speculative; photocopying for educational uses usually lacks any direct profit motive; and injunctions and impoundments may be easily circumvented, or may be too costly in attorneys' fees, or may yield bad publicity for copyright owners when asserted against educators.

Recognizing the deficiency of standard remedies, the Copyright Act allows "statutory damages" of $500 to $20,000, as the court may determine, without proof of actual damages to the owner or of actual profits to the infringer.[64] Moreover, proving a "willful" violation can boost statutory damages to $100,000,[65] and criminal penalties may reach $250,000 and five years imprisonment for even the first offense.[66] These penalties may attach to a university or to individual faculty, librarians, or staff members. On the other hand, Congress shielded "innocent" infringers and persons relying on "fair use" for education. First, the 1976 act allows courts to reduce statutory damages to as low as $200 if the "infringer was not aware and had no reason to believe that his or her acts constituted an infringement of copyright."[67] Second, Congress potentially eliminated statutory damages for educators and librarians who act in good faith:

> The court shall remit statutory damages in any case where an infringer believed and had reasonable grounds for believing that his or her use of the copyrighted work was a fair use under section 107, if the infringer was . . . an employee or agent of a nonprofit educational institution, library, or ar-

chives acting within the scope of his or her employment who, or such institution, library, or archives itself, which infringed by reproducing the work
in copies or phonorecords. . . .[68]

Injunctions and impoundments remain possible. Actual damages and profits may still be recovered. Statutory damages may apply to "noninnocent"
or willful infringements and to uses not within "fair use" or not involving
the reproduction of "copies or phonorecords." But for most reproductions
for teaching and research, Congress drastically reduced the potential consequences in recognition of the unique value of education and research.
Congress shielded the academe and seemed to doubt that much "good
faith" copying actually harmed authors and publishers.[69] Some possibility
of monetary damages nevertheless continues.

Public universities seemed to escape even that possibility for a short
time. In the late 1980s a few courts ruled that the Eleventh Amendment to
the U.S. Constitution prevented copyright lawsuits for monetary damages
against state universities.[70] The Eleventh Amendment protects states from
most liabilities in federal courts, with the underlying purpose of securing
state coffers from federal intrusion.[71] Yet federal law mandates that
all copyright infringement cases shall be filed in federal courts.[72] Thus, in
BV Engineering v. University of California, Los Angeles,[73] a software
developer brought an infringement action against UCLA when a faculty
member allegedly made several copies of a computer program. The Ninth
Circuit Court of Appeals held that state universities were immune
from damage claims in federal court, and the Supreme Court declined to
hear the case. The public university was momentarily free from liability,
and the copyright owner was left with few rights to pursue. Congress
amended the Copyright Act in 1990 to allow such actions to proceed.[74]
Congress would not allow educators to escape liability completely, and it
made clear that public and private institutions were equal candidates for
infringement lawsuits.[75]

SCOPE OF ACTIVITIES UNDER COPYRIGHT LAW

Although photocopying remains the cynosure of copyright on campus, the
law applies to diverse information resources at educational institutions:

Off-air videotaping: In 1984 the U.S. Supreme Court ruled that recording
television broadcasts for later home viewing is not an infringement,[76] but
a lower court found an infringement when a school system recorded television broadcasts to build a permanent collection of videotapes for classroom use.[77]

Performance and display: One of the copyright owner's exclusive rights is the performance or display of protected works, including the projection of motion pictures, the performance of dramas, and the playing of copyrighted songs by a marching band at football games. Section 110 of the 1976 act allows educators to "perform or display" these works in classrooms, but most other uses remain within the copyright owner's domain.[78]

Software duplication and modification: Section 117 expressly permits backup copies and some modifications of software,[79] but some experts argue that fair use offers no additional rights to software users.[80] Left in doubt is the legality of such common practices as loading software on multiple machines, circulating software from libraries, and even sharing one software package among several users.

Database creation and downloading: Copyright implications for database development and use are unavoidable. Making an electronic copy of a protected work for storage or analysis is itself a duplication, and the resulting "database" may be further reproduced or "downloaded" almost without limit on common computer equipment.[81] Flagrant instances may be easy to judge, but the uncertain parameters of user rights may inhibit full exploration of the technology.[82] Existing databases of text and factual records are now widely used on campuses, and their producers often seek protection through copyright law and contractual limitations. A notable example of database copyright and the confusion it engenders arose when OCLC, a national database of bibliographic records from numerous libraries, registered its copyright with the Copyright Office in 1984.[83] Participating libraries argued that they were the real "authors" of the computer files, and that copyright threatened beneficial uses of the resources that they helped to construct.[84] OCLC mollified the controversy by clarifying its purposes and by extending clear rights to participating libraries.

These are only examples of copyright's extensive role at American universities and the problems of utilizing materials while attempting to obey an unclear and unsettled law. This brief introduction to copyright law also reveals basic dilemmas involving universities and the law. First, copyright law can enhance the creation and availability of information resources, but it can also restrict their uses. Second, limited uses of copyrighted material may be allowed, but the standards are vague and therefore difficult to enforce. Third, the conflict between universities and copyright owners is not merely one of allowing or disallowing certain uses. It is a conflict between practical methods of sharing information and the desire or need of authors and publishers to control or to realize economic gains from their efforts.

Despite these conflicts, the rights of owners and users are increasingly intermingled in many respects. Many individual faculty are simultaneously owners and users of copyrighted works, and users' rights help define the scope of rights constitutionally appropriate for owners. Moreover, a few recent proposals have suggested that claims of ownership by the university or by faculty authors can help resolve some doubts about fair use privileges for educational needs. These proposals would either have universities assert an ownership interest in faculty writings or require faculty to retain all or part of their copyright privileges when publishing articles in scholarly journals. As a result, the faculty member or the institution would own rights of reproduction and would presumably then grant permission to educators and librarians to make copies for teaching and research.[85] Although these suggestions may be unwieldy and possibly detrimental to many journals, they nevertheless demonstrate that universities have not fully probed or managed their potential opportunities under copyright.

Universities also need to comprehend the significance of copyright beyond their own narrow, practical needs. Barbara Ringer, former Register of Copyrights, highlighted the larger significance of copyright law in the information processes: "As this society moves deeper and deeper into that phase of economic life called 'post-industrial,' where livelihoods are earned predominantly through the sale of information, expertise, and personal services, the extent to which copyrightable creations are protected by exclusive property interests can become central to national growth."[86] In a society where information processing and the advancement of knowledge are of growing importance, the extent to which information is made available to others is likewise vital to economic growth and educational prosperity. Universities must find the balance in copyright law that encourages creativity while simultaneously facilitating optimal access to information and the advancement of knowledge. In reality, both sides of this balance have something in common: both of them should promote the progress of knowledge as the Constitution directs.

The Foundation of Policies: The Meaning of Fair Use

The uncertain scope of fair use that Congress left in the 1976 act was nothing new. Fair use originated exclusively as a judicial doctrine, uniquely applicable to the facts of each case and without strict precision. It was inherently flexible, and any practical meaning usually required a lawsuit or a negotiated agreement. One of the first attempts to interpret fair use for education was the so-called "Gentlemen's Agreement" of 1935, stemming from the new technology for "photoduplicating" copyrighted works.[87] In the early 1900s many libraries offered manual copying services, or they referred patrons to copyists who transcribed materials by hand for a living.[88] By the 1930s, libraries broadened access to collections with photoreproduction services for duplicating full pages of text, but the equipment was relatively expensive and required steady servicing.[89] By 1935, the machinery and uses had developed to such a stage that researchers and publishers agreed to a set of guidelines detailing allowable copying under fair use.

The Gentlemen's Agreement ultimately did little to clarify fair use. Its central function was to permit libraries to make a "single photographic reproduction" of part of a copyrighted work and to deliver it to a "scholar." The agreement exempted the library from liability, but it required written confirmation that the copy was solely for research and that the "scholar" still risked infringement liability. Libraries gained assurance of avoiding some risks, and publishers acknowledged some copying that they would not treat as infringements. The guidelines also affirmed that fair use for personal research copying could go beyond the traditional brief quotations in scholarly works. The agreement opened new doors, but it also cautioned that publishers intended to scrutinize private activity.[90] The Gentlemen's Agreement remained the only major copying standard for almost a quarter of a century, when the long process leading to the Copyright Act of 1976 began in earnest.[91]

THE LEGISLATIVE HISTORY OF SECTION 107

In 1960 and 1961 the Register of Copyrights—after five years of preparation—fulfilled a congressional directive by delivering a set of thirty-four studies on copyright law and a report proposing a copyright revision act.[92] These works became the foundation of sixteen subsequent years of meetings, hearings, bills, and reports, leading to passage of the current copyright statute in late 1976. This "legislative history" of the 1976 act documents the interests, arguments, and strategies of publishers, authors, librarians, scholars, and other groups with strong interests in the shape of copyright law. The legislative history also reveals congressional resistance to specifying certain rights and congressional urging that interested parties develop mutual guidelines to detail their understanding of user privileges. These developments are chronicled in the hearings and reports, and they illuminate the intended effects and underlying principles of current copyright statutes.

From the earliest report of the Register of Copyrights in 1961, every proposed copyright bill included express rights of "fair use."[93] Several bills from the early 1960s only mentioned the doctrine without elaboration,[94] but pressure from user groups persuaded Congress to add the four criteria that survive in today's statute: purpose, nature, amount, and effect.[95] Congress also narrowed fair use generally to teaching, research, scholarship, and other social purposes in one of the early bills.[96] Beyond these developments, three subtle, but important, changes in Section 107 emerged during congressional reviews and hearings: fair use was expressly applied to the *reproduction* of materials; it permitted multiple copies for classroom use; and the nonprofit character of a use became an explicit factor in the fair use equation.

Throughout the debates, educators were most concerned about whether fair use applied at all to making actual copies of protected works.[97] Courts had sanctioned quoting, but early law was silent on rights to make facsimiles, such as photocopies. Indeed, the 1961 Register's report listed examples of fair use for educators, with only a short mention of the right to copy a "small part of a work."[98] Much of the record from the early 1960s revealed the doubts of many parties that reproducing an entire work would be fair use.[99] For example, in 1963 a consortium of library organizations recommended that libraries should be able to make single copies of articles for patrons,[100] but the publishers' reaction was "violent."[101] When librarians later recommended that they be allowed to copy an entire work after a reasonable search of the market, copyright owners threatened that the proposal could undermine all efforts to achieve a balanced law. According to Irwin Karp, representing the Authors League of America: "I think this is potentially one of the most dangerous provisions you're writing into this new law, and it might render all these other rights included in the law nugatory in the future."[102] Nevertheless, in 1967 Congress accepted the argument of educators that Section 107 should embrace "reproduction in copies or phonorecords."[103] If not a change in existing law, the provision was undoubtedly an important clarification of fair use rights.[104] The amount of copying was not stated, but at least fair use was not confined to mere quoting.

The second important change in the wording of Section 107 came shortly before passage of the final bill. Educators argued that effective teaching requires multiple copies of some works. Congressional reports previously acknowledged a limited right of multiple copying for educators, but teachers feared that any privileges could be lost in future judicial rulings if not expressly stated in the statute. In the final month before passage of the act, Congress expanded the bill's language to approve multiple copies for teaching.[105] The House report also made clear that multiple copies would normally be confined to excerpts of works, or perhaps the entirety of a short news article, a short poem, a map from a newspaper, and other brief works. Congress did not explain whether multiple copies of entire journal articles and book chapters were allowable.[106]

The third significant change also occurred shortly before the bill's passage. Educators, scholars, and librarians noted throughout the 1960s and 1970s that judicial decisions on fair use almost always involved commercial uses, but Congress was never willing to grant a blanket exemption for nonprofit endeavors.[107] In the end, however, the fair use statute did specify that a nonprofit purpose was a valid consideration in the fair use analysis.[108] That modification of the bill gave new significance to educational objectives. It strengthened that aspect of fair use rights, and it was a slight withdrawal from reliance on market effects as the leading factor. Market value may be the most appropriate gauge in commercial disputes, but it may not be most meaningful in the academe.[109] Implying exactly that shift in emphasis, congressional reports dropped the following controversial language that had appeared in earlier House reports: "Where the unauthorized copying displaces what realistically might have been a sale, no matter how minor the amount of money involved, the interests of the copyright owner need protection."[110] Academicians attacked the emphasis on market value and on the apparent right of owners to receive payment for all uses, even "minor" ones.

At nearly every opportunity in its development of a fair use statute, Congress maintained relentlessly that it intended to effect no change in existing fair use law. The intent was neither to freeze the law nor to change it, but only to assure its existence as a fluid set of principles; courts and private parties should continue reevaluating the doctrine for constantly changing circumstances,[111] such as photocopying for teaching and research and evolving technologies.[112] According to a 1966 House report: "The fullest possible use of the multitude of technical devices now available to education should be encouraged." Despite its denials, Congress was unquestionably changing the law.[113] Any statutory provision was itself a significant change in the law; a statute could grant a privilege that a court could hardly revoke. The final version eliminated any remaining doubts that fair use could extend to duplications or to multiple copies. It also hinted that nonprofit educational needs might receive priority treatment.[114]

This evolution of fair use reflects significant advances for education and research.[115] Fair use gained statutory recognition; its broad application to teaching and research was unequivocal if not absolute; Congress expressly allowed reproductions, and even multiple copies for teaching; four general factors were highlighted for evaluation; and the nonprofit purpose of a use was emphasized. Congress repeated at every opportunity that it was only clarifying existing law for important social purposes: "The committee sympathizes with the argument that a teacher should not be prevented by uncertainty from doing things that he is legally entitled to do and that improve the quality of his teaching."[116] Congress also credited educators with shaping the final version of the fair use statute: "The specific wording of section 107 as it now stands is the result of a process of accretion, resulting from the long controversy over the related problems of fair use and the reproduction (mostly by photocopying) of copyrighted material for educational and scholarly purposes."[117] Short of a full exemption from liability,[118] the only significant defeat for educators in shaping Section 107 was the remaining ambiguity of fair use for copying entire articles or book chapters. But at least fair use was securely in the statute.

THE EMERGENCE OF THE CLASSROOM GUIDELINES

Beyond important developments in the wording of Section 107, Congress was not willing to detail exact rights and limits of fair use. Yet educators demanded specificity. To advance their demands, a consortium of professional organizations—ranging in number over the years from twenty-five to more than forty—formed the "Ad Hoc Committee on Copyright Law Revision."[119] Its spokesperson, attorney Harry N. Rosenfield, testified that existing fair use emerged from commercial disputes, leaving the unique needs of educators inadequately addressed. He urged Congress not only to fulfill these needs, but to provide specific guidance as well:

> What education needs is a statute which will enable teachers easily to know when they can use copyrighted materials. Proposed Section 6 [on fair use] does not give this certainty, but means that a teacher in preparing every single lesson must either consult a lawyer or act at her risk. The fair use doctrine both under present law and proposed Section 6 not only fails to give assurance when copyrighted matter can safely be used, but also fails to give assurance as to how much can be copied or how many copies can be safely made. If fair use can be the controversial bone of contention that it is among sophisticated copyright lawyers, in this room and elsewhere, is it any wonder that teachers find less practical value in the application of fair use in education than might be deemed the case?[120]

The quest for greater specificity and assurance of educators' rights would propel the Ad Hoc Committee throughout the revision process.[121] Yet Congress regularly urged the interest groups to develop their own mutually acceptable guidelines,[122] and by mid–1966, educators and publishers were conferring on fair use.[123] The earliest reports from the Copyright Office included examples of fair use rights,[124] and congressional reports in 1966 offered "principles" for interpreting the law: copying should be spontaneous and at the teacher's own volition; anthologies were not allowed; single copies of articles were permissible; and multiple copies should embrace only extracts or less than a full "self-contained" work.[125]

These principles were distilled from the testimony of various groups. The Ad Hoc Committee proposed that the law allow single copies of poems, charts, essays, and articles.[126] The Authors League of America countered that copies be permitted only after assessing the "cumulative" effect of all copying and the "spontaneity" of the request or need.[127] With this gradual elucidation of fair use, educators and copyright owners appeared to have reached a preliminary agreement by 1969 on photocopying for classroom use,[128] and the Ad Hoc Committee of educators readily adopted these "principles."[129] Educators were the main proponents of specific guidelines, overcoming some objections from copyright owners.[130] According to the Ad Hoc Committee: "teachers want and need the certainty of knowing when a given use of copyrighted material in the course of teaching is legitimate." And: "teachers do not want to condone under-the-table uses."[131] A publishers' group, however, cautioned that specific rights may imply that other uses are not permitted, thereby narrowing the full potential of fair use.[132] As early as 1960, copyright expert Melville Nimmer warned about detailed guidelines: "Such arrangements like any detailed statutory codification would not be sufficiently flexible to meet the demands of particular situations."[133]

Despite these cautions, the final report from the U.S. House of Representatives accompanying the new copyright act included the text of fair use guidelines on photocopying for research and classroom purposes. Entitled "Agreement on Guidelines for Classroom Copying in Not-For-Profit Educational Institutions" (see Appendix B), the standards were presented as an agreement among the Ad Hoc Committee, the Authors League of America, and the Association of American Publishers.[134] Congress eagerly received these "Classroom Guidelines"; they delineated fair use well beyond the detail Congress was willing to put in the statute. They may have been within the spirit of fair use, but the guidelines are narrow in scope and rigorous in application, requiring diligent users to count all copies and even the number of words reproduced. Full compliance may be first and foremost an unrealistic nuisance.

In summary, the guidelines allow single copies of articles and parts of larger works for research or classroom preparation. They also allow multiple copies for classroom distribution, if the copying meets meticulous standards regarding "brevity," "spontaneity," and "cumulative effect." For example, a teacher can distribute to each student in one course a copy of an article which does not exceed 2,500 words, but only within other overall limits on total copying and on the frequency of copying from one author or one periodical. Most scholarly articles exceed 2,500 words, and limits on the amount of copying from one author sharply burden specialized literature courses.[135] These limitations surely must have satisfied authors and publishers, and their specific "answers" were exactly what the Ad Hoc Committee of educators had sought.

The guidelines were also consistent with congressional hopes. They were a "voluntary arrangement" as Congress had urged; they incorporated many principles of fair use that interest groups and congressional reports had distilled; and they did not directly undercut the full scope of rights granted by the new statute. Indeed, the guidelines were expressly "minimum standards of educational fair use under Section 107."[136] Additional, although unexplained, copying was still permissible. Nevertheless, the American Association of University Professors and the Association of American Law Schools attacked the guidelines as "too restrictive with respect to classroom situations at the university and graduate level."[137] In separate letters to Representative Robert W. Kastenmeier, chair of the House subcommittee reviewing the bill, the AAUP and the AALS urged him not to print the guidelines in the congressional report. Portending their actual implementation at many universities, these academic organizations warned that the guidelines would in practice be misapplied as maximum limits with sweeping prohibitions that would ultimately constrain fair use as established in Section 107.[138] Congress was unsympathetic; the House report dismissed critics by underscoring the possibility of further copying and affirming that the guidelines were only examples of rights and were not mandatory restrictions.[139]

With this congressional blessing, the Classroom Guidelines became an important part of understanding and applying fair use, and numerous publications reprinted them.[140] They compensated for a statute that lacked specifics and for court rulings that rarely dealt with educational needs. For universities working with the law, the guidelines were a model policy to follow. Moreover, they implied a "safe harbor": stay within these limits to avoid risks of infringements. A second set of guidelines for reproducing music appeared in the House report, also with the same implication of avoiding liability risks.[141] In 1981, Congress fostered yet another set of guidelines for using videotapes recorded from television broadcasts.[142] None of these guidelines is law, but they gained congressional approval as reasonable interpretations of fair use, and they engendered wide public perception as "safe harbors" from liability. In the absence of alternative interpretations and of judicial rulings to clarify the law, these guidelines also became the most important part of the foundation on which universities began developing their copyright policies.

The Foundation of Policies: The Meaning of Library Copying

Contemporary librarians may challenge copyright as a constraint on their fundamental services,[143] but they once viewed the law as an ally in acquiring new materials. The "legal deposit" provision of American copyright requires publishers to deposit copies of new works with Library of Congress,[144] and the director of that library wrote in 1876 of "the intimate relation that exists between the growth of great national libraries and the law of copyright. . . . "[145] The Smithsonian Institution was also building a "national library" from legal deposits during the nineteenth century, and its 1871 report declared a general principle of copyright that modern librarians often overlook: "The results of the labors of the mind, which form the basis of all human improvement, ought not to be appropriated without remuneration, any more than the labors of the hand or of the machine."[146]

International copyright developments also garnered librarian support a century ago. Librarians endorsed America's entrance into its first copyright treaty, which came in 1891. The treaty extended copyright protection to foreign works and gave popular authors, such as Charles Dickens, the benefit of American markets.[147] The new protection also encouraged the availability of foreign books for American libraries and readers. To console domestic publishers and printers, however, Congress adopted the "manufacturing clause," which severely limited the importation of works "manufactured" in other countries. Librarians organized a "Library Copyright League" early this century to oppose import limits in any form.[148] These positions were properly rooted in library missions: international copyright protection enhanced the availability of publications, but limited imports could restrain the growth of library collections and access to the intellectual endeavors of worldwide authors.

Close ties between libraries and copyright continue. The Library of Congress still benefits from legal deposit, and international treaties encourage distribution of foreign works. Moreover, the manufacturing clause expired in 1986, opening access to more foreign materials.[149] Technological developments in photoduplication, however, have turned library attention away from copyright as a fountainhead of information to copyright as a restraint on service. The law's perceived constraint on duplication and distribution has overshadowed its benefits. This transition did not result from changing laws or changing library missions; it resulted instead from new technologies and the service opportunities they facilitated. For today's libraries, the copyright challenge is to make full use of available technology in furtherance of their mission to acquire, maintain, and provide access to information resources; the vague and uncertain parameters of copyright are perceived as a damper on that pursuit.

That problem regenerates with each innovation, including the advent of computers and videotapes. From the outset of debates on copyright revision, however, attention centered on photocopying. When the Copyright Office submitted its initial studies to Congress in 1960, it surveyed library needs and recommended a library photocopy right. The studies also set a sympathetic tone for the ensuing debates:

> The various methods of photocopying have become indispensable to persons engaged in research and scholarship, and to libraries that provide research material in their collections to such persons. Effective research requires that the researcher be informed of the findings and opinions of others and have an opportunity to study the materials written by them. These materials are often very extensive and appear in a large number of publications. It is here that the libraries provide an indispensable service to research by furnishing the individual researcher with the materials needed by him for reference and study.[150]

THE LEGISLATIVE HISTORY OF SECTION 108

As in the evolution of fair use, some mention of library copying rights appeared in nearly every congressional bill from 1960 to 1976. Unlike fair use, the library rights were relatively few and highly specific, although they were considerably ambivalent in the early years. The 1964 bill authorized libraries to make single copies of articles and other parts of works for the research needs of patrons; copies of entire works were allowed only after searching for a copy from trade sources.[151] The 1965 bill, however, dropped the provision altogether, noting "strong opposition on both sides."[152] Libraries argued that the language would actually curtail existing services, and publishers contended that it would sanction rampant copying. The Copyright Office favored only general principles adaptable to changing needs and technologies.[153] These early efforts to establish library rights were confused and belabored.

In the absence of a library copying privilege, user groups demanded express rights for their own needs. The U.S. Department of Health, Education, and Welfare and the American Council of Learned Societies lobbied for rights to copy articles and similar items,[154] and the Harry S. Truman Library Institute advanced the need for facsimile copies of archival manuscripts for sharing with other libraries.[155] Yet library organizations still opposed specific provisions, contending that statutory language can neither anticipate changing technology nor properly balance the interests of owners and users.[156] Detailed terms nevertheless crept back into the bills. Copying of archival materials received early acceptance,[157] and libraries called for more specifics after the formulation of mutual guidelines with publishers appeared impossible.[158] Librarians also testified that some copying was simply inevitable, that it could discourage theft or mutilation of books, and that it ultimately served copyright's constitutional purpose of advancing knowledge.[159] This meticulous and awkward progression finally gained a clear direction in February 1968 when a publisher sued a major library for circulating photocopies of journal articles.

THE *WILLIAMS & WILKINS* CASE

The Williams & Wilkins Company publishes numerous medical journals for physicians, scholars, and scientists. Long concerned about widespread photocopying, the company president once proposed to a skeptical Senate committee that libraries pay a two-cent royalty for each photocopied page.[160] Apparently dissatisfied with progress in copyright revision and with the dismal prospect of mutual photocopy guidelines, Williams & Wilkins took its case to court, alleging that library duplication of journal articles for patrons and for extensive interlibrary "lending" were infringements. The named defendant was the United States government, proprietor of the National Library of Medicine and the National Institutes of Health, where the alleged violations occurred. Although a decision in the case was a few years away, librarians were alarmed, and Congress responded by broadening library rights in the 1970 copyright bill—again sanctioning single copies of articles and other short items for patrons.[161]

Judicial action on the Williams & Wilkins claim did little to resolve the legal uncertainty. Indeed, the circuitous path that the case followed begged for congressional attention. In February 1972 Commissioner James F. Davis of the United States Court of Claims ruled in favor of the publisher, concluding that the library copying was not fair use.[162] No longer could libraries rely on fair use, and the decision intensified arguments in Congress.[163] Statutory provisions on library copying rights grew in length and detail, and publishers resolved anew that photocopying could destroy their business, especially the publication of scholarly journals with their limited markets.[164] Yet Congress seemed more sympathetic to library arguments; Williams & Wilkins was unable to find a functional plan for royalties on copies,[165] and one senator contemplated sorrowfully whether his own photocopies from the Library of Congress might be deemed unlawful.[166]

The commissioner's ruling motivated Congress to support library rights,[167] but in 1973 an appellate panel of the Court of Claims reversed that decision and held that the copies were fair use.[168] The lengthy opinion from the court was a stirring endorsement of library services and the importance of photocopying. The court embraced the nonprofit character of the libraries, which were "devoted solely to the advancement and dissemination of medical knowledge."[169] It was unpersuaded by evidence that photocopying harmed publishers, and the opinion emphasized social benefits: "There is no doubt in our minds that medical science would be seriously hurt if such library photocopying were stopped."[170] The publisher appealed this ominous ruling, but the United States Supreme Court divided evenly four-to-four on the case without issuing an opinion.[171] The Court of Claims decision in favor of libraries was left intact.

Its effusive language notwithstanding, the *Williams & Wilkins* decision was fragile consolation to libraries. The court highlighted the rigorous limits and elaborate standards that these particular libraries voluntarily followed for photocopying. Single copies were allowed only for personal research, and the copies became the patron's property. The library generally limited copying to single articles, and requests for copies from "widely available" journals were routinely rejected if the article was published within the preceding five years.[172] The decision's most profound effect, however, was its demonstration that fair use was an uneasy source of rights. One judicial decision may be favorable, while the next may be adverse. Each ruling is based on the peculiar facts of the case at hand, and judges can interpret the law differently. That uncertainty in fair use enabled librarians to gain express rights of photocopying in future copyright bills.[173] For example, a 1975 bill would have prohibited "systematic" photocopying, but librarians successfully argued that the limitation could obviate rights won in *Williams & Wilkins*. As a result, the 1976 act retains the prohibition on "systematic" copying, but it also expressly sanctions organized interlibrary lending services and the making of single copies of articles for patrons.[174]

The interlibrary lending provision may be the most problematic part of Section 108. At what point does copying articles for "lending" become "systematic"? This principle was at the center of the *Williams & Wilkins* controversy, and Congress recognized its significance. In 1976 the congressionally formed National Commission on New Technological Uses of Copyrighted Works recommended guidelines on photocopying for interlibrary lending.[175] Better known by the acronym "CONTU," the commission proposed that during any one-year period a library may "borrow" from other libraries not more than five copies of articles published within the preceding five years of any one journal title. Relying on the tenet that copies should not substitute for purchase, CONTU implied that if a library needs more than the five copies, it should purchase its own subscription.[176]

This "rule of fives" is unquestionably arbitrary; other numerical limits would also be rational, and peculiar circumstances may demand six copies one year and none ever again.[177] Moreover, the CONTU Guidelines do not place limits on copies from journals more than five years old or from other types of publications.[178] Still, library, publisher, and author groups assented to the CONTU Guidelines, and they were rooted in practices and policies already employed in some libraries, including the National Library of Medicine.[179] The fact that similar standards survived a judicial test in *Williams & Wilkins* ennobled them as lawful measures and fixed them for future adoption elsewhere. Although the guidelines lacked legal force, they gained a congressional endorsement before passage of the 1976 act.[180] The CONTU limits offered some assurance that specific practices could escape liability. Subsequent years of experience also have shown that they neither significantly restrain service nor jeopardize the survival of publishers.[181]

THE CURRENT STATE OF SECTION 108

Section 108 may leave doubts and controversies about the lawfulness of certain copying, but it was unquestionably a tremendous victory for libraries. At one time libraries and publishers jointly opposed specific provisions in the revision bill, but pressures of real needs, dangerous uncertainties, and the unreliability of fair use inspired libraries, researchers, and Congress to reinstate special rights. Throughout the proceedings, Congress affirmed that the new law was not intended to create new rights, but only to clarify existing privileges. In reality, as with fair use, the library copying provision grants rights that many experts did not believe were allowed under previous law.[182] Most fundamentally, Section 108 allows copies of entire articles, and even entire books under some conditions. Experts previously diverged on any right to copy entire articles and similar "self-contained" works.[183]

The specificity of Section 108 also reassured libraries. Congress was responding to the failure of librarians and publishers to agree on photocopy standards. Congress had urged interested parties to formulate mutual guidelines, rather than to rely on statutory measures,[184] but as late as 1975 authors, publishers, and librarians met with little success in conferences sponsored by the Copyright Office and the National Commission on Libraries and Information Science.[185] In the end, Section 108 sets forth guidelines that are far more specific than the general fair use standards of Section 107. Section 108 does leave some room for interpretation, but it principally details allowable copying under given conditions. Single copies of archival materials may be made for preservation or security or for transfer to another library. Articles may be copied for patrons, and even entire works may be duplicated after a market search. The fair use statute is devoid of such details.

Section 108 may not describe every circumstance for library copying, but for the issues it does address, the provisions are immediately usable at most academic libraries with a minimum of analysis or interpretation. Parties still dispute important details, such as the nature of the copyright notice to be placed on copies and the relationship between Section 108 and fair use.[186] Nevertheless, the text of Section 108, the CONTU Guidelines, and a warning notice promulgated by the Copyright Office, taken together, form practical guidance for libraries.[187] These primary sources alone can form a useful copyright policy for libraries. Recognizing that Section 108 was innovative, Congress originally mandated a review of the law every five years. The first report, in 1983, was contentious. The second five-year report that the Copyright Office issued in 1988 noted some compliance problems, but it generally affirmed that Section 108 functions adequately and demands no major revision.[188] While Section 107 leaves users with many difficulties, Section 108 apparently has been an acceptable success from the perspective of most owners and users. Acknowledging the quieting controversies, Congress in 1992 rescinded the obligation of further five-year reports.[189]

The Fountainhead of University Policies: Litigation from NYU to Kinko's Copies

The NYU settlement overlooks the historic flexibility of copyright and fair use. The balancing of copyright owners' and users' interests contained in the copyright clause of the Constitution that is developed in the common law doctrine of fair use and codified in the Act's section 107 is not found in the terms of the NYU settlement.

Eric D. Brandfonbrener, attorney (1990)[1]

The settlement was an attempt to establish a mechanism that would be fair to the creators and owners of copyrighted works and also to the users of those works. It both acknowledged the right of copyright owners to determine the use of their works and provided certain exceptions for users under the doctrine of fair use.

Sheldon Elliot Steinbach, American Council on Education (1988)[2]

The legislative history of the 1976 Copyright Act reveals a sympathetic Congress that responded to the concerns of researchers, educators, and librarians. Congress also reiterated at every opportunity that it did not intend to change existing law, but in truth the 1976 act affirmed user rights that previously had been uncertain at best. Moreover, Congress added language to Sections 107 and 108 at the behest of educators and librarians over resounding distress from publishers and authors about their ability to survive. After 1976, however, Congress had completed its basic duty, and the meaning of copyright statutes was placed in the hands of courts and private parties. The 1976 act went into effect on 1 January 1978, and since that time many privileges that educators and librarians apparently won in Congress have been nearly lost. Universities have failed to adequately assert their claims, and a few isolated cases have garnered national reactions, usually with adverse results.

President Ford and J. D. Salinger

Few judicial opinions directly address educational needs. Controversies worthy of litigation almost exclusively have involved commercial uses of copyrighted works. Commercial violators are logical targets for lawsuits; they seek profits and compete directly for the monetary value of copyrighted works. These defendants may also lack public sympathy and may be able to pay actual damages. Yet many commercial disputes have produced judicial interpretations of copyright that transpose poorly to the academic context. In 1985 the U.S. Supreme Court ruled that *The Nation* magazine committed a copyright infringement when it printed substantial excerpts from President Gerald Ford's yet unpublished memoir.[3] The Court rejected the fair use defense, underscoring that the excerpts in fact prevented the sale of reprint rights to *Time* magazine. The unpermitted publication usurped the market value of the original manuscript.[4] The Supreme Court downplayed arguments that reprinting the excerpts served the public interest in receiving important news; the Court instead reaffirmed potential market effects as a leading factor in the fair use analysis.[5] The legislative history of Section 107 seemed to weigh "noncommercial purpose" as a most important factor, but the high Court reestablished the emphasis on economics.

In that same case, the Supreme Court declared a sweeping principle that would directly shape many academic uses of copyrighted works. The Court stated that the right of fair use for unpublished materials—such as Ford's manuscript—is narrower than the rights applied to published works. The Court opined that authors should determine the circumstances of first publication and that unpublished materials may include confidential information deserving additional protection.[6] The resulting sharp restriction on unpublished works has come to haunt the most fundamental needs of historians and other researchers.[7] This limitation was dramatically enforced by the Second Circuit Court of Appeals in 1987 when it ruled that a biographer could not even paraphrase unpublished letters written by reclusive author J. D. Salinger, despite open access to the letters in research archives.[8] The same court in 1989 seemed to eradicate even the last vestiges of fair use for unpublished manuscripts, but a 1991 decision allowed some rights under stringent conditions.[9] The net result of these cases has been the imposition of severe restrictions on access to personal papers, and publishers have canceled projects that utilize manuscript resources.[10]

Not all court cases have been a burden for education. In 1984 the Supreme Court extended fair use to home recordings of television broadcasts.[11] That ruling may serve individual needs, but a lower court has resolved that schools cannot record broadcasts for long-term retention.[12] Nevertheless, the 1984 decision—widely known as the "Betamax" case—shows that fair use rights can extend to the newer media of copyrighted works and can continue to allow single copies for personal or research needs. While educators may find a variety of cases influencing their activities, a well-planned strategy of legal pressure has been applied directly and cautiously on the academe itself.

The New York University Case

The most important legal action affecting fair use for education is the infringement suit brought against New York University (NYU) in 1982. Supported and organized by the Association of American Publishers (AAP), this suit charged that photocopies of book chapters, reproduced and sold for classroom use, violated copyrights held by an assortment of publishers. Defendants included the university, several individual faculty members, and an off-campus photocopy shop. This bold effort against a major university has received enormous attention, but it did not occur in isolation. Its full significance lies not only in its strictly legal implications, but also in the events leading to the case and the misunderstandings that subsequently emerged.

Long before filing the suit, publishers had approached many universities to urge adoption of the Classroom Guidelines as the official university policy.[13] Although educators were the original proponents of standard guidelines, the AAP became the main advocate of the Classroom Guidelines as the limit of fair use. The strategy was to shape the patterns of behavior that universities would follow. Some education lawyers have called these patterns a "campus common law."[14] They are the trends and customs on which parties rely when the traditional sources of law—statutes, cases, and regulations—do not fully expound on the unique circumstances of higher education. In 1980 and 1981, the AAP sponsored two lawsuits against private, off-campus photocopy shops to attack the copying they allowed as a service to nearby colleges and universities. Both lawsuits were settled when each shop agreed to follow the Classroom Guidelines.[15]

Acceptance of the guidelines by a few commercial photocopy shops was an important symbolic victory with limited practical significance. If the guidelines should prove too burdensome, most university neighborhoods offer numerous other shops that might not follow the guidelines and that would be ready to accept the university's business. Moreover, constraints on commercial shops are not necessarily a bar on copying by academic institutions themselves. According to one analysis:

> Both of these cases . . . may have unsettled some in the educational community since teachers' ability to have needed materials quickly and inexpensively copied might have been somewhat impaired by the outcomes of the litigation, but the cases should not have caused undue alarm. The defendants were, after all, commercial establishments, not nonprofit educational institutions, and so a possible court determination that fair use for classroom copying was not intended to extend as broadly for them as it would for teachers was not overly threatening to educators' interests. [16]

A piecemeal effort against all shops would likely prove time-consuming and expensive, and probably even impossible, but actions against commercial shops demonstrated that settlements on AAP terms were possible. They also advanced the Classroom Guidelines as the fair use standards that publishers would enforce and on which educators may rely as at least a "safe harbor" to avoid liabilities. Yet in cornering the shops to stay within the guidelines, the AAP had converted them from "minimum" standards to maximum limits. The original guidelines mentioned some unspecified additional copying allowable under fair use, but the settlements effectively eradicated it.

With these relatively easy successes, the publishers were ready to tackle a major university. By extending their strategy to a university directly, the plaintiffs could effectively destroy the attitude of "just going to another copy shop," and they could apply the Classroom Guidelines directly to noncommercial copying. The publishers filed their lawsuit against NYU in December 1982. The claim was settled only four months later when NYU accepted the Classroom Guidelines as the university's policy. Once again, the original clause that acknowledged some additional copying was omitted in the settlement agreement. The guidelines thus again became "maximum" standards—the upper limits of fair use for teaching and research. Faculty and staff at NYU could exceed the guidelines only with permission from copyright owners or from the university counsel. [17] No longer could faculty members simply take their copying to another shop; they were now subject to a university-wide policy enforceable directly against them. The university's disciplinary system was tacitly enlisted as an intermediary for supporting owners' rights; only by strictly adhering to the policy could faculty obtain the benefits of the university's defense and indemnification. No longer would individuals analyze fair use under unique circumstances; all interpretive authority shifted to the legal counsel. The flexibility of fair use was replaced at NYU by the rigidity of quantitative evaluations entrenched in the Classroom Guidelines.[18]

The lawsuits against the commercial shops and NYU were valuable public relations breakthroughs for the publishers. Discussions about copyright began focusing on the guidelines and on potential infringements, and the one university lawsuit ultimately influenced action at multiple institutions. Even before filing the action, press reports disclosed that the AAP was contemplating a lawsuit against a major university in the northeast.[19] That word alone probably motivated widespread reassessments of photocopy standards and chilled many activities. The chair of the AAP's copyright committee said that the case would show the need for colleges and universities to adopt copyright policies, and indeed the settlement compelled a full reevaluation of university practices nationwide.[20] Press reports expounded on NYU's predicament, and the AAP immediately notified hundreds of colleges and universities to recommended adoption of the guidelines in order to avoid incurring NYU's legal fate.[21]

To borrow from the general principles discussed in chapter one, the external forces of copyright infringement threats overwhelmed NYU's internal obligations to best promote teaching and research. The opportunities of fair use were sacrificed to the strictures of litigation and the fear it exudes. The AAP copyright chair summarized that the overall litigation strategy should "frighten people on and near campuses into understanding that publishers will defend their rights."[22] Through carefully targeted lawsuits, favorable settlements, and effective public relations, the AAP had begun transforming the guidelines into standard interpretations of Section 107 for all educational copying. Even at universities where no legal action was taken or threatened, versions of the Classroom Guidelines became local copyright policies.[23] In order to avoid possible lawsuits, these universities were deferring to external pressures for a definition of "fair use."

The Wisconsin Reaction

One university that refused to be passive about copyright standards was the University of Wisconsin, and its early resistance would prove influential at a few other universities. John C. Stedman was a copyright expert on the Wisconsin law school faculty. Born in 1904, he joined the Wisconsin faculty in 1934.[24] The university was closely associated with copyright reform through its local member of Congress, Representative Robert W. Kastenmeier, who chaired the House committee responsible for copyright matters.[25] Stedman himself served from 1955 to 1960 as associate counsel to the Senate subcommittee that oversaw copyright developments.[26] Beginning in 1967 he chaired the copyright committee of the American Association of University Professors. In that capacity he testified before the Senate subcommittee that a fair use statute should be flexible for future needs and technological developments. He also spoke eloquently on the need for special treatment of educational uses: when the law limits uses or raises costs, the public suffers; when a school chooses not to make the use at all, the copyright owner suffers.[27]

As the fair use provision approached its final form, Stedman urged its passage and recommended that Congress clarify a broad application of fair use for educators. Silence from Congress could lead to narrow privileges, and higher education depends on limited uses of copyrighted works:

> In seeking to assure the application of traditional fair use doctrine through express statutory recognition coupled with supportive legislative history, we are moved by the essential importance of the availability of copyrighted materials in teaching and research. First and most basic is the fact that the higher education community, college and university administrators and their faculties, are primarily the institutions in which the ultimate task of transmitting and advancing knowledge is reposed.[28]

In general, though, Stedman agreed with some emerging principles of educational fair use: multiple copies should be at the teacher's own volition, spontaneous, and for temporary use. He also accepted the premise that the "compilation of anthologies would be outside the ambit of fair use."[29]

Stedman's cooperative spirit seemed to wane after 1976. He accepted the fair use statute, but he led attacks against the Classroom Guidelines.[30] Opposition from the American Association of University Professors and the Association of American Law Schools appeared in the House report,[31] and Stedman worked with his home institution—the University of Wisconsin—to avoid the guidelines, which he saw as too restrictive and as representing only the publishers' views.[32] In 1976 and 1977 Stedman's law school colleague, Stuart G. Gullickson, was serving as the Special Assistant to the Chancellor with responsibility for legal matters. The unique views of Stedman, Gullickson, and Chancellor Edwin Young converged to form a proactive voice on copyright.[33]

Gullickson taught civil procedure and litigation classes at the law school.[34] He knew the risks of litigation and its possible consequences for the university. To Gullickson, those risks were either small or worth incurring. From his administrative post, he perceived that the institution had conflicting interests: avoiding liability and serving academic needs. In interpreting copyright law, his priority was clear: to serve the academic interests of the university community. Chancellor Young was willing to take risks to support the university's teaching and research mission. He was willing to adopt innovative copyright interpretations, and he refused to let adverse economics or public relations overshadow accomplishment of the university's fundamental purpose. The actual risk of a lawsuit appeared slight, and Gullickson and Young were willing to defend their interpretations against legal challenges.[35]

Gullickson did his own research on copyright, and he drafted a policy on photocopying for teaching and research. He firmly believed that the policy followed the law and that he needed to assert the university's academic interests. He also believed that his interpretations were essentially balanced: the university and its faculty were themselves copyright owners, and he did not want to undermine their rights. Stedman supported the policy with his copyright expertise, and another assistant to the Chancellor—Arthur Hove—used his close ties to the faculty to evaluate the policy's likely effects on their needs and habits. These officials made suggestions and revised portions of the draft. Gullickson returned to his law school position at the end of 1977, and with the chancellor's approval he completed and issued the university's copyright policy in February 1978.[36]

The Wisconsin policy is similar to the Classroom Guidelines in allowing single copies of articles and other short works for research and teaching, but the policy makes two significant breaks from the guidelines. First, it describes unrestricted copying. Users may freely copy materials that were never copyrighted or that have expired copyrights.[37] In particular, publications of the U.S. government are generally without copyright protection.[38] The Wisconsin policy advises the community that these materials could generally be duplicated without permission and without limit. The Classroom Guidelines never mention them. Second, the Wisconsin policy abandons the detailed quantitative standards on multiple copies for classroom uses. The Wisconsin policy applies more general standards, allowing multiple copies for classroom distribution so long as the quantity is "selective and sparing." Faculty still have to follow a few procedures, such as placing a notice on copies and avoiding repetitive uses, but the specific need to count words, pages, and authors is eliminated. Gullickson supplemented these copyright standards with some practical and informative guidance on requesting permissions from copyright owners and on penalties for infringements.[39]

The American Library Association Model Policy

The Wisconsin policy remained generally of local interest until Nancy Marshall shared it with the American Library Association (ALA).[40] Marshall was a high-ranking librarian at the University of Wisconsin who participated in developing the local policy. One of Marshall's early duties had been as director of the Wisconsin Interlibrary Loan Service, where she expressed concern about copyright as a restraint on sharing photocopies of journal articles.[41] From 1978 to 1984 she chaired the ALA's Ad Hoc Copyright Subcommittee, and she advocated the full exercise of fair use. She argued against "minimum" standards and refuted the publishers' argument that all copying is barred unless specifically allowed. Marshall believed instead that all uses are allowed unless specifically prohibited.[42] Either one of these "all-or-nothing" positions is probably inappropriate under a fair use statute that specifies virtually nothing, but as publishers began asserting their claims in court, academic institutions were assuming a firmer stance. Even Stedman's views became more extreme. In a 1982 letter to the Copyright Office he concluded that copyright interpretations based on the rights of proprietors are irrelevant; creators have only those rights that Congress chooses to give them. According to Stedman, American law "supports the right of everyone to use the published writings of others to one's own benefit except to the extent that Congress has decreed otherwise. . . . "[43]

Marshall endorsed the Wisconsin policy and added a few introductory paragraphs; it then moved through the committee structure of the ALA. It was modified and expanded, and a section on reserve room copying was added, but the underlying standards for teaching, research, and classroom photocopying remained intact. The policy also retained its innovative components that would be helpful to educators: explanations of unrestricted copying, instructions on writing for permissions, and a summary of legal penalties. After a final review by Mary Hutchings Reed, then legal counsel for ALA at a Chicago law firm, a revision of the Wisconsin policy became the ALA's "Model Policy Concerning College and University Photocopying for Classroom, Research and Library Reserve Use" in early 1982.[44]

The ALA Model Policy was widely distributed while the lawsuit against New York University was pending, and while apprehensions about copyright were elevating. As the Classroom Guidelines received new publicity in the wake of the NYU settlement, various organizations noted the ALA and Wisconsin policies as possible alternatives. A 1983 newsletter from the National Association of College and University Business Officers reprinted the Wisconsin and ALA policies, emphasizing that policymakers have alternatives to the Classroom Guidelines.[45] A 1984 publication from the Association of Research Libraries recommended the ALA Model Policy,[46] and the American Association of Law Libraries eventually disseminated it to members in 1988.[47] A clearinghouse of sample policies retained by the National Association of College and University Attorneys shared the Wisconsin policy on request.[48] Nevertheless, this dissemination was modest compared to the tremendous attention given to the Classroom Guidelines in 1976 and after the NYU case, but at least many university officials had a chance to discover that they had a choice. Indeed, since 1983, the legal counsel at the University of Wisconsin has received numerous requests from other universities and colleges for permission to adopt the Wisconsin policy. Permission was always granted.[49]

Comparing the Two Model Policies

These two "model policies" on photocopying for educational purposes— one advanced by the AAP and the other from Wisconsin and the ALA— are the most significant copyright policies publicized for adoption at other universities. They represent two different interpretations of fair use, and their backgrounds reflect the two competing objectives in the formulation of copyright policies. The Classroom Guidelines are a "safe harbor" purportedly for avoiding liability, even though not every publisher or copyright owner may subscribe to the standards. The ALA Model Policy— which is substantively similar to, but more elaborate than, the Wisconsin policy—has the express purpose of interpreting the law to serve the university's academic mission. Although the Copyright Office has endorsed the Classroom Guidelines,[50] the Register of Copyrights made this surprising remark to the American Association of Law Libraries about the guidelines in 1977:

> I am going to say something now that I may regret. It does seem to me that this [the Classroom Guidelines] was written with elementary, secondary situations in mind. I am not suggesting that you can go very far beyond this in the law school situation, but it does seem to me that although these guidelines were endorsed by Congress in the Conference Report, that there is a realistic borderline beyond these guidelines that in a law school situation you could probably apply. I am saying that you do not need to regard these as the law of the Medes and the Persians, that in fact, you can go beyond this within a certain realistic area, but you are going to get to a point where you have to say "no."[51]

The Classroom Guidelines and the ALA Model Policy differ fundamentally from one another in four crucial respects. They first differ in their scope of coverage. Both policies address only photocopying of print materials primarily for teaching and research, but the ALA policy includes provisions on reserve room copies.[52] Although reserve operations are routinely housed in libraries, many commentators believe that they are extensions of classroom teaching and that fair use and implicitly the Classroom Guidelines are applicable there as well.[53]

The second difference is the ALA's additional discussion of unrestricted copying, requests for permissions, and legal liabilities. The section on

unrestricted copying underscores an important but subtle difference between the policies. The ALA policy directs users to many lawful uses of
information resources. It is a positive gesture that identifies rights belonging to the public. The ALA policy also explains the theory and source of
fair use and the need for such a policy. The Classroom Guidelines, by
contrast, take a negative approach. They describe only one confining
sphere of copying that may be safe from lawsuits. The guidelines never
mention other unequivocal rights secured by law; their purpose is clearly
not to provide full help to users.

The third difference is the Classroom Guidelines' statement of "minimum" standards and their effective conversion to "maximum" standards in
the NYU case. The ALA policy counters this trend by listing examples of
copying that are outside the guidelines but that could be regarded as fair
use. The ALA policy attempts to identify some additional fair use privileges that the Classroom Guidelines avoid. The ALA policy comments on
the Classroom Guidelines:

> These minimum standards normally would not be realistic in the University
> setting. Faculty members needing to exceed these limits for college educa-
> tion should not feel hampered by these guidelines, although they should
> attempt a "selective and sparing" use of photocopied, copyrighted mate-
> rial.[54]

The fourth difference is the ALA's break from a highly quantitative fair
use analysis. Both policies permit faculty to copy limited portions of publications for research or for preparing class lessons. Faculty may also distribute copies to students in a course, subject to limitations on frequency,
spontaneity, and the amount of copying. The ALA policy acknowledges
the quantitative standards in the Classroom Guidelines, but it also emphasizes that they are "the most conservative guidelines."[55] The ALA standards instead make clear that full articles may be copied, without necessarily counting words and authors.

The most critical difference between the Classroom Guidelines and the
ALA Model Policy is the breadth of user rights discerned under fair use.
The ALA policy—and its Wisconsin source—allow copying that the
Classroom Guidelines alone would preclude. Most significantly, ALA allows multiple copies of entire journal articles for classroom distribution
and reserve rooms, while the Classroom Guidelines at most confine multiple copies to excerpts. The ALA policy also removes limits on the frequency of copying from individual authors and the elaborate tests of "brevity" and "spontaneity." The omission of such technical measures of fair use
have been the leading argument of publishers against the ALA Model Policy.[56] These differences affirm that universities have two fundamentally

different model policies available for possible adoption. Relative to one another, the ALA policy is a lenient interpretation, while the guidelines are by contrast strict.

Kinko's and the Failure of Model Policies

One characteristic that the Classroom Guidelines and the ALA Model Policy share is their desperate need for a fresh evaluation and revision. The 1991 decision in *Basic Books, Inc. v. Kinko's Graphics Corporation*, in particular, tacitly calls both model policies into question. The Federal District Court ruled that photocopies of book chapters, compiled into anthologies for classroom use, were infringements.[57] The court scrutinized each excerpted item individually, applied the fair use factors, and specifically refused to prohibit all "anthologies" of copied materials.[58] To that extent, the *Kinko's* decision is neither surprising nor unduly complex. The court used the statutory factors and easily found nearly every argument militating against fair use in the for-profit context. The only support for Kinko's is a seemingly token conclusion that copying from "factual works" is more permissible than copying from fiction; most of the copied materials were from nonfiction textbooks.[59] Judge Motley's fair use analysis is otherwise a rousing condemnation of the policies and procedures at Kinko's.

The opinion assails the claim that the photocopies were for nonprofit educational purposes: "The use of the Kinko's packets, in the hands of the students, was no doubt educational. However, the use in the hands of Kinko's employees is commercial."[60] The central issue, therefore, was Kinko's purpose for making the copies. The inescapable conclusion was that its purpose was to profit. The amount of copying also overwhelmed the court, with the opinion underscoring that the copies amounted to five to twenty-five percent of each book, and that the copying of entire book chapters amounted to "a complete representation of the concept explored in the chapter." The opinion almost summarily concludes that this substantial copying has a strong effect on the publisher's potential sales of the books and receipt of photocopy permission fees: "While it is possible that reading the packets whets the appetite of students for more information from the authors, it is more likely that purchase of the packets obviates purchase of the full texts."[61]

Despite the court's fair use analysis, many readers of the *Kinko's* decision will conclude simplistically that all "anthologies" now violate federal copyright law.[62] Judge Motley unequivocally assured, however, that anthologies of photocopies are not themselves unlawful. She specifically rejected pleas from the publishers for such a ruling. Indeed, the decision is unquestionably directed primarily against Kinko's and its profit motive within the framework of fair use. As a for-profit shop, the Classroom Guidelines, as a measure of fair use, technically did not apply to Kinko's; they were developed and approved only for nonprofit educational institutions. Although the court stated clearly that the guidelines were not law and were applicable to educational institutions, the judge nevertheless found their use in this case "compelling."[63] Turning to their elaborate limits on words and circumstances for lawful copying, the court again had little trouble finding no fair use.

Kinko's was only the second judicial decision to utilize the Classroom Guidelines.[64] Eight years earlier, in *Marcus v. Rowley,* the Ninth Circuit Court of Appeals ruled that a teacher exceeded fair use when she copied portions of a booklet on cake decorating into her classroom materials.[65] The plaintiff had written a thirty-five-page booklet that she sold at a profit to students in her adult-education courses. The defendant taught other decorating classes and assembled a twenty-four-page manual; eleven of those pages, however, were copied directly from the plaintiff's work. The defendant made no profit on her manual, but she also gave the plaintiff no acknowledgment and never sought permission for the copying.[66]

Although the infringement occurred before the 1976 act took effect, the court applied the four factors now in Section 107 to conclude that they "weigh decisively" against fair use.[67] The court then turned to the Classroom Guidelines, noting carefully that they were not controlling, but that they were instructive. The court specifically declined to adopt the guidelines as "law." It ruled nonetheless that the defendant's practices were not fair use by that measure as well.[68] The narrow and unusual facts of the *Marcus* case prevented it from gaining the widespread attention and provoking the immediate response comparable to *Kinko's,* but the case gave the guidelines their first judicial credibility.

The problem with both the *Kinko's* and the *Marcus* cases is that the readers' attention focuses on the Classroom Guidelines and overlooks the more careful fair use analysis actually employed. The simple presence of the guidelines in each case tends to equate them with legal standards; if they are used in court they invariably gain the appearance of law. Yet the *Kinko's* case in particular, while seemingly endorsing the guidelines, is actually demanding their reconsideration. Judge Motley couches her decision in cautious language, but her decision suggests that the Classroom Guidelines can apply universally to classroom copying—whether in the nonprofit or profit sectors—and that exceeding their limits creates a presumption of no fair use. For the wary and untrained policymakers at many universities, those suggestions will no doubt distract from any other comprehension of fair use.

The *Kinko's* decision also distorts the Classroom Guidelines by simultaneously using them and eviscerating them. The court found them "compelling," but it rejected their blanket prohibition against all anthologies—a provision that was in the guidelines from their inception and that had been advocated vociferously by the publishers. The court gave the guidelines credibility, but it showed that they deserve close scrutiny, and that not all of their terms will survive a true fair use test. But amidst the rampant fears of litigation that the decision has produced, superficial readings of Kinko's will no doubt focus on the Classroom Guidelines in toto and will infer a rigid rule against photocopied anthologies. A closer examination of the case instead demands a new critical questioning of all details in the Classroom Guidelines.[69]

The Kinko's decision also draws the ALA Model Policy into question. The case never addresses that policy, but the court obviously would curtail multiple copies more rigorously than the ALA's standard of "selective and sparing" copying. That vague measure is no longer an adequate response to the legal principles established in Kinko's. Even a nonprofit educational institution can easily divine from the ruling that some photocopying—especially anthologies of book chapters—must be judged by tighter standards. Nevertheless, as this study will show, almost all university copyright policies are based on these two model policies.[70] They are therefore the key to understanding fair use at universities. Given their substantive differences, the selection of one of these model policies can reveal how the policymaker understands the nature of fair use and perceives the institution's objectives in responding to the copyright system.

Amidst this confusion, the Kinko's decision will spur a reevaluation of fair use and initiate development of new copyright policies at colleges and universities across the country. The Classroom Guidelines will receive renewed attention, and the misperception that they are law will no doubt grow. Universities have been in this position before. In many respects it is a repeat of events leading to and stemming from the NYU case. The next four chapters of this book will analyze copyright policies actually in force at major research universities. That analysis will show not only the influence of the Classroom Guidelines, but also the paramount effects of a single legal action—the lawsuit against New York University—on copyright policy-making at universities throughout the nation. In the wake of the more recent Kinko's decision, the lessons of the recent past offer badly needed insights on the law, on university decision making, and on the influence of environmental forces shaping the academe's perception of its own fair use privileges.

④ University Policies in Force: Motivations and Responsibilities

By and large information processing in higher education is improvised, not planned.
Organizational Communication and Higher Education (1981)[1]

Our policy should ensure compliance with the law without, we hope, disruption to effective teaching and research at the University.
Copyright policy, University of Pittsburgh (1978)[2]

University copyright policies may ideally balance competing interests, but their actual accomplishment of that objective never has been tested. This study accordingly probes the nature of university decision making by analyzing policies from surveys of ninety-eight research universities throughout the United States (see table 4.1).[3] Those policies—and sometimes the absence of policies—reveal the official responses to copyright concerns. The analysis will demonstrate whether university policymakers respond to internal or external forces, and whether they are able to find a balance between these sometimes conflicting obligations. The universities within this study were selected by their participation in one or both of two major research university associations: the Association of American Universities (AAU) and the Association of Research Libraries (ARL). The surveys specifically sought copies of the policies in use; thus, this study focuses on written standards. It does not systematically explore personal attitudes and undocumented responses, although interviews sometimes elucidated those less-formal positions, and they were insightful to show how a formal policy may emerge and affect the academic community.

Identifying "Research Universities"

Both AAU and ARL are dedicated to serving the needs of research universities. To accomplish its purposes, the AAU "serves its member institutions through activities designed to encourage timely consideration of major issues affecting the quality of academic research and graduate and professional education and to enable member institutions to communicate more effectively with the federal government."[4] Originally founded in 1900 with fourteen members—constituting all American universities then offering the Ph.D. degree—the AAU today has fifty-four member universities in the United States.[5] All but five of them also belong to ARL. The ARL mission is more specific, but also sweeping: "to strengthen and extend the capacities of its member libraries to provide access to recorded knowledge and to foster an environment where learning flourishes, to make scholarly communication more effective, and to influence policies affecting the flow of information."[6] ARL was founded in 1932, and as of the surveying for this study it had 117 members, ninety-three of which were libraries at United States universities.[7]

The broad purpose of AAU encompasses nearly every university concern, including copyright, while the ARL statement focuses on the education, communication, and information problems that copyright especially affects. ARL defines member "university libraries" as "those whose parent institutions broadly emphasize research and graduate instruction at the doctoral level and grant their own degrees, which support large, comprehensive research collections on a permanent basis, and which give evidence of an institutional capacity for and commitment to the advancement and transmittal of knowledge." More specifically, the university must offer the Ph.D. degree in a minimum number of disciplines, which in the 1984–85 academic year was thirty-one different fields. Other membership criteria are based on library collection and staff size, expenditures, and rate of new acquisitions. Even many of these quantifiable standards are inexact, with the emphasis apparently placed on how well the university and its library share the research and information ideals of current ARL members.[8]

Definitions of "research university" may vary, but selecting these ninety-eight universities by virtue of their participation in either or both of ARL and AAU assumes that members of these organizations are leaders

Table 4.1

American Research Universities

University of Alabama	Georgia Institute of Technology
University of Arizona	Harvard University
Arizona State University	University of Hawaii
Boston University	University of Houston
Brandeis University	Howard University
Brigham Young University	University of Illinois
Brown University	Indiana University
University of California, Berkeley	University of Iowa
University of California, Davis	Iowa State University
University of California, Irvine	Johns Hopkins University
University of California, Los Angeles	University of Kansas
University of California, Riverside	Kent State University
University of California, San Diego	University of Kentucky
University of California, Santa Barbara	Louisiana State University
California Institute of Technology	University of Maryland
Carnegie Mellon University	University of Massachusetts
Case Western Reserve University	Massachusetts Institute of Technology
Catholic University	University of Miami
University of Chicago	University of Michigan
University of Cincinnati	Michigan State University
Clark University	University of Minnesota
University of Colorado	University of Missouri
Colorado State University	University of Nebraska
Columbia University	University of New Mexico
University of Connecticut	New York University
Cornell University	State University of New York at Albany
Dartmouth College	State University of New York at Buffalo
University of Delaware	State University of New York at Stony Brook
Duke University	University of North Carolina
Emory University	North Carolina State University
University of Florida	Northwestern University
Florida State University	University of Notre Dame
Georgetown University	Ohio State University
University of Georgia	University of Oklahoma

Table 4.1

(*continued*)

Oklahoma State University	Temple University
University of Oregon	University of Tennessee
University of Pennsylvania	University of Texas
Pennsylvania State University	Texas A&M University
University of Pittsburgh	Tulane University
Princeton University	University of Utah
Purdue University	Vanderbilt University
Rice University	University of Virginia
University of Rochester	Virginia Polytechnic Institute
Rutgers University	University of Washington
University of South Carolina	Washington State University
University of Southern California	Washington University
Southern Illinois University	Wayne State University
Stanford University	University of Wisconsin
Syracuse University	Yale University

in refining and improving academic activities. Moreover, participation in ARL assures that the university has a relatively large and professionally active library. Libraries are the information centers of research universities, and this study will confirm that librarians frequently are responsible for developing and applying copyright policies, not only for their library administrative needs, but for more general teaching and research needs as well.

Obtaining the Policies

Contacts with university officials to obtain their policies and additional information extended over a period of more than two years in the late 1980s. The policies and attitudes manifested here therefore reflect the state of copyright law in the several years following the controversial lawsuit against New York University, but before the legal action against Kinko's Graphics Corporation. The timing of this study is fortuitous in many respects. Ample time had passed for the NYU case to have its effects. The policies here were also written before the *Kinko's* case arose, so that lawsuit had not yet had the slightest consequences. Therefore, this study is able to focus on NYU as a possible predictor of post-*Kinko's* developments, and the insights here can help guide future policymakers in their response to events such as *Kinko's* and the inevitable future legal actions affecting higher education. Moreover, the survey is untainted by the trepidation that *Kinko's* has compelled. A survey today would likely be afflicted with a veil of confidentiality and might encounter widespread retraction and reevaluation of current policies. Other, more recent survey attempts have stirred suspicions about the ultimate uses of the data.

A series of surveys, follow-up letters, and telephone interviews for this study (as detailed in Appendix C) reached at least one official from each university. Only sixteen institutions indicated that they had no written copyright policy.[9] Officials at a few of those universities sometimes alluded to familiar standards, such as the CONTU Guidelines or the ALA Model Policy, but they offered no written evidence of a copyright standard. The remaining eighty-two universities submitted a total of 183 distinct copyright policy documents.[10] Many universities obviously have more than one "policy," and their documents vary greatly in scope and diversity. They address an enormous range of issues, from photocopying to software duplication and from off-air video recording to displays and performances of dramatic works.

The policies also vary greatly in form, sometimes manifested as formal policy measures, informal memoranda, letters, or procedural instructions relevant to copyright matters. "Policies" for this study also include "recommended guidelines" and not merely enforceable mandates. Whatever the character of the policy, each of these statements embodies the university's position on at least some copyright issues.[11] Each statement is the product of someone's awareness of issues, perspective on copyright interpretations, and perceived need to issue the given statement for other members of the university community to follow.

A lack of thorough planning and coordination in policy-making revealed itself from the earliest inquiries. The original request for policies went to both the legal counsel and the library director at each university. Multiple respondents at one campus often submitted contradictory and conflicting documents as their university's "copyright policy." For example, a policy issued at the University of California, Davis, in June 1986 allows multiple copies of full articles for classroom distribution, but another policy adopted a few months earlier established tighter limits. Developers of the June policy were at that time not aware of the earlier policy; they now dismiss the differences as insignificant.[12] Both policies remain officially in effect. The conflicts are sometimes even more blatant. One respondent from Indiana University said that the university had no formal policy, while another respondent submitted an elaborate manual on several copyright matters.[13] Multiple responses from any one university were rarely identical; each official was aware of different policies, revealing that copyright responsibilities are diffused and poorly coordinated across campuses. Rarely did one officer oversee all copyright concerns, and even "Directors of Patents, Trademarks, and Copyrights" apparently were unaware of policies employed by legal counsel and librarians elsewhere on campus.

Despite the often piecemeal approach to copyright policy development, the 183 policies reveal some clear patterns in their content, their scope of application within the university, their developers, and their dates of issuance. The emergence of these basic patterns discloses much about the influence of environmental forces on university governance and the relationship of copyright policies to the academic mission.

Scope of Issues in Copyright Policies

Just as policies exist in many forms, so do they address many different issues. Photocopying for personal research, classroom needs, and reserve rooms are the most common copyright problems that policies encompass (see table 4.2). Also frequent among the policies are provisions on copying for various library needs and for interlibrary lending of photocopied articles. Less prevalent are policies for software, videotapes, and music. Each of these issues will be defined and explored in subsequent chapters of this book.

Certain policy issues appear with comparable frequencies. Research, classroom, and reserve copying policies appear at approximately the same number of universities. Indeed, nearly three-fourths of the universities with a policy on any one of these three issues also address the other two. Similarly, policies on library copying and interlibrary lending occur with nearly identical frequency, and nearly eighty-five percent of the universities that address either of these issues also address the other. By contrast, policies on videotapes, music, and software were submitted from nearly the exact number of institutions, but seldom does any one university address any combination of these concerns.

The joint appearance of research, classroom, and reserve issues is not surprising; all three are primarily concerned with the common activity of photocopying from printed works. The closer examination of these issues in subsequent chapters will link these concerns for a host of other reasons, notably their joint appearance in model policies. The close correlation between library copying and interlibrary lending issues is also not astonishing; here, too, the issue is typically photocopying, and these issues appear together in the 1976 Copyright Act. They are also recurring copyright problems for every library. On the other hand, the lack of correlation

Table 4.2

Frequency of Issues Addressed in University Copyright Policies

Issue	No. of Policies	No. of Universities
Classroom Photocopying	73	61
Research Photocopying	67	57
Reserve Room Uses	81	61
Library Copying	57	44
Interlibrary Lending	54	43
Music	34	28
Videotapes	32	28
Software	29	27

among videotape, music, and software policies is not surprising; the copyright activities are not functionally the same, and they do not necessarily occur together. Off-air videorecording, reproducing music, and duplicating software disks are physically not the same processes. They are not likely to occur at the same location or to be conducted by the same individuals. The legal considerations are also disparate; limits on software duplication offer relatively little guidance for music duplication. The relatively low occurrences of these policies also suggest that the issues may arise infrequently, or may be poorly identified or defined, or may simply not be a crucial problem for universities.

The near dearth of comprehensive policies—covering most or all possible issues—suggests a variety of situations. New demands, new legal developments, and new technologies give rise to copyright problems on an uneven and unpredictable timetable. Different units of the university may also need only a specialized policy; few constituents may require a comprehensive approach. The resulting array of policies, however, ultimately demonstrates the lack of coordinated position within the university. The remainder of this chapter will categorically show that policy-making is spread among diverse groups and is seldom overseen with uniformity by central officials.

Scope of a Policy's Application within the University

A copyright policy may apply to the entire university, or it may be a directive for only one department or other campus agency. Because this study centers on policies obtained primarily from university counsel offices and library directors, nearly all of the 183 policies apply either throughout the university or throughout the library system. Legal counsel reasonably concentrate on university-wide matters, and librarians are generally responsible only for policies with immediate significance to themselves. The full set of policies divides almost exactly evenly between applying to the entire university and applying only to the libraries.[14]

That split evidences the perception of copyright both as a university institutional issue and as an information management tool. A copyright policy functions as guidance and support, as a means for avoiding infringements, and as a standard for utilizing the information resources housed in university libraries. When a policy encompasses different types of "library copying," it sets standards on the utilization of the vast resources contained in libraries. The prevalence of library policies also underscores the awareness and sensitivity that librarians have about copyright. The important and close link between librarians and copyright will be reaffirmed in many ways throughout this book.

Identity of Principal Policymakers

Responsibility for formulating copyright policies is scattered across the university community, with most policies developed by administrators, legal counsel, and librarians. Faculty members may serve on committees overseeing copyright matters, but they have had a surprisingly small role in the policy-making process. Several policies were adopted by a Faculty Senate, such as at Tulane University, but Tulane's legal counsel originally formulated and proposed the terms.[15] Occasionally an identified professor with copyright expertise assumes a leading role in drafting the policy or in responding to questions that may arise in understanding or applying a policy. Of the 183 policies, librarians were identified as the principal developers of eighty-nine (or 48.6%) of them; administrators developed forty-nine policies (or 26.8%); legal counsel formulated twenty-nine (or 15.8%) of them; and faculty had a primary role in developing only six policies (or 3.3%). The developers of ten policies (or 5.5%) were unidentified.

The lack of faculty leadership in formulating university copyright policies suggests an institutional view of copyright as a managerial matter, rather than an academic concern. In the history of university management, central administrators have assumed primary responsibility for policies with management objectives, particularly policies affecting external affairs. If general expectations about universities hold true, the high level of copyright responsibility among administrators and legal counsel would suggest that copyright policies are viewed as management tools, serving objectives arising outside the university. The driving force behind copyright standards may therefore be primarily the legal rights of copyright owners and concerns about institutional liability. Another common generalization is that faculty control academic policies. The paucity of faculty involvement in copyright matters therefore suggests that the relationship between copyright and academic objectives is overshadowed by other issues or is simply overlooked in the policy-making process.

The identification of policy developers also bears an important relationship to the policy's scope of application. The most significant revelation is the role of librarians. They have virtually no leading role in developing university-wide policies, but they have almost exclusive domain over library policies (see table 4.3). University copyright policies comprise virtually two independent worlds: librarians are responsible for library policies, and administrators and legal counsel handle campuswide standards. Additional university constituents often participate in developing many policies; some officials were consulted for their expertise, or they served on committees overseeing and shaping the policy. Yet reaffirming the isolation of librarians on university copyright matters, they are identified among these "secondary" participants at only seven universities where other constituents led the policy effort.

While librarians seldom participate in making nonlibrary policies, they frequently depend on other university officials in setting library-related standards. First, legal counsel reviewed, approved, or contributed to more than one-fourth of the copyright policies developed by librarians. Second, many university-wide policies include provisions directly—and sometimes exclusively—pertinent to library activities. Thus, central administrators are developing policies with obvious consequences for libraries and are probably preempting the opportunity for librarians to establish their own directives.

Nevertheless, a paramount role for central officials is appropriate. Central oversight can facilitate greater coordination, and it can nurture the diverse concerns within the institution. For example, policies applicable to libraries are not merely procedural concerns for one segment of the university. They affect the availability and utility of information resources for most of the community. Librarians may well be masters of their own fate on stating copyright positions, but their policies are clearly intertwined with the university's broader academic mission. Each policy also has obvious legal implications, so the involvement of legal counsel is especially appropriate. The participation of legal counsel, however, suggests that the policies may gravitate toward avoiding liability. This study will test that expectation and will reveal a surprising tendency, especially among university legal counsel.

Table 4.3

Principal Policy Developers and Scope of Application

Scope	Administrators	Counsel	Librarians	Faculty
University-wide	47	27	4	5
Library only	0	2	82	1
Total:	47	29	86	6

Dates of Policy Development

Passage of the 1976 act, with its new provisions on fair use and library copying, offered immediate awareness that copyright law governed university pursuits, and it raised the specter of potential liability. Faculty, staff, and other members of the university community needed to know about the new law and how to avoid its pitfalls. Thus, university copyright policies became a means for sharing information and for recommending appropriate behavior in response to the new law.[16] The law became effective on 1 January 1978, and that year the number of new copyright policies immediately peaked, with thirty policies issued at twenty-six universities. Policy development slowed during the next four years and then surged again in 1983, when New York University settled its infringement lawsuit with considerable publicity. In 1983 alone, twenty-three universities issued twenty-eight policies. Policy development remained active in subsequent years, but has gradually declined (see table 4.4).

The effect of the NYU case is not merely an inference; eleven policies expressly refer to it or allude to "recent litigation" in 1983.[17] These policies split nearly evenly between accepting or rejecting the terms of the NYU settlement, but the lawsuit nevertheless motivated creation of the policies or at least shaped some of their terms. In addition, interviews with officials at the University of Massachusetts and at the University of California revealed that their policies—both issued in 1986—were also responsive to the NYU case.[18] Most reactions to NYU came in its immediate aftermath, but NYU's effects clearly lingered for years.

Another apparent consequence of the NYU case is a shifting of responsibility for policy development. The terms of the NYU settlement underscored liabilities and established for NYU's legal counsel a direct role in interpreting and applying fair use standards. Librarians led in policymaking before 1983, and they continue as key players, but legal counsel and administrators have assumed an increasing role in the wake of NYU. Once again, the external legal implications have taken hold of the copyright question (see table 4.5).

Table 4.4
Number of Policies Issued and Number of Issuing Universities in Year Groups,
1977–89

	No. of Policies	No. of Universities
1977–79	47	34
1980–82	18	14
1983–85	63	47
1986–89	51	41
Total:	179	—

Stated Purposes of the Policies

While university copyright policies actually serve a dichotomy of conflicting purposes, the policies themselves often state a single purpose. Interviews with university officials disclosed further understandings of policy
purposes. Avoiding infringements and utilizing resources are mentioned
from time to time, but most policies purport to encourage "compliance"
with the law or simply to "inform" users about the law. These claimed
"purposes" reveal how university officials articulate the role of their own
standards.

A typical statement of anti-infringement purpose comes from the University of Miami: "To inform the University community of possible liabilities resulting from infringement upon the Federal Copyright laws."[19] The
policy ostensibly "informs," but it informs users about infringements. Not
all policies are even that direct. A Cornell policy alludes to educational
needs, but it ultimately emphasizes liability risks: "To achieve for faculty
members greater certainty of procedure, to reduce risks of infringement or
allegations thereof, and to maintain a desirable flexibility to accommodate
specific needs. . . . "[20] Perhaps the most extreme anti-infringement standard is the Brown University software policy. It has no express purpose
statement, but the entire one-page policy is little more than a litany of civil
and criminal penalties for copyright infringements. The policy offers virtually no guidance, only threats of fines and imprisonment.[21]

A benign "compliance" with the law is the most common stated purpose. A Boston University policy is typical: "The University's copyright
policy may be succinctly summarized as compliance with the copyright
law."[22] "Complying" with the law may imply the need to avoid infringements, but it is by itself noncommittal or neutral as long as the law is open
to interpretation. If pressed, every university official would probably claim

Table 4.5

Principal Policy Developers in Year Groups, 1977–89

	Administrators	Counsel	Librarians	Faculty
1977–79	9	2	35	0
1980–82	1	6	10	0
1983–85	18	13	25	3
1986–89	21	8	16	3
Total:	49	29	86	6

to "comply" with the law, and indeed they should. Several other policies similarly carry a neutral tone and purport to "inform" the community of rights and limits under copyright law. Yet to "comply" and to "inform" are fundamentally different from one another. To "comply" means to meet given standards; to "inform" means a sharing of information, with decision making implicitly left to individuals. A university policy could do both. It could offer full information, while also identifying relatively specific standards to follow.

A few policies recognize the potential conflicts in copyright law and reflect the competing pressures of avoiding legal troubles while exercising full rights of use. For example, a University of Pittsburgh policy states: "Our policy should ensure compliance with the law without, we hope, disruption to effective teaching and research at the University."[23] A photocopy policy adopted throughout the University of California system opens with this guidance: "In many cases, photocopying can facilitate the University's missions of teaching, research, and public service. The University therefore wishes to encourage the appropriate use of such material within the spirit and the letter of the United States Copyright Law."[24] These purposes manifest the significance of copyright at universities, yet one must look to the substantive policy standards themselves to determine how the university actually balances avoidance of infringements and fulfillment of the academic mission. Chapters five through seven of this book will make that exploration.

Universities without Written Policies

Rarely does an institution admit to absolutely no written or unwritten "copyright policy" by any definition. The legal counsel at Arizona State University emphasized that the university lacks even informal standards for case-by-case reviews; copyright simply has not been an issue. The only indicia of copyright "policy" she could identify were the customary signs on photocopy machines.[25] An employee at Catholic University similarly stated flatly that it has no copyright policy.[26] Columbia University attributed its lack of policy to the difficulty of defining fair use, although the legal counsel described a "conservative, cautious" approach in resolving copyright matters. As a lawyer, she explained, she wants to avoid lawsuits and therefore prefers to err on the side of "undercopying" rather than "overcopying."[27] The copyright officer at Carnegie Mellon University evaluates questions individually based on information from a standard text on copyright and fair use, and she prefers a conservative stance.[28]

At least six universities look to familiar publications and guidelines—such as the Classroom Guidelines and the CONTU Guidelines—but without incorporating them into any institutional directive. Respondents from the University of Alabama,[29] California Institute of Technology,[30] Case Western Reserve University,[31] and Temple University,[32] alluded to such standards, but they never submitted for this study any written evidence of the exact standards espoused.[33] Librarians at Howard University claimed to follow various American Library Association publications and regarded their position on copyright as "very strict and rigid" in order to avoid legal problems. Librarians at the University of Kentucky also look to various published guidelines, but they prefer liberal interpretations in order to serve teaching and research needs.[34]

A simple ordering of priorities at the local campus is apparently the main reason for not having a policy.[35] None of the university officials interviewed preferred to be without a policy; they simply had not taken the time to draft a statement.[36] Librarians at Clark University admitted to once having had a policy, but it is now deemed obsolete and no longer in effect. They also claimed inadequate experience with copyright matters to assess current practices.[37] Without further motivation, a new policy may be a long time in coming. Lack of knowledge, lack of experience, and lack of controversy at the home campus all lead to the lack of a copyright policy. Nevertheless, this study will show that controversy elsewhere can motivate policy-making at home. The New York University lawsuit is a classic example; action at one university inspired changes at others.

An actual lawsuit is also not necessary to prompt copyright concerns. For example, librarians at the University of Minnesota have drafted an elaborate new policy with an overt concern for avoiding infringements and liability, despite language in a preface that claims to espouse relatively liberal standards issued by the American Library Association. The librarians perceived that the "environment is heating up," and that they must "be as conservative as possible." Those observations did not stem from lawsuits or any dilemmas occurring on campus. Rather, the librarians attended conference presentations on copyright and heard publishers voice responsibilities under the law. Those perspectives fueled a particular awareness that shaped Minnesota's copyright policy.[38] A simple shaping of the copyright environment thus directly influenced both the need for the policy and the policy's content.

The Power of Congressional Guidelines: Photocopies, Videotapes, and Music

> The Committee [on the Judiciary] believes the guidelines are a reasonable interpretation of the minimum standards of fair use. Teachers will know that copying within the guidelines is fair use. Thus, the guidelines serve the purpose of fulfilling the need for greater certainty and protection for teachers.
>
> House report accompanying the Copyright Act (1976)[1]

> These minimum standards [in the House report] normally would not be realistic in the University setting. Faculty members needing to exceed these limits for college education should not feel hampered by these guidelines, although they should attempt a "selective and sparing" use of photocopied, copyrighted material.
>
> Model copyright policy, American Library Association (1982)[2]

Law and Policies for Photocopying

The simple, common, and familiar act of making photocopies for research or classroom use is the key issue in the relationship between universities and copyright. To some observers, the copies may seem too ordinary or too thoroughly addressed elsewhere to truly be ripe with controversy and fresh insights. Yet photocopying was the object of the 1991 case against Kinko's, which has further exacerbated the university-copyright relationship.[3] Moreover, photocopying most certainly remains the most common activity on campus that stirs copyright dilemmas—despite the growing importance and attraction of software and videotapes.

Most important, however, is that universities have had the opportunity to grasp the issues and to implement policies responding to the obligations and privileges surrounding photocopies. Photocopying is the issue on which most policies are built, and it offers the best available forum for discerning the institution's comprehension of its responsibilities and objectives. A thorough understanding of photocopy issues will set the ground rules for the next generation of copyright policies that must respond to newer technologies. The strong reliance on congressional guidelines for photocopying—and for video and music issues—will also demonstrate that policymakers look to easily available solutions, rather than probe anew the complexities of technology and law.

Photocopying, particularly for research and classroom purposes, is one of the most common issues in copyright policies for several reasons. It is first of all a common activity on campus that regularly stirs copyright questions. It was also a prominent topic in the legislative history of the 1976 act, and it is the subject of the Classroom Guidelines (see Appendix B). The two particular issues of research and classroom copying almost invariably appear together in university policies; virtually every university policy that addresses one of these issues also includes the other. They were debated together through the evolution of the 1976 act, and they appear side-by-side in the Classroom Guidelines, in the seminal University of Wisconsin policy, and in the American Library Association model policy (the ALA Model Policy).[4] They are the principal testing ground for university responses to copyright dilemmas.

PHOTOCOPIES FOR RESEARCH NEEDS

Nearly every member of the university community relies on photocopied articles, chapters, and other extracts to conduct "research" in the broadest sense of the term. Professors maintain files of articles, students copy materials for study, and administrators duplicate works for their professional needs. Although widespread, and undoubtedly totaling multitudes of copies, most research demands are apparently satisfied with isolated single duplicates of specific works. This "research copying" is a common and important part of teaching, research, and service. It was also an object of major debate leading to the 1976 Copyright Act. As chronicled in chapter two of this book, early efforts toward copyright revision began with some doubt that copying an entire journal article or book chapter—even a single copy—could be fair use. By 1976, however, most parties agreed that single copies of such materials for teaching or research were lawful without permission from copyright owners.

The Copyright Act expressly applies fair use to research copying, and the Classroom Guidelines describe these "minimum" standards:

> A single copy may be made of any of the following by or for a teacher at his or her individual request for his or her scholarly research or use in teaching or preparation to teach a class:
> A. A chapter from a book;
> B. An article from a periodical or newspaper;
> C. A short story, short essay or short poem, whether or not from a collective work;
> D. A chart, graph, diagram, drawing, cartoon or picture from a book, periodical, or newspaper.[5]

As a "safe harbor," the Classroom Guidelines can assure that single copies of most short works are not copyright infringements. Although the guidelines refer only to "teachers" and to copying for scholarly research or teaching, they would likely extend to administrators and staff as well, so long as their copies ultimately advance the university's mission.

The 1976 act gives strong credence for broad rights of single copies for individual needs. Section 108 permits libraries to copy from their collections "no more than one article or other contribution to a copyrighted collection or periodical issue" for delivery to a user for "private study, scholarship, or research." Libraries may even copy an entire work if another copy "cannot be obtained at a fair price."[6] Section 108 evolved as an elaboration on rights that libraries arguably already had under fair use. Thus, if Section 108 allows librarians to make single copies for patrons on request, the inference is that fair use allows similar copying outside of libraries.

COPIES FOR CLASSROOM DISTRIBUTION

Copyright implications compound when duplication grows from single copies to multiple copies for classroom distribution. The fair use statute expressly allows multiple copies for teaching, but it offers no exact limits.[7] The Classroom Guidelines sanction multiple copying only within narrow and meticulous standards:

> Multiple copies (not to exceed in any event more than one copy per pupil in a course) may be made by or for the teacher giving the course for classroom use or discussion; *provided that:*
> A. The copying meets the tests of brevity and spontaneity as defined below; *and,*
> B. Meets the cumulative effect test as defined below; *and,*
> C. Each copy includes a notice of copyright.[8]

Under the tests of "brevity," "spontaneity," and "cumulative effect," copies from articles generally may not exceed 2,500 words; the "inspiration and decision" for the copying must be so close to the time of need that permission may not be reasonably obtained; and not more than one work may be copied from the same author for each class. The full guidelines offer many more rules, all of which must be met to find a place in the "safe harbor." Full compliance with these guidelines requires users to count every word, to keep track of authors, and to retain records of the frequency and dates of copying. In addition, the guidelines specify prohibitions that may in no event be breached. For example, the guidelines prohibit creation of "anthologies," the copying of workbooks and other "consumable" materials, copying in lieu of purchase, and sales of copies to students beyond actual costs.[9]

The *Kinko's* case, however, reveals the confusion between these interpretations and actual law. The judge used the quantitative standards as a "compelling" tool for testing Kinko's actions, even though the guidelines were plainly not intended to gauge copies made for profit. Judge Motley also specifically rejected the guidelines' sweeping prohibition of all "anthologies," choosing instead to evaluate each item in the collection.[10] The guidelines are thus far from "law"; they are only part of the legislative history, and the court was not bound to follow them. Yet they seemed to be the only instructive source to fill the fair use vacuum. Just as the judge in *Kinko's* was drawn to the Classroom Guidelines, so have universities resorted to adopting them, usually without openly questioning their appropriateness.

THE INFLUENCE OF THE CLASSROOM GUIDELINES

The Classroom Guidelines are the single most significant influence on the content of university copyright policies. They are the foundation for the policies at approximately eighty percent of the universities that address either classroom or research copying. These policies reiterate the guidelines either verbatim or with little substantive variation in form or content. The Classroom Guidelines gained an enormous boost in 1983 with their incorporation into the settlement of the NYU lawsuit. In the next few years, universities across the country accepted them, often with reference to the NYU case, and with the stated intent of avoiding potential liabilities. With much less fanfare, the University of Texas also settled an infringement claim on similar terms. The resulting policy is virtually identical to the NYU settlement: both policies require permission from copyright owners or approval from the university legal counsel before exceeding the once supposedly "minimum" guidelines.[11]

Now in the second decade after passage of the 1976 act, the Classroom Guidelines continue to have broad acceptance and continue to be a strong force on understanding copyright law. In 1986 the University of California developed a policy for all U.C. campuses that closely follows the Classroom Guidelines, with selective elimination of a few quantitative measures deemed impractical to apply or enforce.[12] The 1986 policy was a sharp break from a 1977 memorandum written by the legal counsel cautioning that the Classroom Guidelines should not be allowed to "unduly" harm classroom teaching.[13] The NYU case intervened, and the earlier leniency was no longer heeded. The University of Colorado similarly issued a policy in 1978 that simply reiterated the guidelines and noted some flexibility under fair use. Colorado's 1986 policy, however, restructured the appearance of the Classroom Guidelines in a more onerous fashion, putting the general limitations and prohibitions at the beginning and even expanding some of them beyond the original wording.[14] The university was apparently putting aside flexibility and dwelling instead on mandates. Copyright concerns obviously sharpened between 1978 and 1986.[15]

Despite individual attributes among these policies, one trend is clear: the Classroom Guidelines have shaped the fair use standards at a vast majority of American universities, and most of these universities adopt the guidelines with little change in their central provisions. Only a few universities have made significantly lenient deviations from the guidelines. In particular, five universities emphasize that the guidelines are "minimum" standards by elaborating on some additional copying permitted beyond the narrow, quantitative limits. Those elaborations, however, are usually vague or are of limited scope.[16] Policies at Harvard and Princeton adopt the guidelines, but they add broad explanations of fair use that ultimately give faculty considerable flexibility and discretion.[17]

Widespread use of the guidelines does not mean complete support. The House report that originally contained the Classroom Guidelines in 1976 noted criticisms from two academic associations about the appropriateness of the guidelines for higher education.[18] Similar concerns appear in twenty-two of the university policies, even though most of those policies ultimately adopt the guidelines. By contrast, no university policy is any more restrictive than the Classroom Guidelines, and no policy even suggests that the guidelines are too permissive. The Classroom Guidelines continually emerge as the standard of choice, and they have largely ossified university thinking on fair use for common photocopying.

THE WISCONSIN AND ALA POLICIES

The University of Wisconsin was the leader in resisting the Classroom Guidelines entirely, and it issued an innovative alternative policy in 1978.[19] Two other universities within this study eventually adopted the Wisconsin policy as their own.[20] The Wisconsin policy was also the foundation of the American Library Association's model policy (see Appendix B), and eleven policies are based on the ALA example for both research and classroom copying.[21] Thus while some eighty percent of policies are rooted in the Classroom Guidelines, most of the remaining twenty percent are based on either the Wisconsin or ALA standards.

The Wisconsin standard differs slightly in language—but little in substance—from the Classroom Guidelines with respect to "research copying." The ALA policy, however, describes single copies as "the most conservative guidelines for fair use" and offers these principles and examples for evaluating additional research copying:

> The following demonstrate situations where increased levels of photocopying would continue to remain within the ambit of fair use:
> 1. the inability to obtain another copy of the work because it is not available from another library or source or cannot be obtained within your time constraints;
> 2. the intention to photocopy the material only once and not to distribute the material to others;
> 3. the ability to keep the amount of material photocopied within a reasonable proportion to the entire work (the larger the work, the greater amount of material which may be photocopied).[22]

The "classroom copying" provisions in the ALA and Wisconsin policies break almost completely from the Classroom Guidelines. Wisconsin fully and deliberately abandoned the enumeration of words and authors, declaring this brief and flexible standard:

> For one-time distribution in class to students, a teacher may make, or have made, multiple copies if he or she:
> a. makes no more than one for each student; and
> b. includes the notice of copyright (writes it on the first sheet or copies the page on which it appears); and
> c. is selective and sparing in choosing poetry, prose and illustrations; and
> d. makes no charge to the student beyond the actual cost of the photocopying.

The Wisconsin policy includes a few specific prohibitions—such as avoiding repeated copies in successive terms, or copying from unpublished works—but nowhere does it mandate the rigors of counting words, authors, and every instance of copying. The ALA policy similarly recommends the simple and flexible standard established at Wisconsin: fair use allows "selective and sparing" copying.[23] The ALA Model Policy attacks the awkwardness of the Classroom Guidelines for higher education, asserting instead that copyright limitations must be based on all circumstances, not merely the precise amount of copying.

The nearly complete absence of original copyright policy standards dra-

Table 5.1

Source of Classroom Copying Policies and Identity of Principal Policy Developers

	Administrators	Counsel	Librarians	Faculty
Classroom Guidelines	22	14	18	3
ALA Model Policy	6	3	1	1
Wisconsin Policy	0	3	0	0
Total:	28	20	19	4

matically reveals the influence of model policies. Of the seventy-three pol-icies addressing research or classroom copying on any terms, only two are not traceable to the Classroom Guidelines, the ALA policy, or the Wiscon-sin policy. The University of Delaware has a cursory memorandum of five diverse rules, including some rules reminiscent of the Classroom Guide-lines, but the guidelines are not necessarily the wellspring of Delaware's policy.[24] The University of Michigan has an internal memorandum from the legal counsel's office criticizing and rejecting the Classroom Guide-lines, preferring instead a lenient "case by case" review.[25] Rarely do poli-cymakers exhibit originality, and these few examples are only sketchy or skeletal. The lack of originality also implies that policymakers seek only to create a policy; they do not necessarily pursue the best policy.

Policy Content and Policymakers

The clear pattern in policy content is closely linked to the identity of the particular university official developing the local policy. If the general prin-ciples in chapter one of this book hold true, faculty and librarians should prove most likely to adopt the relatively lenient ALA or Wisconsin poli-cies, while administrators and legal counsel would tend toward the stricter Classroom Guidelines. Yet the evidence about actual university policies reveals a surprising conclusion. Contrary to expectations, administrators and legal counsel have infused the greatest flexibility into the guidelines, and they—not librarians—have been most responsible for adopting the ALA Model Policy. Of the eleven instances where the lenient ALA stan-dards became university policy, librarians were the leading developers of only one. Moreover, all three policies adhering to the Wisconsin standards were developed by legal counsel (see table 5.1).[26]

All groups of policymakers have shared in adopting the Classroom Guidelines, and widespread reliance on them results in generally large numbers of "strict" policies (see table 5.2). But policies on classroom

Table 5.2
Relative Strictness or Leniency of Classroom Copying Policies and Groupings of
Principal Policy Developers

	Administrators and Counsel	Librarians and Faculty
Strict Policies	36 (75%)	21 (91.3%)
Lenient Policies	12 (25%)	2 (8.7%)
Total:	48 (100%)	23 (100.0%)

copying developed by librarians are rooted almost exclusively in the guidelines, boosting their statistical tendency to write the strictest policies of all
campus constituents.[27]

Although librarians are not principal developers of most university policies based on the ALA Model Policy, they often had a secondary role.
Librarians brought ALA standards to the attention of other policymakers
at three universities who ultimately adopted them.[28] At three more universities, librarians also served on policy committees that accepted the ALA
standards.[29] Librarians may not have been the principal developers, but
they nonetheless influenced more than half of the university copyright policies based on the ALA Model Policy.

Another important trend among classroom copying policies is that responsibility for their development has shifted markedly away from librarians and toward administrators and legal counsel since 1983, the year
NYU settled its lawsuit.[30] Librarians wrote twelve policies on classroom
copying in the three years after passage of the 1976 act, ten of them being
issued in 1978 alone (see table 5.3). But beginning in 1983, the NYU suit
apparently prompted administrators and legal counsel to assume most
policy-making responsibilities. As in the overview of all policies (see
tables 4.4 and 4.5), two waves of policy development are clear: accompanying implementation of the new law in 1978, and in the years following settlement of the New York University lawsuit in 1983.[31] Given the
predominant influence of the Classroom Guidelines, these patterns suggest
that policymakers were not merely made aware of the need for policies in
general; they were compelled to accept the Classroom Guidelines in particular. The copyright environment brought the issue to the universities,
and it largely directed each university's response. Moreover, the environment's main feature in 1983 was the NYU lawsuit—an unequivocal reminder of potential liabilities.

What causes a university to choose a particular position on copyright
matters? This analysis suggests that if librarians or faculty—rather than

Table 5.3

Principal Developers of Classroom Copying Policies in Year Groups, 1977–88

	Administrators	Counsel	Librarians	Faculty	Total
1977–79	9	2	12	0	23
1980–82	0	4	2	0	6
1983–85	6	10	1	2	19
1986–88	13	4	4	2	23
Total:	28	20	19	4	71

administrators or legal counsel—are in charge of policy-making, the resulting standards tend more often to be "strict." That finding is an astonishing rebuke of fundamental expectations. One possible reason for the
greater leniency among legal counsel in particular may be that lawyers are
trained in the law and should be familiar with its potential for interpretation and flexibility. They should recognize the difference between "law"
and recommended guidelines. Legal counsel may therefore be most aware
that they have alternatives when implementing copyright standards. Moreover, faculty and librarians have a record of demanding "answers" to their
copyright dilemmas. Educators, in particular, led the demand for the
Classroom Guidelines by insisting on specific answers to their questions.
They seemed to overlook that the law may have more constructive effects
when it fosters flexibility and encourages an evaluation of circumstances,
rather than points in one narrow direction.

Regardless of distinctions among policymakers, the overwhelming influence of the Classroom Guidelines is inescapable. The prevalence of
strict policies, the frequent acceptance of the Classroom Guidelines as a
"safe harbor," and their resurgence after NYU all point toward crucial
understandings of copyright with implications reaching far beyond photocopying. In the practical endeavor to write a policy, universities respond
primarily to the objective of avoiding potential infringement liabilities.
Serving the academic mission is at best a secondary concern. Policy-
making is a response to environmental demands, rather than internal
needs. The environment, in turn, can be shaped by legal interpretations
that appear "official" and by strategic legal actions that instill fear of litigation and advance a specific position on fair use.

Congressional Guidelines Revisited: Videotapes and Music

The Classroom Guidelines are the most prominent of all fair use interpretations, but guidelines on music duplications and videotaping that also

appeared in congressional reports reaffirm the power of "official" standards. These guidelines may not be so well known, but they have enjoyed strong influence over universities addressing the pertinent issues. Videotapes and musical works can be reproduced and used in many different ways and for many different purposes. Like software, entire videotapes or music recordings may be reproduced expeditiously and with a quality comparable to the original. Portions can be excerpted and compiled into "anthologies," and copies can be made from television and radio broadcasts. Music has the additional peculiarity of being published both as sound recordings and as printed sheet music. Like other printed works, multiple copies of sheet music may be important for research, teaching, performances, reserve rooms, and other needs. Unlike many other printed works, an entire work of sheet music is often just a few pages or less; the copyright owner's entire work may be easily reproduced in single or multiple copies at only slight cost, and the copy may be useful only if it is complete.

THE MUSIC GUIDELINES

Photocopying of music was not a prominent issue in debates leading to the Copyright Act in 1976, but the House report that promoted the Classroom Guidelines nevertheless included "Guidelines for Educational Uses of Music" (see Appendix B).[32] Like the Classroom Guidelines, these "Music Guidelines" were devised by various interest groups at the urging of Congress. Two trade associations of music publishers, three professional associations for music teachers and schools, and the "Ad Hoc Committee on Copyright Law Revision" jointly developed the Music Guidelines and submitted them for congressional approval.[33] They appeared in the House report with little comment and without the specific objections that the Classroom Guidelines engendered.

Like the Classroom Guidelines, the Music Guidelines were offered as "minimum" standards, with acknowledgment that other copying may be permitted, and with hope that they might be "helpful" in clarifying fair use "as it applies to music." The Music Guidelines were also a relatively minor concern as Congress revised the law, and they were formulated in little time. The developers did not convene until after the Classroom Guidelines were submitted to Congress in March 1976, and the Music Guidelines were ready by the end of the next month.[34]

These standards posit five specific rules for limited copying of printed sheet music, for recording student performances of copyrighted music, and for reproducing sound recordings for teaching purposes. All rights are limited to teaching purposes only, and specific "prohibitions" mandate against "anthologies" and copying from "consumable" works. The guidelines also require a copyright notice on each copy. Despite their narrow

scope, the Music Guidelines are nearly devoid of strictly quantitative standards, such as the precise counts of words, authors, and numbers of copies
found in the Classroom Guidelines. One rule generally limits copying to
ten percent of an entire work, but the quantity is based primarily on a
"performable unit" from the music. Copying limits are not defined by arbitrary numerical limits, but instead by a measure of intellectual creativity
that may better reflect the utility of the originals and the copies.

No brief set of guidelines can anticipate the multifaceted copyright
problems of sound recordings. Composers receive copyright protection on
original music, and arrangers and lyricists may have rights to their independent contributions. All of these interests may vest jointly in one musical work, whether in printed or recorded form.[35] These creators possess
not only rights of reproduction and distribution, but also exclusive rights
of public performance.[36] Moreover, once a musical work is recorded, the
performer holds additional copyright interests. An educational institution
may have a limited performance privilege for educational purposes, but it
does not have a clear right to record and make copies of that performance
without permission from the owner of the underlying music rights. Universities also have no specific privilege to record or to reproduce recordings of other people's performances, other than through some possible
interpretation of fair use. The Music Guidelines are an effort to apply fair
use to at least a few such circumstances.

THE OFF-AIR GUIDELINES

The Classroom Guidelines and the Music Guidelines appeared together in
the 1976 House report, which then noted:

> The problem of off-the-air taping for nonprofit classroom use of copyrighted
> audiovisual works incorporated in radio and television broadcasts has
> proved to be difficult to resolve. The Committee [on the Judiciary] believes
> that the fair use doctrine has some limited application in this area, but it
> appears that the development of detailed guidelines will require a more thor-
> ough exploration than has so far been possible of the needs and problems of
> a number of different interests affected, and of the various legal problems
> presented. Nothing in section 107 or elsewhere in the bill is intended to
> change or prejudge the law on the point. On the other hand, the Committee
> is sensitive to the importance of the problem, and urges the representatives
> of the various interests, if possible under the leadership of the Register of
> Copyrights, to continue their discussions actively and in a constructive
> spirit. If it would be helpful to a solution, the Committee is receptive to
> undertaking further consideration of the problem in a future Congress.[37]

The pursuit of guidelines for off-air videotaping lasted another five
years, and on 14 October 1981 the "Federal Guidelines for Off-Air Re-

cording of Broadcast Programming for Educational Purposes" appeared in the *Congressional Record* (see Appendix B).[38] Unlike the Classroom Guidelines or the Music Guidelines, these "Off-Air Guidelines" were the product of numerous points of view. The earlier congressional guidelines were prepared by relatively few associations, while nineteen associations and private firms contributed to and approved the Off-Air Guidelines.[39] The only criticism came from a few copyright owners known for aggressively protecting their exclusive rights.[40]

In summary, the Off-Air Guidelines provide that nonprofit educational institutions may record television programs that are transmitted without charge to the general public. The tapes may be retained for no more than forty-five days, and may be used only once for teaching purposes during the first ten "school days" of that forty-five day retention period. One "reinforcement" use of a tape is permitted, with further uses limited to evaluation for future needs. Additional rules prohibit alterations of the programs or their reconstruction into "anthologies." The guidelines also limit teachers to one recording of a program, even if it may be broadcast repeatedly. The implications are clear: if repeated uses are anticipated, or if the use is more than ten "school days" into the future, teachers must seek permission from copyright owners before taping, retaining, or using the television program.

Video and Music Issues in University Policies

The Off-Air Guidelines and the Music Guidelines are not themselves "law," and neither has been tested in court.[41] But both model policies offer innovative interpretations of fair use without significant opposition, and both derive the all-important semblance of law by virtue of their congressional approval. For these reasons, and for their promise of liability avoidance, both model policies have virtually monopolized the field. Three-fourths of all policies encompassing any video or music issues whatsoever rely on these model guidelines with little substantive variation or challenge.[42] Moreover, these congressional guidelines are virtually the sole understanding of copyright employed for the specific issues they include.

No other model policy competes with the Off-Air or Music guidelines. A few universities limit the retention period to only seven days if the recording is from the Public Broadcasting Service. PBS has advocated that somewhat tighter standard since 1975. In 1986 the American Library Association attempted to clarify library rights and responsibilities in a model policy for videotape use, and it addresses issues beyond off-air recording (see Appendix B).[43] Only three university policies reflect the 1986 ALA policy.[44] These interpretations of fair use have received only a fraction of the attention bestowed on the congressional guidelines, affirming the influence of official standards on university policy-making.

The common traits among all congressional guidelines are revealing. They carry the lawmakers' imprimatur and the promise of a "safe harbor" from infringement liability. They were developed by consortia of interest groups and widely circulated for implementation at colleges and universities. The main difference among them is timing. The Music and Classroom guidelines appeared in the House report accompanying the 1976 act. They were available to policymakers when interest in copyright and the development of university copyright policies was at a peak; the Off-Air Guidelines were not available until 1981. Another difference is that the Classroom Guidelines apply to the more common concern of photocopying, and they have been used in actual litigation. Timing, litigation, and the promise of official approval thus have become leading factors shaping the environment and directly influencing university responses to copyright concerns.

Congress as a Policy Source: Library Copying and Reserve Rooms

> The results of the labors of the mind, which form the basis of all human improvement, ought not to be appropriated without remuneration, any more than the labors of the hand or of the machine.
> Annual Report of the Smithsonian Institution for 1871[1]

> Where his own official activities are concerned, a librarian must now increasingly view copyright as a form of exterior control which threatens serious limitations of his library's freedom to put its collections to work in the service of its users.
> Verner W. Clapp, former Acting Librarian of Congress (1968)[2]

For librarians, the perception of copyright has shifted in recent decades from being a fountainhead of creative works to a spearhead of restrictions and limitations. Judging by their literature, one could easily conclude that librarians most often see copyright as a constraint on their socially beneficial service—the law limits the public's access to information resources, all apparently for the benefit of relatively few copyright owners or their publishers. Copyright law undoubtedly encourages authors and publishers to create and disseminate new works, but those benefits are often overlooked as librarians pursue their daily struggles to meet complex and uncertain legal limits. Just as many advocates of owners' rights disregard fair use, so do many librarians give little attention to the merits of copyright.

Copyright in libraries is today intrinsically enmeshed with the growth of innovative library services and the availability of new technologies. Fax machines send copies of materials to remote locations, computer databases connect libraries to a wealth of information, CD-ROM media allow libraries to preserve images of books that are rapidly crumbling on the shelves, and resource-sharing programs enable libraries to cancel some expensive purchases and to rely on interlibrary loans. The ambiguities of copyright limits leave uncertain restrictions on many of these endeavors, with librarians and copyright owners often left in an unproductive standoff. The parties increasingly respond in terms that simply circumvent the need to define specific copyright principles. License agreements with database providers establish limits on the nature of allowable uses, and many journal publishers are simply increasing their subscription prices to offset the apparent number of sales lost from library resource-sharing arrangements.[3]

In the years preceding passage of the 1976 Copyright Act, however, the main library issue was once again photocopying, generally for individual patron needs, for preservation, and for seemingly modest interlibrary lending. Congress listened closely as librarians detailed their dilemmas, and the 1976 act accordingly includes specific provisions—notably Section 108—granting many libraries substantial copying rights under specified conditions.[4] The photocopy issues outlined in Section 108 and the problem of placing copies of articles and other materials on reserve are still among the most common copyright situations that librarians face. The frequency that these issues arise and the peculiar legal difficulties they engender combine to make them highly problematic issues for university officials developing and implementing policy statements.

Law and Policies for Reserve Rooms

Typically located in libraries, reserve rooms retain materials for current teaching needs. The immediate and often short-term demand by entire classes of students usually requires that several copies of an item be placed "on reserve." Purchasing multiple items for only temporary use is often impossible or impractical, so many reserve facilities instead turn to photocopies of articles and book chapters. Despite the obvious legal pitfalls, the copyright implications of reserves received little attention in the legislative history of the 1976 Copyright Act, leaving policymakers and legal analysts to disagree even on the applicable law. These legal uncertainties handicap the ability of university officials to formulate reliable policies and to advance institutional needs and objectives.

One argument is that reserves are an extension of the classroom, and thus should be treated like classroom copying under fair use.[5] Specific standards may in turn be based on the Classroom Guidelines, on the American Library Association's model policy (the ALA Model Policy), or on another fair use interpretation. The reserve room may alternatively be a library function, and the copies are simply in service to patrons. Thus, reserve copying should be limited to rights under Section 108, such as making one copy of an article for research or study, or copying an entire work after searching the market for a purchase. In any event, multiple copies for individual patrons are not allowed under Section 108, while fair use does allow some multiple copies for teaching.[6] A conceptual understanding of reserve operations can accordingly affect the choice of legal theory—which can then affect the scope of rights allowed. Whatever the legal theory employed, reserve room copying is the single most prevalent copyright issue addressed in university copyright policies. Eighty-one policies from sixty-one universities expressly address reserve room copying.

The leading legal analysis of copyright and reserve rooms came from John C. Stedman, the University of Wisconsin professor who marshaled efforts to criticize the Classroom Guidelines and who moved the University of Wisconsin to formulate its influential policy on research and classroom copying. Stedman wrote a seminal article in 1976 on copyright and educational needs in general; he wrote another article in 1978 on the reserve problem alone.[7] Stedman put little faith in Section 108 as a legal foundation for reserve copies. He noted its logical possibilities (If the library can make one copy for each student, why not several copies for an entire class?), but Section 108 presented too many technical "chuckholes" for assured reliance.[8] He preferred instead a fair use approach, arguing that libraries seldom photocopy in quantities that significantly affect copyright owners and that faculty would make no copies at all if reprints were expediently and economically available.[9] Stedman concluded: "a balancing of the burdens upon users (in terms, not only of financial costs, but also of uncertainty, delay and *non*-use) of denying the right to engage in reserve photocopying, against the minuscule benefits likely to accrue to copyright owners, supports a conclusion that reserve copying, within reason, should be deemed a 'fair use' under section 107."[10]

Stedman never specified exact amounts of reserve copying that fair use allows, but he clearly would have permitted multiple copies of full articles. Stedman also dismissed once again the constraining standards of the Classroom Guidelines, including word limits and the demand to seek permissions whenever time allows.[11] Despite Stedman's obvious interest in reserve copying, the 1978 policy he helped develop at the University of Wisconsin makes no mention of reserve rooms.[12] Reserve issues, however, do appear in a separate Wisconsin policy that was also issued in 1978, but which was developed at the library.[13]

The Wisconsin reserve policy provides that libraries may make or accept multiple copies, but it does not detail the types or amounts of materials that may be duplicated. It concludes that reserve operations are classroom extensions, and states liberally: "If it is 'fair use' to make 100 copies for the use of 100 students in a face-to-face teaching situation, it would appear equally 'fair' to make 5 or 10 copies to be put in a Reserve Collection for the use of those same students." Few universities would follow Wisconsin's example of allowing "100 copies" in the first place, even though they may well allow the five or ten copies for reserve use. Indeed, the 1991 *Kinko's* decision should bring Wisconsin's sweeping generosity into question; the court made clear, for example, that under almost any circumstances multiple copies of book chapters could easily brush the limits of fair use.[14]

THE ALA MODEL POLICY

Although Wisconsin librarians were instrumental in developing the ALA Model Policy, the ALA policy ultimately does not adopt Wisconsin's open-ended standard, placing instead a "reasonable" limit on the number of reserve copies. The ALA Model Policy also affirms that reserve rooms are extensions of the classroom, and that copies may be made either in accordance with the "classroom" standards for multiple copies or the right to make single copies for research use. Thus, single copies of entire articles, book chapters, and poems are not infringements according to this interpretation, and multiple copies should adhere to the following rules:

> 1. the amount of material should be reasonable in relation to the total amount of material assigned for one term of a course taking into account the nature of the course, its subject matter and level, 17 U.S.C. §107(1) and (3);
> 2. the number of copies should be reasonable in light of the number of students enrolled, the difficulty and timing of assignments, and the number of other courses which may assign the same material, 17 U.S.C. §107(1) and (3);
> 3. the material should contain a notice of copyright, *see,* 17 U.S.C. §401;
> 4. the effect of photocopying the material should not be detrimental to the market for the work. (In general, the library should own at least one copy of the work.) 17 U.S.C. §107(4).[15]

The ALA standard resolves that a "reasonable number" of copies would "in most instances be less than six," but circumstances may allow more.

ISSUES FOR RESERVE ROOM POLICIES

The array of policies employed at universities reveals that reserve room copying is more complex than simply selecting a model policy or a legal theory. Reserve operations often involve elaborate procedures, and policies smack of copyright challenges as well as the practical problems of handling and monitoring thousands of books, articles, and other materials. The distinction between a copyright limit and a practical limit is not always clear.[16] For example, a University of Colorado policy endorses Stedman's recommendations, but it limits faculty to six copies of any item.[17] The limit, however, stems not from copyright, but instead from space limitations at the reserve facility. In their efforts to formulate workable standards amidst such diverse legal and practical constraints, many policy developers thus have broached some or all of the following ten concerns:

1. Will the library make any copies at all, and will it make only single copies or multiple copies?

2. Will the library accept any photocopies from a faculty member, and will it accept only single copies or multiple copies?

3. May copies be placed on reserve that apparently have been read or used before?

4. May copies be placed on reserve while awaiting permission from the copyright owner?

5. Who has responsibility for copyright compliance: the library or the faculty member?

6. Must the faculty member certify compliance with copyright?

7. May copies be allowed only from materials owned in the library's collection?

8. Must a notice of copyright be placed on each copy?

9. Must the notice be a formal copyright notice or merely a general statement that copyright law may apply?

10. Are blanket licenses available from select journals or publishers?

These questions are widely debated in library journals and appear with varying frequencies in the policies themselves. Hardly a single policy, however, treats all issues, and even the ALA Model Policy takes a position on only a few.

THE CHARACTER OF UNIVERSITY STANDARDS

Despite the potential for elaborate or complex reserve room policies, the crucial copyright aspect of a policy is the amount of copying allowed from a single work—whether a book, article, or otherwise—and the total number of copies permitted. Some policies allow only single copies. Others— like the ALA Model Policy—allow multiple copies. Seventeen reserve room policies (or approximately twenty-one percent) are based on the ALA standards.[18] Still other universities allow multiple copies only within the confines of the Classroom Guidelines. Because the Classroom Guidelines do not expressly cover reserve copying, they do not dominate the university copyright policies on this issue. Only twenty-four (or approximately thirty percent) of the eighty-one policies are based on the Classroom Guidelines in one manner or another.

Reliance on the Classroom Guidelines has been troublesome. The University of Notre Dame adopted the guidelines in 1978, but it interpreted them to prohibit all multiple copies on reserve. In 1983 the university reaffirmed its strict standard and allowed multiple copies only with permission from the copyright owner.[19] The Notre Dame library also implemented a "blanket permission" program to secure advance rights of duplication from journal publishers. Still, a 1986 survey of faculty revealed deep opposition and a perceived interference with effective teaching:

> Significant numbers of those who responded indicated that the new policy had caused them to change their teaching methodology. Forty-five percent said that the change in the way the University Libraries handled photocopies of copyrighted materials had an effect on their style of teaching. Sixty-eight percent had reduced the number of items they placed on reserve, while 35% reduced the amount of required readings. Further, 46% also reduced the amount of supplemental readings that they assigned. Thirty-nine percent increased the number of books that their students had to buy for the course.[20]

The complete prohibition on multiple copies at Notre Dame is among the most restrictive policies at any university, and several faculty members mentioned in the library's survey that they were accustomed to less-restrictive standards at other universities. Yet, the library staff concluded that no other policy would comply with the law and that faculty complaints about reserve copying are commonplace.[21] The Notre Dame study showed no evidence of having reviewed the ALA Model Policy or policies from other universities.[22]

Forty reserve policies are not based on either the ALA Model Policy or the Classroom Guidelines. Apparently not influenced by any model policy, these original policies have little in common with one another. To varying extents they respond to one or more of the ten questions stated above. Some policies are cursory memoranda on single points. Other policies are ambitious attempts at covering the full range of copyright problems, replete with detailed guidance. Despite their tremendous variation, they can be grouped according to their central copyright positions.

Policy Content and Policymakers

The most significant copyright trait among reserve room policies is the amount of copying allowed without permission from copyright owners. The wide range of reserve room policies may accordingly be grouped into three categories: (1) twenty-eight policies allow only single copies of items; (2) twenty-two policies allow multiple copies, but only in accordance with the Classroom Guidelines; and (3) thirty policies allow multiple copies of entire articles, book chapters, and other such works.[23] The last category includes the seventeen university policies based on the ALA Model Policy. In relative terms, the first two groups may be called "strict," while the third group is "lenient." Identifying the middle group as "strict" is also consistent with the treatment of "classroom copying" policies based on the Classroom Guidelines.

Relating the character of the reserve room policies to their principal developers reaffirms important trends found among the classroom copying standards. All members of the university community share in developing reserve policies, with faculty bearing only slight responsibility, despite their clamor for less-restrictive policies at Notre Dame and elsewhere. As might be expected, librarians have assumed most responsibility for developing reserve room policies; reserve rooms are almost exclusively located within library systems and are operated by library staff (see table 6.1). Indeed, librarians had primary responsibility for nearly three-fourths of the reserve room policies. By contrast, they were primary developers of only about one-fourth of the "classroom copying" policies (see table 5.1). Legal counsel were primary developers of only five reserve policies, but they served a secondary role as advisor or consultant on at least fifteen additional policies, twelve of which were developed primarily by librarians.

Reserve rooms are overwhelmingly viewed as a library responsibility, regardless of their arguable function as "classroom extensions." Librarians also have developed reserve policies fitting all categories of description, with the Classroom Guidelines and other restrictive standards figuring prominently. Librarians again have proved more willing than other policy developers to keep duplications of copyrighted works within only "minimum" standards. While policies developed by administrators and legal counsel divide nearly evenly between strict and lenient, almost two-thirds of all policies developed by librarians are strict.[24]

The ironies of copyright at American research universities are once again exposed. The greatest challenge in copyright analysis and application lies not with legal counsel and administrators, but instead with librarians. University employees who are not lawyers are grappling with the most difficult copyright law problems. They are called upon to analyze, interpret, and apply the law. Moreover, librarians in particular tend to implement the strictest legal interpretations, despite the potential constraints on library service, and despite their professed concerns about the law's inhibiting force. These conclusions are closely related to one another. Li-

Table 6.1
Relative Strictness or Leniency of Reserve Room Policies and Groupings of
Principal Policy Developers

	Administrators and Counsel	Librarians and Faculty
Strict Policies		
(Single copies or		
Classroom Guidelines)	8 (47%)	36 (63%)
Lenient Policies		
(Multiple copies)	9 (53%)	21 (37%)
Total:	17 (100%)	57 (100%)

brarians often find responsibility for copyright problems thrust upon them.
They are rarely eager to pursue policy-making, but they recognize its
need, and often no one else is willing to take the initiative. Thus faced
with an unwanted and extraordinarily difficult challenge, the reluctant policymaker takes the easily available route. For reserve copying, often that
route is either accepting the Classroom Guidelines or simply limiting the
user to a single copy of any item.

CHRONOLOGICAL TRENDS IN POLICYMAKING

Librarians have held the leading role in developing reserve room policies
ever since passage of the 1976 Copyright Act (see table 6.2). Reserve
room policy-making by administrators and legal counsel increased slightly
after the NYU suit in 1983, but even their few policies were usually only
supplements to broader statements on classroom copying. The most remarkable revelation is the expediency with which librarians discharged
their policy-making duty. Librarians issued a peak of twenty policies in
1978, when the 1976 act took effect.[25] In 1983 alone, the year of the NYU
case, librarians issued another nine policies. By contrast, administrators
and legal counsel gained a more prominent role after the NYU case, but
their efforts are more scattered over the next several years.

THE DILEMMA FOR LIBRARIANS

The immediate response among librarians most probably results from their
central role in the copyright dilemma. Faculty approach librarians to request or make copies. Students approach the librarians to obtain those
copies. The more copies, the more satisfied the users, and the less criticism librarians receive. The more copies, however, the more likely the

Table 6.2
Principal Developers of Reserve Room Policies in Year Groups, 1977–89

	Administrators	Counsel	Librarians	Faculty
1977–79	4	0	25	0
1980–82	0	2	5	0
1983–85	3	2	17	0
1986–89	5	1	6	2
Total:	12	5	53	2

possibility of a copyright infringement. In the midst of this conflict, a written policy becomes a useful tool for possibly avoiding violations, or for simply explaining standards and limits. A written policy also facilitates consistent service; all patrons can be subjected to uniform limits, and no one receives less favorable treatment. The efficiency of librarians in formulating policies also suggests a drive toward "professionalism." Library publications kept abreast of the 1976 act and the NYU case. Librarians were made aware that they had duties and privileges under copyright law; compliance was heralded as a librarian's institutional and social responsibility. They may not have savored the task, but it was a unique opportunity for librarians to address legal issues that directly affected the library's mission. It was a chance for librarians to shape responses to a major national concern.

Some of these same reasons may underlie the relative strictness among the librarians' policies. The struggle with "professionalism" might compel the need to "follow the law" and to expound on the latest legal developments. That effort may strengthen their public and professional image, but a hasty and overreaching application of the law may also inhibit their duty to provide optimal access to library collections. Librarians are also caught in the middle between patrons and higher-level administrators. A lenient policy may serve patron needs, but it may incur administrative wrath if it invites a legal challenge. Librarians also perceive steady pressure from publishers; they are compelled to show utmost respect for copyright and to avoid liabilities.[26] They also need simply a positive working relationship with their suppliers of copyrighted works. Lenient positions may only stir animosities.

Another dilemma for librarians is that innovative applications of fair use under these complex conditions require legal analysis and interpretation, a task for which few librarians are trained. As a result, only the basics of copyright and established model policies may gain prominent attention amidst such fogginess. Limited expertise allows limited capacity for innovation. In the end, the immediate managerial demands of librarians may take precedence. If few copies are allowed, then the library has fewer duties of maintenance and distribution. Practical limits are a reality, but if librarians confuse them with copyright, they will erode fair use and constrain the university's options for serving the educational mission. Once again, the objectives of administrative duties conflict with academic pursuits.

Blanket Licenses for Reserve Operations

Some universities are now attempting to sidestep the copyright intricacies of reserve operations with ambitious "blanket license" programs. The library at the University of California, Davis, issued a policy in May 1985 that placed new limits on reserve copying.[27] The policy required a year to develop, but according to one librarian, "It took much less time for some faculty to express their outrage at our limitation of their ability to teach."[28] With support from the university administration, the library sought to ease complaints by obtaining "blanket permissions" from select journal publishers to make copies for reserve room use. By the end of 1986, publishers of nearly eight hundred journals had either granted the permission requested or provided information about paying fees to the Copyright Clearance Center, an organization that grants photocopy rights on behalf of thousands of publishers. According to one librarian, "many" journals participating in the CCC still gave the requested permission without cost. The program has eased tensions and increased use of the reserve facility.

Concerns about reserve room copying spearheaded development of a "Photocopy Permissions Manual" at Dartmouth College.[29] A large portion of the manual is given to listing nearly two hundred fifty journal titles, over half of which have granted "blanket permission" for multiple copies, whether for reserve or classroom use. The remaining journals allow copying with varying stipulations or only after obtaining permission for each use. Policies from at least two other universities mention blanket-license programs, but only Davis and Dartmouth submitted evidence of large-scale programs. Copyright arguments surrounding reserve rooms put libraries in tension with both faculty and publishers. But blanket licenses enable publishers to protect their interests, and they may improve relations between faculty and libraries.[30] A variety of such "collective arrangements" have emerged in recent years, and they will receive closer attention in the final chapter of this book.

Library Copying and Section 108

Unlike the reserve standards, policies on library copying and interlibrary lending are remarkably consistent. Section 108 of the 1976 Copyright Act expressly addresses the following litany of copying rights, among others, and university policies often encompass the same issues:

Section 108(b): copying of unpublished works for preservation or security or for deposit at another library.

Section 108(c): copying of published works for replacing a damaged, deteriorated, lost, or stolen copy, if an unused replacement is not available at a fair price.

Section 108(d): copying of articles or contributions to collections for a patron's private study, scholarship, or research.

Section 108(e): copying of an entire work for a patron's private study, scholarship, or research, if a copy is not available at a fair price.

Section 108(f)(1): copying by patrons on unsupervised machines where notices are posted.[31]

These rights, especially the making of single copies for patrons, form the basis of much "interlibrary lending" as well. Indeed, Section 108 affirms that libraries may make copies to fulfill requests from patrons not physically present at the library, but no copying under Section 108 may amount to the "systematic reproduction or distribution of single or multiple copies."[32] Librarians argued that the "systematic" limitation might be construed to shut down interlibrary lending programs. Congress sympathized and added this proviso:

nothing in this clause prevents a library or archives from participating in interlibrary arrangements that do not have, as their purpose or effect, that the library or archives receiving such copies or phonorecords for distribution does so in such aggregate quantities as to substitute for a subscription to or purchase of such work.[33]

All rights under Section 108 are subject to a few general conditions: rights are limited to single copies made without commercial advantage, only at libraries open to the public or to outside researchers, and only so long as the copy includes a notice of copyright.[34] Further, these rights to make copies for library patrons generally do not apply to musical, pictorial, graphic, or sculptural works, or to motion pictures or other audiovisual works;[35] Section 108 is principally for photocopying of printed works and has been so regarded in most university copyright policies. Within these parameters, Section 108 clears the way for libraries to perform specified services without the copyright owner's consent and without fears of infringements. Unlike fair use, Section 108 is detailed; it of-

fers functional meaning for narrow but common situations, without resort
to significant interpretations. Given the broad scope of Section 108, this
chapter will make separate examinations of "library copying" and "interlibrary lending."

Library Copying and Policy Standards

Fifty-seven policies from forty-four universities address one or more aspects of library copying—other than interlibrary lending—and all but four
of the policies are explicitly based on at least some part of Section 108.
The heavy reliance on Section 108 reflects the utility of the detailed statute
and the relative lack of controversy and lawsuits it has produced. The most
common "library copying" provision in university policies is the immunity
privilege that libraries enjoy simply by posting notices on unsupervised
copying machines.[36] That broad privilege is probably exploited at nearly
every educational institution across the country, without necessarily appearing in a written policy.[37] Several universities post similar notices or
warnings on computer equipment, advising users that software may be
subject to copyright protection.[38] Indeed, the 1976 act allows libraries to
avoid infringement liability if general warnings appear on all "reproducing
equipment," not merely on photocopy machines.[39]

Despite Congress's effort to enact specific library rights, parts of the
law are open to some interpretations and reasonable differences of opinion.
For example, the obligation to search for a copy of materials at a "fair
price" begs further guidance.[40] How thoroughly must the library conduct
the search? What is a "fair price"? The American Library Association
recommends that a "reasonable effort" include a search of customary trade
sources, bibliographies, catalogs, and sales outlets. If the work is out of
print, librarians should inquire with the publisher or copyright owner.
Only after exhausting these avenues may the library make a complete
copy, whether for its own collection or for a patron's use. The ALA generally regards "fair price" to be "as close as possible to the latest suggested
retail price," if the copy is unused.[41] Only two university policies expressly
rely on these interpretations.[42] One university requires only a search of
Books in Print before copying an entire book, rationalizing that such requests are sufficiently infrequent to harm publishers.[43] Various analysts and
policymakers may have differing views, but Section 108 is yet to be tested
in court.[44]

Section 108 also requires a "notice of copyright" on each copy, but the
nature of that notice is in dispute.[45] The American Library Association
concludes that the "notice" could be merely a general statement that copyright may apply to the work,[46] while other groups promote using the for-

mal copyright notice found at the beginning of most publications—usually a copyright symbol, the year of publication, and the owner's name.[47] Like many other copyright issues, this difference of interpretation remains unresolved. The dispute over the notice may also be of declining significance; since March 1989 the law no longer requires protected works to carry a formal copyright notice. Because the notice is now only optional, libraries may not be reasonably expected to include it on all copies, and the absence of a notice will not jeopardize copyright protection. On the other hand, the formal notice is a useful reminder of copyright's protections, and librarians must surely acknowledge that it often includes important bibliographic information.

THE FIVE-YEAR REPORTS

Significant debate over Section 108 is manifested primarily in the "five-year reports" issued by the United States Copyright Office. Congress enacted Section 108 with a clear awareness of its experimental provisions and uncertain consequences. To gain insights on these new rights and responsibilities, the statute originally mandated that every five years the Register of Copyrights shall consult with interested parties and "submit to Congress a report setting forth the extent to which this section has achieved the intended statutory balancing of the rights of creators, and the needs of users."[48] The Copyright Office completed "five-year reports" in 1983 and 1988 before Congress repealed the requirement in 1992.[49]

Both reports are based on extensive hearings and written testimony, together with empirical studies. Widespread criticism came particularly from librarians in advance of the 1983 report, when a study sponsored by the Copyright Office concluded that libraries regularly engaged in photocopying that could be infringements. The study—conducted by King Research, Inc. and known as the "King Report"—found that ten percent of all library copying could "arguably" be infringements, and that more than twenty-five percent of all photocopying by librarians involved two or more copies of an item.[50] These findings outraged librarians, and the entire 1983 report reflects nearly universal tension between librarians and publishers.

For all the important insights that the 1983 report uncovered, it has been largely ineffectual. The statutory revisions it recommended were never implemented, and the report apparently has had little effect on university copyright policies. The second report, in 1988, was considerably less ambitious. Financial constraints prevented extensive studies, and five additional years of experience had brought some acceptable balance to relations between users and owners. Librarians, publishers, and other observers generally agreed that the law should remain unchanged. Opposing groups had not cooperated to formulate mutual guidelines, but the combination of legal threats from publishers and independent copyright policies within libraries had worked to find a middle ground.[51]

Although interpretations and controversies persist, the more settled response to library copying reflects two factors. First, the statute's relative specificity gives direct guidance without significant interpretations. Second, copying under Section 108 apparently has not posed a serious threat to publishers and authors. Arguments will always arise that Section 108 undermines the survival of creativity and publishing, but single copies for research, preservation, and similar needs thus far have not compelled major reexaminations of the law. The relative lack of controversy may in turn be responsible for the varying degree of reliance that policies have placed on Section 108; if the issue is not in controversy and not in need of clarification, perhaps it need not be highlighted with a formal statement of university standards.

VIDEOTAPING NEWS BROADCASTS

Confirming the usefulness of Section 108, ten university policies refer to a Section 108 provision that allows libraries to record and to lend copies of televised news programs.[52] It was a late addition to the 1976 act in order to rescue one university in the home state of an influential U.S. senator. Vanderbilt University established a Television News Archive to record and index broadcasts and to share the tapes with scholars and researchers.[53] When a commercial television network challenged the plan, Senator Howard Baker proposed an amendment to allow news taping and to shield Vanderbilt from liability. Although the amendment was applicable to all libraries eligible for Section 108 privileges, the Copyright Office confirmed that Baker's proposal was not "broader than is necessary to validate the Vanderbilt operation."[54] A timely challenge and a powerful senator came together to secure a specialized opportunity. Few universities manifest the privilege in their copyright policies, perhaps because the statute is so clear that a reaffirming policy would be superfluous. Moreover, probably only a few universities have ambitious programs for taping broadcasts that necessitate such a policy.

In the end, the most significant aspect of Section 108 is that no formal "guidelines" appeared in the legislative history, and interest groups have not greatly influenced any interpretations. Policy-makers instead have looked directly to the statute and to a few supporting regulations for a policy source. The specificity of Section 108 may deprive the law of flexibility, but it also has avoided the confrontations and tensions that surround fair use at American research universities.

Overview of Interlibrary Lending

One of the most significant aspects of Section 108 is its interlibrary lending provisions. "Lending" is often a misnomer. Libraries sometimes actually "lend" materials to one another, but the materials transferred are increasingly photocopies, with no expectation that they will be returned. Copies of articles, book chapters, and other works are shuttled all over the world as a practical means for opening one library collection to researchers in almost any location. The use of photocopies preserves original works and keeps them available at their home libraries. The copies customarily become the property of the user.

At first glance, interlibrary lending of photocopies may appear little different from a library making single copies for patrons under Section 108. Why should the law differ just because the patron is not physically present? Yet the growth of interlibrary lending means that reliance on photocopies is more than isolated instances of research needs. Networks of libraries, shared catalogs of library holdings, and the affordability of photocopying have no doubt replaced subscriptions to many journals. Knowing that photocopies are reasonably available, a library may forgo a purchase when the contemplated demand is only modest and when copies are easily obtained elsewhere. A basic tenet of copyright law is that copying should not substitute for purchase, yet publishers warn that interlibrary "lending" is especially an increasing substitute for subscriptions.

The actual effects of interlibrary lending on publishers are the object of enormous dispute. Studies from publishers contend that journal subscriptions have declined, and that the survival of many periodicals is at risk—all from expanded photocopying.[55] Studies by librarians have argued that photocopying generates a new demand for materials that never would be filled by purchasing originals.[56] Academic libraries today are increasingly confronted with tightened budgets and the imperative to meet growing demands with shrinking funds. One prominent librarian has asserted, however, that an efficient "document supply system" does not lead to reduced budgets for subscriptions; rather, the reduced budgets effect an improved system.[57] The real cause of lost subscriptions, therefore, is simply the lack of money.

The evidence for almost any position on these issues is weighty, but inconclusive. The only sure bets are that serial prices are escalating, library budgets are declining, and tensions between librarians and publishers are worsening.[58] Interlibrary lending issues are spilling over into the realm of "resource-sharing"—the coordinated acquisition and access to materials among a group of libraries. Faced with reduced funds, many libraries rely increasingly on obtaining little-used publications from other institutions. Each library participating in a consortium can avoid a purchase with assurance that the materials will be available elsewhere. No library is likely to cancel many purchases of commonly used materials with modest prices, so most resource sharing bears most heavily on periodicals with small circulations and relatively high prices. If sales of such works decline significantly, prices will surely rise even further, and the survival of some works may be at risk.

Few observers would dispute either the value of interlibrary lending or of resource sharing, or the need for publishers to survive; the difficulty is deriving an appropriate balance under a copyright law that both separates and links the often opposing camps. A clearer awareness of diverging arguments can help relieve some tension. Libraries have legitimate concerns about escalating prices and shrinking budgets. They are expanding interlibrary services largely from practical necessity; most libraries would undoubtedly prefer to avoid sweeping subscription cancellations that they now face. Publishers also live with understandable distress when sales drop and copying increases. The need is for a copyright standard that permits customary interlibrary operations, but that signals a reasonable limit and indicates when a library should reinstate its own purchase of the original work. In an effort to reach that goal, Section 108 allows single copies and interlibrary arrangements, but it prohibits "systematic reproduction or distribution" of copies. The challenge is to bring practical meaning to that ambiguous limit.

THE CONTU GUIDELINES

Guidelines prepared by the National Commission on New Technological Uses of Copyrighted Works (CONTU) in 1978 interpret "systematic reproduction and distribution" by proposing a "rule of fives" now familiar to many librarians: during any calendar year, a library may "borrow" not more than five photocopies of articles from the most recent five years of any journal title. CONTU presumed that any library needing the journal on six or more such occasions should have its own subscription.[59] The "CONTU Guidelines" emerged with support from authors, publishers, and librarians, who jointly accepted both the reasonableness of the standards and the feasibility of adopting and monitoring them. In addition, several empirical studies have found that CONTU limits pose minimal interference either with the researcher's access to information or with library operations.[60] Actual university copyright policies manifest a general acceptance of the CONTU Guidelines. Fifty-four policies from forty-three universities address interlibrary lending, and all but eight of those policies are rooted in the CONTU Guidelines. Those eight policies usually do not propose alternative standards, but rather avoid stating any particular limit at all.[61]

The CONTU Guidelines are the only "model policy" to gain prominence on this issue. They have suffered little criticism and have overwhelmed the understanding of relevant copyright limits. The most notable variations on CONTU are merely supplements and enhancements. For example, the CONTU Guidelines apply only to journal articles that are less than five years old. They do not address older journals or any other works, and universities may develop local standards to fill those voids.[62] In addition, the CONTU Guidelines permit five copies from a journal title, but they do not tell how to handle the sixth request.[63] A few policies indicate alternatives upon reaching the five-copy limit.[64] Some policies require permission, or require a fee paid to the Copyright Clearance Center. Responsibility for paying the fee or for obtaining permission is usually on the patron.[65] With or without these elaborations, the CONTU Guidelines are the centerpiece of nearly every interlibrary lending policy.

Summing Up the Library Policies

University copyright policies for library copying and interlibrary lending have many similarities. Librarians have predominant responsibility for policy-making on both issues, leading the development of approximately seventy percent of all such policies. Like "reserve room copying," these issues are largely viewed as library functions and are primarily the concern of librarians. Librarians must respond to the needs, requests, and expectations of patrons. When faculty or students come to the library seeking copies of journal articles and other copyrighted materials, librarians are confronted with the dilemma of fulfilling the service to every extent possible, while adhering to copyright limits. Librarians have an obvious and immediate need for written standards of practice.

As with their policies on "reserve room copying," librarians are virtually alone in creating statements that deal primarily with these library-oriented concerns. Indeed, every policy on either library copying or interlibrary lending that is developed by a nonlibrarian relegates these issues to a secondary position and gives greater prominence to classroom copying issues. Librarians are the only policymakers to award these library issues any priority, with individual attention and independent policy documents. Moreover, librarians have remained the leading policymakers on these issues ever since passage of the 1976 act, even after the New York University lawsuit, when the specter of liability arose and responsibility for policies on other copyright issues generally shifted to administrators and legal counsel (see table 6.3).

The legal substance of policies on library copying and interlibrary lending also have much in common. Most remarkable is their nearly uniform dependence on the text of Section 108 and the CONTU Guidelines. These

Table 6.3

Principal Developers of both Library Copying and Interlibrary Lending Policies in Year Groups, 1977–89

	Administrators	Counsel	Librarians	Faculty
1977–79	10	2	37	0
1980–82	0	5	5	0
1983–85	2	3	20	0
1986–89	3	0	11	4
Total:	15	10	73	4

trends confirm the importance of model policies. A model policy is certain to be incorporated into university copyright policies, if it has official stature, if it is sufficiently specific, if it addresses actual needs and practices, and if it has withstood testing by the university community. Several studies during the past ten years have shown, for example, that the CONTU Guidelines do not significantly hinder library practices, and the most recent—and the last—"five-year" study from the Copyright Office evinced a general acceptance of Section 108 by most parties.[66] By contrast, the Classroom Guidelines have been criticized since their inception, and their meticulous provisions can discourage or befuddle even the most law-abiding citizens. Experiences with Section 108 also show that effective standards can come from Congress itself and from congressional commissions, not only from negotiations among disparate interest groups.

The lesson for lawmakers, academicians, and copyright owners is crucial: copyright standards that are attuned to practical needs and to university operations, and that gain congressional approval, will find overwhelming acceptance. University policymakers are not looking for complex solutions. They accept copyright standards that other groups have developed, particularly standards endorsed by lawmakers—such as the Classroom Guidelines or the CONTU Guidelines. Ultimately, then, Congress has the most significant role in shaping university copyright policies. Congress passed Section 108, which has directly shaped university standards. Congress also established CONTU, and its recommendations have been the leading influence on interlibrary lending policies. These developments parallel experiences surrounding classroom copying, where Congress endorsed the Classroom Guidelines, and they subsequently dominated university policies. Congress may have wanted user rights to be flexible for changing circumstances. But the players responsible for copyright decisions have instead relied almost exclusively on every specific signal and clue from Congress about the law. Rather than adapting to dynamic forces, policymakers instead look for readily available "answers." Without question, the "answers" from Congress retain the most significant role in shaping university copyright standards.

The Weakness of Innovation: New Technology and the Lack of Policy Direction

The bill endorses the purpose and general scope of the judicial doctrine of fair use, but there is no disposition to freeze the doctrine in the statute, especially during a period of rapid technological change.

House report accompanying the Copyright Act (1976)[1]

[T]he "fair use" doctrine normally has little applicability to Computer Software.

Draft copyright policy, University of Hawaii (1988)[2]

Computers and software have become a mainstay in nearly every part of American universities. Faculty, staff, and students write papers, process data, and communicate ideas with personal equipment on campus or at home. Central facilities—in libraries and elsewhere—also make computers and software available to the entire university community. The enormous growth of the software industry underscores both the practical value and the financial value of computer programs—and the need to secure the rights of software writers and producers. Software is protectible under the 1976 Copyright Act, and many of its uses on campus give rise to infringement possibilities. Many uses also stir claims of fair use, but the legal parameters of rights and privileges are almost wholly unresolved.

Unique copyright issues surround the duplication, circulation, or even just acquisition of computer programs. Unlike most other materials, each disk may be easily, cheaply, and repeatedly copied in full, and each copy is fully as useful as the original. While photocopies of printed works may replace a book or article of relatively modest price, commercial programs may retail for hundreds of dollars. Moreover, the only meaningful software copy is ordinarily a complete copy; portions or excerpts are usually of little use to anyone. The difference between photocopying of printed works and duplication of software is fundamental to understanding university copyright standards. By legal standards, software is an infant. Users and producers reveal few common perceptions of either the nature of the copyright issues or of their solutions. The result is a vacuum of knowledge, and no statute or model policy has significantly shaped software copyright issues. By contrast, earlier chapters of this book demonstrate that the Classroom Guidelines and the ALA Model Policy are at the root of almost every copyright policy on classroom photocopying. Years of experience with photocopying have produced some general understandings of legal rights—regardless of lingering debates and disputes. That depth of experience is yet to exist for software, and its absence leaves universities to search for new legal meaning.

The Growth of Software and the Uncertainty of the Law

Software producers are acutely aware of copying, and they often point to universities as perpetrators of infringements or "piracy."[3] Copyright owners and universities alike contend that policies can calm some legal concerns and can encourage easier availability of software. Yet of the ninety-eight American research universities within this study, only twenty-seven demonstrated the existence of a policy on software use; they submitted a total of twenty-nine written statements.[4] Reasons for the paucity of software policies are seldom clear. Timing alone is certainly important. Personal computers and the accompanying software are relatively new creations, proliferating swiftly from technical laboratories to such diverse departments as history, business, art, and sociology. Universities may simply not have had time to implement policies. In fact, most statements have been issued only in recent years; twenty of them were issued between 1986 and 1989. Software's recent arrival also means that policymakers may not yet comprehend its utility or the potential copyright implications. Disks are loaded for word processing, statistical analyses, and database development, but the nuances of downloading, uploading, file serving, and front-end modifications may not be so evident. If actual uses are uncertain, so will be the terms of a meaningful policy.

Perhaps the most important reason for the sparsity of policies is he fluid state of applicable law. The Copyright Act of 1976 indicates little about software, and traditional doctrines of fair use often do not seem germane.[5]

Judicial rulings have been few and not comprehensive, leaving policy developers to apply, at best, an unsettled law. What can policymakers tell users when the law offers only vague notions? Congress recognized this dilemma, and in 1980 it revised Section 117 of the Copyright Act to sanction two common uses of software: making "archival" or "backup" copies for use in the event of damage to the originals; and making copies as an "essential step" in software utilization.[6] The latter provision allows some modifications of programs, transfers from floppy to hard disks, and simply the "loading" of a program—which actually involves copying it from the disk to the computer memory. "Archival" copies under Section 117 may be used in the event of electronic damage to the original disks; the privilege is intended specifically to counter software's unique susceptibility to quick and total destruction.[7]

The revised Section 117 encompasses only a few narrow uses, but it represents major congressional action. Congress was not prepared to address software problems at all in 1976, preferring instead to await advice from the National Commission on New Technological Uses of Copyrighted Works (CONTU), the same group that proposed guidelines for interlibrary lending of photocopied articles.[8] The current Section 117 comes directly from CONTU recommendations.[9] Like Section 108 for "library copying," Section 117 is a specific and practical guide for users—but only for the few circumstances it describes. Eighteen university copyright policies mention the right to make "archival" copies.[10] Eight policies refer to "essential step" copying.[11]

THE EDUCOM BROCHURE

Another reason for the lack of policies is the lack of influential models for universities to emulate. Many model policies for software use have been proposed, but only two of them have had any apparent consequences for university standards.[12] The first, *Using Software: A Guide to the Ethical and Legal Use of Software for Members of the Academic Community,*[13] was originally issued in 1987 and revised in 1992 by EDUCOM, a consortium of over six hundred colleges and universities (see Appendix B).[14] At its core is a succinct "code" affirming "respect for intellectual labor and creativity" and warning that violations may lead to unspecified penalties and sanctions. The original 1987 brochure was a sharp discouragement of any copying. That version referred to "unauthorized" copying, but it inadequately explained what copying might be "authorized" by law or by the copyright owner. Readers might easily have concluded that all copying was illegal under any circumstances, despite Section 117 and fair use. It alluded to "backup" copies and to the utility of uncopyrighted "freeware" only in fine print at the end. The 1992 version is an enormous and welcome improvement. It offers prominent and detailed descriptions of rights to use shareware, freeware, and public domain software. The new brochure answers some common questions about software use, and it even acknowledges a "cloudy" right of fair use and presents a better balanced perspective.

The original brochure was a curious and disappointing position for an academic organization. A professional society representing educational institutions might be expected to describe and secure rights of use at every opportunity.[15] Several factors may have shaped its restrictive posture and the false start at developing a truly helpful policy for serving the academic mission. For example, administrators—particularly directors of computing services—represent many colleges and universities in EDUCOM activities.[16] The general principles reviewed in chapter one of this book suggest that administrators often exercise undue caution on legal matters. EDUCOM also depends on over one hundred computer and software producers who participate in EDUCOM's "Corporate Associates" program and underwrite many of its expenses.[17] Representatives of these firms attend EDUCOM functions and at times outnumber officials from colleges and universities. Software producers are not known for emphasizing user rights.

Another possible reason is that the brochure is actually a joint effort with a trade association of computer and software companies once called "ADAPSO" and now known as the Information Technology Association of America (ITAA).[18] The prominent role of a producers' group probably meant the inevitable subordination of user rights. Indeed, an ADAPSO officer who contributed to the brochure declared in 1987 that "the college community is a hotbed of piracy."[19] The president of EDUCOM also referred to the original brochure as part of a commitment to "software security and to sustaining the rights of authors and publishers."[20] Owners' rights need protection, but they should not consume the entire copyright debate, lest the law's delicate balance be lost. In the end, a leading reason for the restrictive mood may simply be the common lack of known specifics about users' rights regarding software. The 1992 version reflects an evolving understanding of the law. It appropriately asserts owners' rights, but it softens the aggressive rhetoric and highlights a few public privileges.

EDUCOM reports that its 1987 brochure gained powerful acceptance, but the university copyright policies obtained for this study hardly acknowledge it. Only at Washington University did an interviewee disclose that copies of the brochure were shared on campus, but only when a software supplier required their distribution.[21] Recent policies at Rice University and at the State University of New York at Albany incorporate the brochure's central "code."[22] Nevertheless, the EDUCOM brochure has been widely circulated, with more than 500,000 copies of the 1987 edition reportedly reaching faculty and students at more than 1,200 educational institutions.[23] According to EDUCOM reports, faculty and students wishing to use the computer facility at Mills College must complete an application form that asks questions based on the brochure.[24] Before borrowing software at Drew University and Swarthmore College, students and faculty must sign a document based on the brochure.[25]

EDUCOM also has reported that several universities within this study—including Brown, Michigan, Princeton, and Syracuse—have relied on the brochure, but that use is unconfirmed here.[26] The policies obtained for this study seldom reflect the brochure, probably because its adoption may be confined to the computing facilities most closely associated with EDUCOM; only on rare occasions has it become part of the broad-based policy adopted by university-wide administrators or by the central library. Those rare appearances—despite the many brochures in circulation—further underscore the lack of overall policy coordination within universities. Moreover, the copyright perspective of computer facilities is apparently not influential up the administrative hierarchy.

THE 1986 ALA MODEL POLICY

The second model policy, *Library and Classroom Use of Copyrighted Videotapes and Computer Software,* was developed by the American Library Association's legal counsel in 1986 (see Appendix B).[27] It offers specific provisions on a few matters of library concern, such as circulation of software, reserve room use, and software availability at computer facilities. This model policy also addresses the making and use of "archival" or "backup" copies and includes procedures for responding to license restrictions that software producers may impose. Throughout the policy are specific guidelines and standards applicable to particular circumstances. This "1986 ALA Model Policy" may not be comprehensive, but it addresses several actual needs with clear guidance. This policy also reflects the ALA objective of optimizing access to information by identifying rights granted under the law. Like the EDUCOM "code," only two university copyright policies adopt the 1986 ALA Model Policy for software issues.[28] At Vanderbilt University, the ALA standards became library policy in March 1986. A 1988 policy from Rice University includes both the 1986 ALA Model Policy and the EDUCOM code, a strategy which details user rights while affirming respect for intellectual property.

Original Policy-Making and the Search for Legal Meaning

Because model policies have had limited influence, and because Section 117 embraces only two issues, most policymakers have turned primarily to original language and standards. These original policies may include some provisions from the statute or from model policies, but in general, policymakers have searched for their own understandings of even the most familiar software concerns. Original policy terms demonstrate the challenge of responding to an uncertain law, to the demands for utilizing computer resources, and to the growing importance of license provisions. The following examples illustrate the difficulty of formulating useful policies.

HARD DISK LOADING

Only two policies mention the common occurrence of loading a program onto a computer's hard disk.[29] Shifting a program from one storage device to another is of growing importance, as hard disks become common computer features, and as different systems use differing disk sizes. Such software transfers seem clearly to be fair use or even an "essential step" for software utilization under Section 117 of the 1976 act, so long as the objective is not to create multiple copies for simultaneous uses. Given the combined possibility of floppy disk damage and hard disk "crashes"—losing all programs and data—the hard disk copy is usually in addition to the archival "backup." A helpful policy should give guidance for these common needs.

MULTIPLE MACHINES AND MULTIPLE USERS

Also common is the use of a single software package on multiple machines or by multiple users, although not simultaneously. Software license provisions often limit use of a program to just one specific person or even to just one specific machine. Neither the copyright statutes nor court rulings require that limitation. If several readers can share a book, why not also share a floppy disk? Four policies address this issue, but they confusingly intermingle legal rights and rights established under a license.[30] For example, Stanford's policy properly calls for adherence to licenses, but it otherwise permits lending of software so long as lenders and borrowers do not use their programs simultaneously:

> Unless the license agreement is to the contrary, it probably is OK to assume that you can loan the software or "sell" it to another person provided the recipient agrees to be bound to the license agreement. But both of you cannot use it at the same time nor should the borrower make any copies.

No policy addresses the similar case of one person carrying one program to machines at various locations, such as from home to office. So long as a single program serves only one user or terminal at a time, transporting the program should not reasonably be a copyright infringement.

On a related issue, four policies proscribe multiple loading of a single program or entering it into a network available to multiple users.[31] Again, according to the Stanford policy: "One rule of thumb is to assume that only one person at a time may use the software when one copy has been purchased from the vendor." The law on this issue is not firm, but the logic is simple. Multiple or network loading is the functional equivalent of multiple copies. It effectively creates whole copies from only one original; it has the characteristics of a traditional copyright infringement.

LIBRARY CIRCULATION

Software lending is increasingly a major responsibility of libraries and computer centers, and producers regularly attack software circulation as an outlet for uncontrollable duplications.[32] Congress amended the Copyright Act in 1990 to prohibit software lending for profit, but the law specifically sanctions lending within nonprofit educational institutions.[33] Stanford's policy acknowledges the potential liabilities:

> University software lending libraries shall undertake appropriate measures to ensure that patrons are advised that copying of the loaned software is prohibited (unless the software is in the public domain or the owner has consented to copying). Such steps shall include all or some of the following: signed statements by the borrowers, posted signs, labels on software and documentation, and warnings displayed on the computer screen.[34]

These steps generally serve two purposes: to notify users of copyright obligations and to shift responsibility for compliance to the patrons. The Stanford policy thus allows circulation, but it may also reduce the risk of institutional liability. By contrast, the University of Hawaii policy—drafted before the 1990 statutory amendment—implies that circulation is allowed only if expressly granted in license agreements.[35]

A few policies attempt to obviate or modify license restrictions by stating on purchase order forms that the software will be acquired for circulation purposes. The theory is that suppliers are consenting to the use when filling the order. The 1986 ALA Model Policy recommends that approach, and a few universities add this statement to their order forms: "Purchase is ordered for library circulation and patron use."[36] The legal effect is dubious, but the strategy may at least demonstrate the library's good faith intentions.[37]

FREEWARE AND SHAREWARE

Even without venturing deeply into the wilderness of fair use, a policy may serve many needs simply by describing the unrestricted use of public domain software. Many software producers forgo their legal rights by issuing uncopyrighted programs, also called "public domain" software. "Freeware" is copyrighted software that may be circulated to the public without cost, but possibly with some restrictions on further uses or commercialization. Such programs are common and usually may be freely copied. In addition, "shareware" is copyrighted software that the developer permits to be duplicated under stated circumstances, usually for a small fee. Shareware, freeware, and public domain software are important for educational institutions—multiple copies can be immediately available for library, laboratory, or classroom use. A thorough policy should help users to identify them with certainty and to use them with impunity, thereby maximizing the usefulness of available software resources. Only nine policies even mention these valuable opportunities.[38]

These examples of original policy terms reflect the challenge of imputing practical meaning into the vagueness of fair use, and no policy even approximates a comprehensive overview of common software uses. No one policy encompasses all issues described above, and numerous other uses of software give rise to ever more complex copyright issues and policy terms. A more common policy-making practice is to skirt these complexities and to leave even the applicability of any fair use rights for software in doubt. The University of Hawaii openly questions the relevance of fair use:

> the "fair use" doctrine normally has little applicability to Computer Software
> for three reasons. First, Computer Software nearly always must be copied
> or used in its entirety if it is to work at all. Fair use seldom excuses the use
> of a copyrighted work in its entirety. Second, unauthorized copying of Com
> puter Software has a direct and measurable impact on the copyright owner's
> revenue, which tends to negate any claim of fair use. Finally, if the Software
> License Agreement is enforceable, a breach of it is actionable as a breach
> of contract even though the breach may not by itself constitute copyright
> infringement.[39]

By contrast, the University of Rochester policy strains to give fair use some practical meaning. For example, under a claim of fair use, librarians at Rochester may make multiple software copies, if the library owns or has on order an equal number of originals, or if the copies are solely for evaluation before purchasing originals.[40] Although such copies may not actually jeopardize sales, the copies may not be properly monitored or returned, and each copy may itself be further duplicated. Rochester's approach to fair use may be laudable and helpful, but it raises new responsibilities. Without careful oversight, even the narrowest right to make copies opens possibilities of unknown and unseen infringements. Fair use can be both an opportunity and a burden.

The Trend toward Restrictions

While the quest for some practical fair use of software is commendable, universities are overwhelmingly opting instead to disregard these nuances and complexities. Rather than highlighting user needs or rights—even the express rights of Section 117—thirteen of the university software policies ultimately do little more than bar all copying, impose restrictions, and threaten liability.[41] These short and restrictive policy statements epitomize a disturbing trend: universities are ostensibly attacking software piracy, but ignoring user rights. A few of these policies refer briefly to "archival" copies under Section 117 or to using uncopyrighted software or shareware. A draft policy from the University of Hawaii is an extensive discussion of particular uses, but it ultimately allows few of them and generally declines to apply fair use to computer software. With that one exception, all thirteen are brief and imposing statements against copying, and little else.

Typical of these policy provisions is this central statement from Harvard's policy: "Unauthorized copying of commercial software is a form of theft."[42] Or from Brandeis: "Copying of software without the permission of the developer of that software is theft of intellectual property and the University does not condone it."[43] These policies frequently condemn "illegal copying" or "unauthorized copying," but they rarely describe copying that may in fact be legal or authorized, whether by law or by consent of the copyright owner. Members of the university community may logically conclude that all copying is strictly prohibited and will lead to sanctions under either the law or university regulations. These policies rarely fill more than a single page, and they most likely arise from confusion and fear. The law is nearly devoid of guidance, and rights of owners and users are increasingly subject to diverse agreements or licenses. Licenses with each software producer are separately created, resulting in distinct rights and duties for each computer program that are too scattered to itemize in one policy statement. Rather than attempt comprehensive surveys of rights and duties, and rather than creatively explore the law, policymakers have responded with simple statements of prohibition. Instead of carefully preserving rights, universities tend to forfeit them.

Software Policies in Force

This overview isolates salient characteristics of software policies: frequent reiteration of basic Section 117 rights; rare reliance on the 1986 ALA Model Policy and the EDUCOM "code"; occasional innovative responses to specific needs; and common imposition of restrictive and sweeping prohibitions. The overview also shows that generalizations about software

Table 7.1

Relative Strictness or Leniency of Software Policies and Groupings of Principal
Policy Developers

	Administrators and Counsel	Librarians and Faculty
Strict Policies		
(category 1)	9 (50%)	4 (40%)
Section 117 Policies		
(category 2)	6 (33%)	2 (20%)
Lenient Policies		
(category 3)	3 (17%)	4 (40%)
Total:	18 (100%)	10 (100%)

policies are not simple. One policy may sharply prohibit copying, while
including a few user rights. Another policy may be based on the ALA
model, while also alluding to broad limitations on copying. Nevertheless,
twenty-eight of the policies[44] may be separated into three categories based
on each policy's most prominent trait: (1) thirteen policies bar virtually all
activities; (2) eight policies primarily reiterate the terms of Section 117;
and (3) seven policies offer guidance for other specific uses (see table
7.1).[45] Unlike the photocopying issues, however, software use is not necessarily measured by the amount of copying or the ability to make multiple
copies. Instead, the principal differences among these three categories are
the circumstances under which even a single copy—or some other use—
may be allowed.

A policy that identifies specific uses and attempts to construct an effective fair use opportunity is—at least in relative terms—"lenient." A policy
that ultimately prohibits most uses is relatively "strict." Thus, categories 1
and 3 are respectively "strict" and "lenient." Category 2 policies, which
are rooted primarily in Section 117, are essentially neutral responses to
copyright. They simply regurgitate black-letter law, without significant
embellishment or explanation. They imply little about underlying motiva-
tions, and they hint little about their consequences; category 2 policies
cannot be fairly lumped as either strict or lenient. Much of the analysis to
follow will therefore focus only on categories 1 and 3.

Unlike the formulation of photocopy policies, administrators and legal
counsel have taken the lead in developing "strict" policies for software.
The greatest degree of caution about software—unlike the caution surrounding photocopies—emanates from the university's management offi-

cials. Lawyers and administrators have led the movement toward simplistic and narrow policies by issuing nine of the thirteen cursory and confining policy statements. In that respect, the general expectations from chapter one hold true. But in defiance of those expectations, faculty also seem to lean toward strictness. Faculty led the development of only three of the software policies, and all three of them are "strict." Faculty may argue for greater rights to use information resources, but their software policies do not manifest that concern.

The lack of a strong model policy to emulate and the growth of "shortcut" responses to complex concerns have eroded most hope for policy statements on the fair use of software. To break that trend and to expand innovation in copyright, policymakers must embark on a challenging exercise in legal interpretation and creative insight. Developers must assess diverse circumstances and recognize opportunities. Where laws and custom offer few specifics, policymakers must be willing to assert a legally sound position that reclaims fair use privileges. Yet human nature and bureaucratic demands rarely allow development of the ideal, thorough, and balanced policy statement; instead, legal pressures and demands on time more often lead to simplistic policies that minimize risks. Hence, simple policies safe from legal challenge become the norm.

The two most prevalent software policy provisions are, accordingly, the terms of Section 117 and the concise pronouncements against software copying. The influence of Section 117 is reasonable and appropriate. Congress listened to the CONTU recommendations and amended the Copyright Act to sanction important rights with little need for interpretation. When universities reach beyond those specifics, however, their software policies fall into the abyss of sweeping and discouraging generalities. They avoid innovation; they avoid assuring that even the most common and least threatening uses may be lawful. These policies may reduce liability exposure, but they also inhibit the university's fulfillment of its own academic mission.

Why should the treatment of software be stricter than the treatment of photocopying? After all, nearly every photocopying policy allows some duplication of materials, even if under strict limits. If a policy were to bar all photocopying of printed materials, it would be resoundingly attacked on campus; yet software policies that purportedly prohibit all software uses seem to proliferate. The evidence seems to reaffirm the general software problems: the medium is new, its uses are unclear, and the law points to few user rights. The most important reason, however, may be the nature of the medium itself. Software may be duplicated easily, inexpensively, and rapidly. The effect—or potential effect—of copying on the original's value is often easily established, especially when entire programs are reproduced. If courts continue looking to market effect as the most important factor in the fair use equation, and if that factor can apply easily to software, then the scope of fair use will accordingly shrink. Perhaps it should. Users should not make multiple copies. Users should not circumvent rightful purchases with inexpensive reproductions. Yet those legal or ethical obligations should not obviate the quest for an operative meaning of fair use for academic needs.

Rather than work toward a meaningful middle ground, software producers have emphasized the potentially enormous liabilities and the need for restrictive policies; many universities seem willing to acquiesce.[46] When all else fails, a few universities have been sued. In recent years the University of Oregon and the University of California, Los Angeles, have been sued for alleged copying of software.[47] The external forces of litigation and threatened liabilities often seem insurmountable. Creative exploration of rights seems impossible or is forgone. Even the unequivocal rights of Section 117 are sometimes overlooked. The result is a university policy that unduly restricts the utility of information resources and that hampers the value of software for teaching and research. Congress has rarely spoken on software issues, and the lack of even hints of user rights has allowed the copyright environment to become filled instead with the oppressive fears of litigation.

Building for the Future and Lessons from the Past: Taking Control of University Governance

The college or university attorney is vested with the obligation to prevent the unnecessary extension of legalistic factors into the administration of the college or university. The attorney may in fact be the most important and effective advocate for autonomy and flexibility in the administration of academic institutions.
"The Role of College or University Legal Counsel" (1974)[1]

The failure of the university to define and to regulate itself, the argument goes, has left the way open for others outside the institution to do so (indeed has given them ammunition for doing so) in ways that are perhaps harsher and less acceptable to the university than if self-regulation had been attempted.
"Higher Education and the Law" (1973)[2]

The Current Framework for University Copyright Policy Development

Copyright at American research universities is in disarray. University copyright policies are seldom the product of coordinated efforts throughout the institution. Policy-making responsibilities are spread among diverse members of the community, with many universities issuing multiple policy statements and each policymaker often unaware of the others. Most crucial in the policy process, however, is the lack of focus on academic objectives. The policies demonstrate little sensitivity to balancing their potentially conflicting functions: avoiding liability and optimizing use of in-

114

formation resources. University copyright standards are not shaped by the relationship between law and the use of copyrighted materials for teaching, research, and service. They are instead overwhelmingly influenced by "model policies" that offer quick answers and some promise of a "safe harbor" from liability. Excess concern for avoiding infringements outweighs the institution's academic mission. From a more functional view, the tendency to accept easily available solutions has nearly smothered the opportunity for innovative and more beneficial fair use comprehension. In general, the copyright environment surrounding universities is signaling one particular standard as the only appropriate policy. Regardless of its merits or detriments, that single perspective is so pervasive that it suppresses awareness of alternatives that may better serve the university's mission. By acceding to the singleness of that environment, universities are forfeiting legal privileges and eroding the success of their own academic programs.

MODEL POLICIES AND THE STRENGTH OF THE ENVIRONMENT

Universities—and all organizations—are influenced by their environments. For copyright policymakers, that environment includes the law itself. It also includes forces that affect an understanding of the law: proposed interpretations, threatened or actual legal action, and developments emphasized in literature or news reports. Educators and librarians may have enjoyed repeated successes in shaping the 1976 Copyright Act while the bill was in Congress, but once the bill became law, copyright proprietors began achieving enormous success in asserting their perspective and influencing the development of fair use.

Policy alternatives are eliminated or at least discouraged when the environment focuses on particular legal interpretations. When Congress, news media, professional publications, and litigators highlight key "model policies," such as the Classroom Guidelines, competing standards have little chance for comparable attention. Moreover, attention from Congress and courts gives the guidelines the semblance of "law" which must be followed for full copyright compliance. Many university officials have the mistaken impression that the guidelines are law. The influence of key model policies is clear throughout this study. The Classroom Guidelines are incorporated into approximately eighty percent of the policies on classroom copying (see table 5.1). The CONTU Guidelines, the Music Guidelines, and the Off-Air Guidelines have won virtually complete acceptance for the specific issues they embrace. By contrast, no "congressional guideline" applies specifically to reserve room copies or computer software, leaving policymakers to consider diverse possible standards. In the absence of an "official" interpretation, policy-making on these issues is lean, and the relatively few original policies that emerge tend to be simplistic and confining.

Copyright owners have found effective means for directing attention toward their desired interpretations of fair use and toward the Classroom Guidelines in particular. The lawsuit against New York University brought renewed attention to the Classroom Guidelines, which were then adopted at other universities through the 1980s. The 1991 *Kinko's* case probably has given the guidelines their most credible endorsement to date. Moreover, the victory for the publishers in that case has commenced the "second phase" of an enforcement program led by the Association of American Publishers, in which the AAP has sponsored a lawsuit against at least one more private copy shop. That shop supplied photocopied anthologies to three universities in Michigan and employed a self-defined schedule of collecting and disbursing royalties. The defendant has fought the action, arguing that the customary process for obtaining permissions is "unreasonable, costly, and time-consuming." But the publishers thus far have had little difficulty enjoining his activities.[3] Suits against private shops preceded litigation against NYU in 1982; the current program of lawsuits may be a precursor to an action against a university as well. Even without ultimately suing a university, however, the strategy has successfully captured university attention and has highlighted the Classroom Guidelines as apparently the sole means for fending off the possibility of threats at home.

THE TENDENCY TOWARD CONVENTIONALISM

The propensity of universities and other organizations to imitate environmental structures and to conform to established conventions may be inevitable. The Classroom Guidelines, for example, are influential because they have been legitimated externally, from their development by professional organizations, their congressional endorsement, and their implementation in key lawsuits.[4] By adopting these environmental structures, universities may gain the appearance of success and may avoid appearing negligent or irrational.[5] Thus, "official" guidelines operate as a conforming force on university behavior, moving universities toward greater similarity, and further reinforcing their acceptance of standard procedures.[6] Selection of a stereotyped policy statement is not only an efficient means for addressing a difficult issue, but it is also a means for diffusing criticism of the policy. A model policy carries with it a broader context of support—which must share any criticism, and which any successful critic must also beat down.

Rival copyright policies must therefore compete not only against better-known standards, but also against an institutionalized social network involving nearly the whole community of American universities that favors one particular policy.[7] When the bandwagon supporting the Classroom

Guidelines is at full speed, individual universities are unlikely to reject that momentum and opt for innovation. These conventional policies may satisfy immediate needs, but they do not necessarily support the university's internal academic objectives. Moreover, standards such as the Classroom Guidelines survive because their actual effects on individuals are seldom directly tested. Any university policy can be easily circumvented simply by using unsupervised machines or copy shops that follow the policy less stringently or not at all—even though the extent of such behavior may be unethical or even unlawful. Indeed, a university policy may be carefully developed and thoroughly disseminated, but each university constituent is only presumed to act properly.[8]

Copyright activities may be unwatched, and policies may be disobeyed, yet a conventional policy may deter some litigation and demonstrate the university's good faith. At a minimum, policies are the university's equivalent of warning labels on cigarettes or power tools. They are informative reminders, but without rigorous implementation and education they rarely change an individual's behavior. When a lawsuit arises, however, the defendant university can point to the policy—just as the manufacturer points to the warning label—in an attempt to exculpate the defendant from allegations of wrongdoing. Liability for actual damages may still apply, but a cautious policy may preclude exemplary damages or sidetrack charges of willful misconduct.

Concentrating on such indirect functions of policies can waylay their full capability to serve academic needs. The University of Wisconsin, for example, looked directly at the fair use opportunities and openly espoused an innovative and relatively lenient policy in 1978. The university has faced no legal challenge. Indeed, its liberal policy might actually have discouraged litigation. If copyright owners were to lose an infringement suit against the university, its lenient policy—rather than the Classroom Guidelines—would gain notoriety, credibility, and influence.[9] Thus, the Wisconsin or ALA Model Policy may actually offer the immediate benefits of deterring litigation while also giving greater promise to the long-run needs of higher education.

That possibility may now face a test with the issuance of a new copyright policy at the University of Georgia. During the data collection for this study, the legal counsel for the University of Georgia replied that the university had no policy and that copyright issues were simply not a priority concern for the institution. After the closure of surveys—as described in chapter four of this book—the university issued the most extraordinary, the most original, and the most "lenient" of all university policy statements. A committee of faculty, administrators, librarians, and legal counsel issued a 162-page "handbook" and a sixteen-page set of "guidelines" that survey the purpose and history of copyright, that outline the structure of the law, and that detail the law's application to numerous specific situations.[10]

Two members of the committee were professors L. Ray Patterson and Stanley W. Lindberg, whose 1991 book tests the limits of user privileges under copyright and proffers an expansive argument.[11] The Georgia policy is expressly based on their book. In accordance with the legal arguments of Patterson and Lindberg, the Georgia policy identifies generous opportunities of "personal use" and fair use. For example, the policy details that sharing computer programs or transporting the program disk from one computer to another can be lawful. It also specifies that multiple copies of recent newspaper articles may be distributed in class and that course readers or "anthologies" may include "reasonable excerpts from copyrighted works."

The Georgia document is the most ambitious statement from any university on copyright's underlying purposes and on the law's implications for specific circumstances. The policy also tests the limits of copyright interpretation. Some of its standards may be drawn into question by more recent cases, notably the ruling about anthologies in the *Kinko's* case and the decision on copying for individual research needs in the *Texaco* case.[12] Yet Patterson and Lindberg would most assuredly draw attention to the nonprofit education purpose of copying on campus and the profit motive behind the copying at Kinko's and Texaco. They would also probably challenge the propriety of those District Court rulings in the first place. Professor Patterson is not known for conforming to the latest judicial opinions when he can argue that those opinions misinterpret the law and ignore its historical and constitutional foundation.

Few institutions share the boldness of the University of Georgia. The university should be commended for avoiding form policy statements and for identifying the broadest scope of user rights. The Georgia policy is worthy of close study by any university establishing its own standards, but no university should adopt those standards without a careful assessment of their full substantive implications and the possible consequences—both the beneficial and troublesome consequences—of testing the law's limits so extensively.

Faced with the difficulty of exploring the law's potential reach, the temptation to conform to stereotyped solutions is overpowering. When policymakers accede to strict policy standards, however, they are foreclosing opportunities at the expense of their academic mission. They are exposing the university to environmental forces that constrain the information flow vital to teaching, research, and service, and they are failing to create an exchange with the copyright environment that preserves and ultimately extends the academic perspective.[13] Universities must respect the needs and rights of copyright owners, but universities must become more active partners in shaping the survival and future of fair use. A few universities might aggressively pursue user rights by following the Georgia example, but a simpler and safer improvement in policy-making for all universities would be the abandonment of the Classroom Guidelines and other restrictive standards as definitive sources of fair use. These model policies may be helpful minimal measures, but standing alone they are narrow and misleading, and they do stand alone in most university policy statements. Those policies are therefore more a surrender of opportunities than a statement of rights. The problem is finding a suitable replacement.

DIVERSE CONSTITUENTS AND THEIR POLICY PERSPECTIVES

Administrators and legal counsel have proved more willing than any other university constituency to replace the Classroom Guidelines with the University of Wisconsin policy or its related ALA standards for research and classroom copying. The American Library Association publicized its model policy among librarians; in effect, the ALA attempted to shape the environment with a more lenient alternative to the Classroom Guidelines, and librarians are generally expected to prefer relatively lenient standards. But that conjecture has not proved true: administrators and legal counsel have been primarily responsible for virtually every implementation of the ALA policy. The ALA might have been more successful by defying expectations and by promoting its policy among the more receptive administrators and legal counsel. The ALA might advance its future copyright perspectives more effectively by promoting them in partnership with associations of administrators and lawyers.

Overall, librarians and faculty develop the strictest policies. Librarians and faculty together lean most strongly toward lenient policies only with respect to software issues. Forty percent of their software policies are lenient, while only seventeen percent of software policies developed by administrators and legal counsel are lenient (see table 7.1). Legal counsel and administrators lead the recent tendency of universities to issue short, narrow, and restrictive statements on software. Nevertheless, librarians tend to write the strictest policies on all other issues. At least one prominent critic, Irving Louis Horowitz, may have misplaced his focus when he attacked librarians for their disregard of copyright; historian Michael Les Benedict was apparently correct when he characterized librarians as unwilling to exploit user rights.[14] An official at the Association of American Publishers was also correct in observing that library associations may promote liberal standards, but individual librarians generally choose standards more in keeping with the publishers' view.[15]

Numerous explanations may underlie this apparent role reversal among policymakers. The most significant may be the position of librarians in copyright controversies. Librarians may not yet be the target of lawsuits, but they are vulnerable to infringement claims whenever they reproduce materials for patrons, for their own collections, or for transmittal through interlibrary lending. Many libraries also provide supervised photocopy centers where they are responsible for copying on behalf of patrons.[16] Copying in libraries is often more visible, more frequent, and more extensive than copying elsewhere on campus. Library publications are rife with articles about the limits of copyright and the possible consequences of violations—whether resulting from photocopying, off-air recording of broadcasts, reproducing software, or any other means. Publishers and suppliers of library materials also remind librarians of copyright and the need for legal compliance.[17]

When librarians acknowledge the role of copyright and adopt limits on their activities, they are negotiating the sensitive middle ground between the legal rights of copyright owners and the demands of faculty, students, and other patrons. Rather than adopt lenient terms that may test that ambiguous gap, the tendency among librarians is to adopt standard operating procedures—especially model policies that bear congressional approval. Librarians may not necessarily intend to adopt "strict" policies; they may instead be seeking reliable and well-tested measures that minimize local controversy. Conventional policy language that carries congressional support is easier to justify than is original language or are standards endorsed only by the ALA or other professional groups. Librarians also operate enormously complex institutions; standard language can greatly streamline the bureaucratic policy-making task.

Positioned in the middle between owners, users, and university administrators, librarians frequently need to explain and justify their copyright standards. Publishers may balk at a highly lenient policy, and faculty often rail against limits on their ability to obtain copies for teaching and research. A well-established and externally legitimized policy may be the only persuasive response to these combined pressures. When librarians look outside their own organization for copyright policies, the determination of fair use will depend on who has the greatest strength in shaping the copyright environment. Most disheartening, however, is that when librarians have relied on their own creativity to formulate original policies, they tend to be even more strict. Librarians have few resources for withstanding legal challenges against innovative policies, and once challenged, their original efforts may even be disavowed or further attacked by the central university administration.

The fact that librarians tend to adopt strict policies does not mean that legal counsel and administrators are entirely lenient. Indeed, most policies developed by these "management" groups are "strict." But legal counsel and administrators have proved better suited than librarians to exploit flexibility in copyright law. Legal counsel, in particular, should be more knowledgeable about the law and therefore better able to grasp its openness to interpretation. They may be better equipped to realize that the relatively lenient ALA and Wisconsin policies have not been tested in court and have withstood scrutiny by attorneys representing universities and copyright owners without compelling a legal challenge.[18] Legal counsel may also recognize that the 1976 Copyright Act mollifies the potential liabilities of nonprofit educational institutions at virtually every opportunity. A lawsuit still presents serious risks, bad publicity, and substantial attorneys' fees, but actual monetary damages for good faith exercise of fair use are not likely to be onerous.

Another characteristic of managers is that they are not the principal parties who need to live by the policies. Most copyright policies ordinarily address the activities of faculty, librarians, and students. If a policy formulated by legal counsel or administrators is challenged, it will likely be in the context of an alleged infringement committed by someone else. But an attack on a librarian's policy will most likely accompany some infringement allegation against the library itself or its staff. If the policy is too lenient, the library may suffer a double-blow against both its policy and its specific activities. Caution is thus a powerful lure. Moreover, management officials may also not need to answer daily copyright questions, or refuse services for faculty and students, or explain and justify the policy to opposing interest groups on a recurring, face-to-face basis. Managers may resolve many copyright disputes, but they are not on the continual "front line" of copyright controversies. Although distance from the front line might breed some complacency, these officials may have a better opportunity for reflection and for assessing and fulfilling the university's broader mission.[19]

Trends among policymakers are not without exceptions. The policymaking process may depend foremost on the individual in charge and that person's awareness and insight.[20] No member of the university community—whether administrator, legal counsel, librarian, or faculty—has a monopoly on particular copyright perspectives or on the willingness to adopt "strict" or "lenient" standards. Generalizations may be helpful predictors, but they cannot substitute for the careful selection of appropriate individuals for policy responsibilities.[21] Choosing those individuals is a central feature of the university's strategic management of copyright issues. The diverse constituents also have much to share with one another. They need one another's perspectives, and they should actively seek wide support across campus for any new policy. Most of all, no one constituent group should assume that another group carries a given—and undesirable—outlook on copyright. Librarians often assume that legal counsel will be unduly cautious; administrators sometimes dismiss the experience and expertise of librarians. Each group instead provides a rich resource for developing intelligent and functional university copyright policies. A policy that neglects any of these groups may suffer gaps in its content, scope, application, and support.

The Need for Strategic Planning: The Role of the University

The challenge for policymakers is to develop and implement copyright policies that are both legally sound and reassuring of optimal user rights. Policymakers thus need a thorough comprehension of the dual functions of copyright policies. They must be aware of alternatives for copyright interpretations, and they must evaluate the relative merits of "strict" or "lenient" interpretations in light of policy purposes. In the process, developers must also be attuned to environmental forces bearing on policy formulation, and they must consciously determine the extent of environmental forces that they will allow to shape institutional decision making.

A reassessment of university policies requires thorough planning with a focus on institutional goals.[22] Through such strategic planning the university may establish an advantageous position for determining its own future on copyright matters.[23] The first step of strategic planning is to identify the "essence" or purposes of the university; the planner must strike a balance between competing objectives.[24] The planner must identify dynamics within the university and relationships with the environment, as well as the diverging views and needs of university constituents. Strategic decisions based on a broad understanding of university objectives can enable the institution to determine its own position within the environment and perhaps to shape the environment, rather than to be shaped by it.[25] Copyright policies emerging from such a process may better serve the academic mission.

Better serving the academic mission also means better coordinating responses. Universities contain two separate worlds of copyright policies. Librarians write policies exclusively for library application, while administrators and legal counsel write policies for university-wide application. Faculty have little participation at all (see table 4.3). University officials should begin a fresh examination of copyright by coordinating existing efforts; constituents who lack participation should seek a broader role. If faculty are truly concerned about copyright limits, they must assert for themselves a role in policy processes and in decision making beyond their specialized teaching and research duties.[26] They must recognize that copyright policies are related to academic concerns and are not exclusively the administration's domain.

Effective copyright policies are also more than direct responses to a system of legal rights and academic demands. Fair use is just one intellectual property concern of increasing importance at research universities. Also important to universities are the ownership of newly created works, patent rights, trademark privileges, and proper attribution for new discoveries and developments. Established legal systems offer means to address some appurtenant issues, but those systems are shaped largely by commercial interests, where academic needs are easily overlooked.[27] When existing structures prove inappropriate, universities should recommend the needed changes. Copyright law—especially fair use—is frequently attacked as inadequate, but universities must be cognizant of its deficiencies and must participate in advocating any needed reforms both in Congress and in the courts.

One common attack on copyright is skepticism about its actual effects or enforceability; copying is commonplace and difficult to detect. Yet such attacks should not deflate the importance of university copyright policies. Lawsuits surrounding educational interests do occasionally arise, as against NYU in 1983 and against Kinko's Graphics Corporation in 1991.[28] The university community also has an ethical duty to respect rights and to obey the law with or without actual litigation. Regardless of their effect on individual behavior, university policies remain important gestures in the evolution of fair use. The cumulative tendency of universities to adopt strict copyright policies is a disturbing erosion of legal rights. One federal court has stated that industry standards do not determine the scope of fair use,[29] but in other contexts courts have acknowledged a "campus common law" based on behavior patterns at colleges and universities.[30] Model guidelines, private settlements, and trends of behavior are not themselves "law," but in the absence of specific legislation and court rulings, they often become the only available gauge, even if they are ill-conceived. In attacking common misperceptions about user rights, one recent study concluded bluntly: "If such fallacies go unchallenged long enough, they are likely to become a substitute for the truth."[31]

Uncertainties in copyright law are a mixed blessing that demand greater planning. They are opportunities for innovation, and they are unwelcome challenges. The general theory of organizational behavior in chapter one of this book suggests that policymakers will treat uncertainties as burdens to avoid.[32] Organizations resist the need to resolve uncertainties; they will resort to standard operating procedures or to stereotyped responses, rather than devise innovative solutions.[33] Decision-makers will overlook their academic mission simply because complicated situations introduce numerous choice problems with no single resolution:

> They [decision-makers] impose plans, standard operating procedures, industry tradition, and uncertainty-absorbing contracts on that environment. In short, they achieve a reasonably manageable decision situation by avoiding planning where plans depend on predictions of uncertain future events and by emphasizing planning where the plans can be made self-confirming through some control device.[34]

The tremendous uncertainty of copyright will likely lead organizations to issue standard policies or no policies at all. Thus, universities typically greet the unsettled world of software copyright, for example, with cursory statements against copying, rather than exploring the legal and practical complexities.

Reforming the policy-making process and overcoming barriers to fresh and effective policies must begin with the individuals who have decision-making authority and who are affected by the policies. Legal counsel and administrators have the most important role. They develop half of all policies and advise other policymakers. These central officers have the opportunity to coordinate university-wide responses to copyright, and they are in the best position to relate the legal response to academic needs. They need to use their position to comprehend the ability of fair use to better serve the academic community.

The university's chief executive also has a potentially key role. The top official can set an example and delineate priorities. The University of Wisconsin's influential policy statement might never have emerged without early support from the university's chancellor. The most important step for any participant in the process is to demonstrate a keen awareness of alternatives and a willingness to look beyond the environmental demands that can blind universities to their own interests and to the opportunity for intellectual creativity. New technological uses of information demand creative analysis. If educators do not take the initiative on these issues, their perspectives and concerns will have at best a secondary role in shaping the university's response to the copyright environment.

Swapping Systems: The Copyright Clearance Center and Collective Administration

The bewilderment and frustration of grappling with copyright privileges and obligations has fueled the creation of alternative programs intended to ease access to permissions and to assure safety from threats of litigation. The most prominent of these alternatives is the Copyright Clearance Center (CCC). The CCC began operations in 1978 in response to congressional demands that the marketplace provide smooth implementation of the 1976 Copyright Act. It acts as an agent on behalf of thousands of journal and book publishers to grant permission to copy from their works. The publishers set the fees, and users are asked to submit proper information and payment for each copy.[35] The CCC serves an important purpose, but it has had limited appeal on campuses for several reasons. First, it officially preserves no privilege of fair use. The CCC makes no distinction between fair use copying and copying that requires permission. Thus, users are still left with the difficult task of concluding whether each instance of reproducing a copyrighted work is a legal right or a legal violation. Second, utilizing the CCC's service is an administrative and financial burden. Submitting the required documentation is often feasible only for most high-volume users. The CCC has had considerable success with campus libraries and copy shops that can process multiple records simultaneously, but it attracts little interest from individual departments or faculty.

In any event, the fees for many uses can easily jump from modest to prohibitive. Antitrust law prevents the CCC from prescribing a fee structure, so each publisher sets its own costs. Costs per copy can be nominal, or they can be a substantial basic fee, plus a surcharge for each page actually copied. The fee is also per copy. Multiple copies require multiple payments. As a result, the fee for distributing copies of a single article to a classroom of students can be hundreds of dollars. The fees for a common anthology of photocopied materials is often as much as five dollars per issue, but they can easily push the purchase price beyond most practical limits.[36] The price of one "anthology" purchased by students at the University of California, Berkeley, nearly doubled to ninety dollars, reflecting permission fees paid after the *Kinko's* decision.[37] The rights of copyright owners deserve protection, and owners deserve payment for uses beyond fair use. But the current fees often mean that the choice is not between lawful and unlawful uses, but instead between using and not using materials at all.[38]

THE CCC'S UNIVERSITY PILOT PROGRAM

In order to make the CCC's opportunities more palatable to the academic community, the CCC launched a "University Pilot Program" in 1990 to review the nature of materials photocopied on college campuses and to structure a more predictable and more acceptable license fee. Six institutions participated in the initial study: Columbia University, Cornell School of Hotel and Restaurant Management, Northeastern University, Principia College, Stanford University, and Utah State University. The CCC expects to use data collected in the study to develop a blanket license agreement, whereby universities may pay a single annual fee for all isolated copying by faculty, staff, and administrators. The creation of anthologies, however, would still be subject to individual review and fees for each item copied.[39]

The blanket license plan may therefore offer some consolation, but in its expected form it suffers serious deficiencies that may prevent or at least retard its wide implementation. First, the blanket license would apply to exactly the type of activity that is commonly within a fair use definition—copying for individual research and teaching.[40] Because the CCC does not define "fair use," the only recourse for participating institutions is to negotiate a reduced fee to reflect their own understanding of fair use. Thus, the universities must still confront that hoary task of analyzing the foggy law if they are to identify and promote their own best interests. Second, the program does not apply to anthologies and perhaps other photocopying on campus. Participants are not wholly spared the task of conducting individual transactions and making individual fee payments for some of the most common needs.[41] The "blanket license" is not truly comprehensive.

The third constraint on the CCC is that it can license rights only for those publishers that choose to participate. The CCC does represent multitudes of owners, but even the fullest involvement with the CCC does not preclude the need to investigate whether an individual item is on the CCC list.[42] Universities need to make separate arrangements with publishers that are not on the list, lest they face the continued possibility of lawsuits. A few countries have avoided some of these problems by enacting compulsory licensing laws for photocopying. The United States has a compulsory license law only for new recordings of musical works. The music is subject to copyright; even so, nonowners are entitled to perform or record the music without the need to seek permission, but they must pay a prescribed royalty fee. No such provision for copying of printed works has gained much support in this country.[43]

Despite these shortcomings, the CCC offers enormous opportunities and some welcome reassurance for nervous universities in the post-*Kinko's* era. After the *Kinko's* case, the CCC began receiving up to two thousand requests each day for permissions, especially from copy shops making anthologies for classroom use. The CCC implemented an "Academic Permissions Service" to expedite permission from publishers already registered with the CCC and to obtain permission from nonregistrants.[44] But even publishers acknowledged in the months after *Kinko's* that the CCC was not successfully processing all requests on time.[45] The increased demand has spawned competing services. The AAP has begun an electronic mail service for college bookstores called "PUBNET," but at last report only about twenty-five textbook publishers were involved.[46] Other organizations, such as University Microfilms, Inc. and The Institute for Scientific Information, Inc. offer various programs for obtaining copies of journal articles and other materials that are cleared with the copyright owners.

The future viability of collective licensing—and particularly the CCC itself—received an enormous boost in a 1992 Federal District Court decision involving photocopying for research purposes by scientists at Texaco Inc. Not only did the court evaluate the four factors of fair use to conclude that photocopying of articles from scientific journals exceeded fair use, but the court further asserted that the easy availability of permissions through the CCC limited user rights in general. The existence of the CCC strengthened the publishers' argument that photocopying had a harmful effect on the potential revenues from the journal; the ease of obtaining permissions from the CCC relieved the burden of copyright compliance:[47]

> Reasonably priced, administratively tolerable licensing procedures are available that can protect the copyright owners' interests without harming research or imposing excessive burdens on users. To the extent such photocopying was "customary," it has become far less so as many giant corporate users have subscribed to the CCC systems. To the extent the copying practice was "reasonable" . . . it has ceased to be "reasonable" as the reasons that justified it before the CCC have ceased to exist.

These words are not only a ringing endorsement of the CCC, but they directly integrate the CCC's practices with the legal definition of fair use rights. The *Texaco* decision is still a few steps removed from the academic context—where copying is not necessarily for profit, and where some scholarly publications are not so dependent on sales revenues—but the case signals that even individual research copies can be infringements, and the advent of the CCC's university program can be construed as a serious limitation on fair use. The *Texaco* case is therefore not only a warning to universities about potential claims from copyright owners, but also is an admonition that academicians must assert their own copyright interests. The CCC may offer important potential benefits for the academe, but university officials must be watchful that their participation with collective licensing agencies does not become a substitute for fair use opportunities, whether in practice or in the terms of a written license agreement.

THE PROMISE OF NEW TECHNOLOGIES

New technological developments for document storage and retrieval offer new challenges for copyright compliance and new opportunities for collective administration. As the chapter on computer software emphasizes, the fair use limits of reproducing and downloading electronically stored data are uncertain at best. But individual uses of such material might be effectively identified, controlled, and traced through proper programming. Several publishers of technical periodicals have formed "ADONIS," an organization that delivers text through online database systems, where access and use may be controlled and a fee imposed. University Microfilms, Inc. is also experimenting with a "Billing and Royalty Tracking" system—also called "BART"—that charges a fee for printing materials stored on CD-ROMs.[48] The CCC has begun experimenting with electronic delivery of text to universities.[49] One general possibility is the attachment of an electronic "courier" to each item of stored information. The courier "can record all uses of the information so that charges can be applied or it can immediately request permission. . . ."[50] Such systems can streamline the compliance process, but the challenge for universities is to utilize them and to pay the requisite fees only when exceeding fair use privileges. A possible compromise solution is to negotiate a lower fee that realistically reflects the volume of uses that are protected by law.

New technologies offer particularly promising solutions to the situation posed in the *Kinko's* case—the copying of book chapters in anthologies. Several textbook publishers have instituted programs for selling only those chapters of their books necessary for each particular course.[51] For example, McGraw-Hill, Inc. has a "Primus" system of electronically stored copies of textbooks from diverse disciplines. The system can print copies of only those chapters—and even shorter excerpts—requested by the faculty member. The result is a customized textbook with full clearance from the copyright owner. Other publishers offering customized textbooks include West Publishing Co., Allyn and Bacon, Simon & Schuster, and Ginn Press. Early indications are that the customized books are feasible for the publishers and can be available at reasonable prices. Some publishers will include in their customized works original materials and journal articles, subject to obtaining clearances.

By fully exploiting available technology, publishers have the opportunity to deliver materials in the form demanded by their customers, thus obviating much of the photocopying controversy and assuring a payment of reasonable royalties. The changing nature of publishing and disseminating information has lessened much of the pressure to change copyright law. A spokesperson for the CCC has concluded that "existing copyright law provides a perfectly adequate context for the development and elaboration of systems to manage computer-based text."[52] Innovative license agreements and cooperative arrangements between suppliers and users of information resources have begun to address and alleviate many of the difficult copyright problems.[53] Combined with the burden of attempting to change the law, many observers are concluding that the current regime of laws is in fact revealing its flexibility to serve changing needs.[54] Many publishers are also discovering that by changing their means of delivering materials they find greater financial rewards and fewer copyright confrontations.

THE IMPETUS FOR GROWTH

The slow and imperfect evolution of "collective administration" of copyright is certain to expand. As sensitivities to copyright heighten, university officials will seek new means for expediting permissions and for obtaining shelter from litigation. The growth of licensing agencies, such as the CCC in the United States, reflects a worldwide phenomenon. These so-called "Reproduction Rights Organizations" now exist in dozens of countries. The United States also joined the Berne Convention for the Protection of Literary and Artistic Works in 1989. That multilateral treaty affirms that each country may establish a right to use copyrighted works for teaching and research, but an accompanying explanation adds that those rights may be curtailed in countries that offer a "collective license" program.[55] The legal and monetary impetus to create an effective and broad-reaching licensing program is unquestionable.

Yet the utopian development of an ideal collective administration in this country is far in the future. It may never exist. Until it does, however, universities must continue to rely on fair use, as either the main source of their rights, or at least as a supplement to the partial successes of the CCC and other organizations. Various forms of collective administration may ease struggles with copyright, but they cannot replace the need for a sophisticated understanding of rights and obligations. Indeed, some of the CCC's services are useful only after the user has concluded that the proposed copying exceeds fair use. Fees paid for licenses are unnecessary if the copying is already allowed under law, and a university policy remains an important tool for making that determination.

A sophisticated insight on fair use can also better serve the multifold objectives of universities. This book has asserted at length that fair use can be interpreted to serve academic needs and to avoid potential infringements. Fair use can also be a tool for responding to the devastating financial condition that higher education now faces. A balanced and lawful approach should prevent both costly litigation as well as needless payments of royalty fees for copies that are already sanctioned. Like universities that rely on the Classroom Guidelines, institutions that resort exclusively to some forms of collective administration may be failing to recognize legally established opportunities that can further their academic—and financial—objectives. Many institutions seek to swap copyright dilemmas for collective assurance; in reality, universities must enable both systems to coexist, and both systems must be tailored to serve the academic mission.

Reshaping the Environment: The Role of Professional Associations and Congress

With or without collective licensing programs, university policymakers will feel the constant pressure to find "answers" to copyright questions, to protect the institution from liabilities, and to rely on easily available and tested policies. They do not make that quest in a vacuum. Even with the most meticulous and creative planning, environmental effects on universities are inevitable. External agents, from Congress to news reports, will continue to signal understandings of fair use that will make their way into university standards. Given that continued environmental influence, another strategy for shaping university perspectives on copyright is to alter the environment and the signal it sends.

Prominent environmental forces on universities include various congressional guidelines that originated in negotiations among professional and trade associations. They received crucial blessings from Congress, and the Classroom Guidelines in particular gained enormous credibility and influence in the NYU case and the *Kinko's* decision. The leading players in shaping the environment therefore include Congress, the courts, and professional associations with interests in copyright matters. The courts, however, have a significant role only because individual parties bring their cases for resolution. The named plaintiffs in the NYU and *Kinko's* cases were publishers, but their trade association—the Association of American Publishers—oversaw both actions. While individual judges, litigants, and their lawyers are obviously central players in the greater copyright environment, the AAP actually spearheaded the lawsuits and promoted the Classroom Guidelines. The AAP also notified hundreds of colleges and universities of the NYU settlement and recommended that they follow NYU's example. The AAP figured prominently in news reports about *Kinko's*. Without the AAP, the Classroom Guidelines would undoubtedly have had much less notoriety and influence.

The American Library Association, another professional group, has promoted the only significant alternative to the Classroom Guidelines. A few university policies reflect the ALA Model Policy, but it lacks the imprimatur of congressional approval, and no court decision has relied on the ALA standards. Without an endorsement from a lawmaking body, those standards will remain a minority perspective. The power of a congressional endorsement is also made undeniable by the Music Guidelines, the Off-Air Guidelines, and the CONTU Guidelines for interlibrary lending. These model policies emerged with support from diverse interest groups and their professional associations, and Congress endorsed them as valid understandings of user rights. As a result, these model policies nearly monopolize the relevant university standards.

A Central Role for Congress

Professional associations may devise and promote model standards, but Congress is the linchpin in shaping the copyright environment. Congress has enacted provisions—notably Section 108 on library copying and Section 117 on software use—with sufficient specificity to become a direct part of university policies. Congress also has enacted provisions—especially Section 107 on fair use—that stir confusion and that beg for clarification. But Congress then attempted to resolve some confusion by endorsing guidelines that can be transposed into written institutional standards. This paramount role for Congress is appropriate. Congress is fulfilling its constitutional authority to enact copyright measures, and Congress is a diverse body that can represent and deliberate the many perspectives on copyright. The legislative history of the 1976 act demonstrates that Congress listened to opinions on all aspects of the law. Educators can take consolation in the repeated sensitivity that Congress has shown for academic needs.

Yet the role of Congress may exceed even its own expectations. Congress enacted a flexible doctrine of fair use to meet changing circumstances with differing measures of legal rights. Congress endorsed the Classroom Guidelines and other interpretations as reasonable responses to the vagueness of user rights. But Congress specifically affirmed these guidelines as only "minimum" standards; they can be helpful "safe harbors," but they are not the final word. Yet once offered to the public, these guidelines were promoted and accepted as the only legitimate fair use standard for the issues they cover. At New York University, in particular, the Classroom Guidelines effectively became "maximum" standards. The flexibility Congress sought to preserve was lost. Rights beyond the "minimum" were virtually shut out. Moreover, the mere existence of apparently "official" guidelines has stifled any tendency of universities to give copyright issues a fresh analysis and a creative evaluation. Their official stature has also been misconstrued as legal edict.

Congress gave irrefutable credibility to these copyright standards, but it did not give them a corresponding degree of introspection. Congress passed the 1976 Copyright Act after years of hearings and study, yet endorsement of the full Classroom Guidelines came only in the final months, and that endorsement began eroding much of the intended fair use formula. Merely printing proposed guidelines in congressional reports gave them a powerfully persuasive boost. Their appearance as "mandates" has displaced the intended flexibility. Confusion and threats combined to extract flexibility from fair use and to instill rigidity.

The opportunity is ripe for new congressional action. Although fair use is seldom a pressing priority for Congress, and even though Congress may ultimately move slowly, Congress should commence a review of the law and the Classroom Guidelines. Members of Congress may believe that the 1976 act continues to reflect a workable fair use doctrine, that the Classroom Guidelines are still a voluntary statement of "minimum" rights, and that the marketplace is better able to give the law meaning in diverse circumstances. But at the local level, where fair use is given its daily application, these ideals no longer hold true. Not only has the "marketplace" instilled rigidity in the law, but the 1991 *Kinko's* decision has utterly confused the issues. That one case has renewed fears and ratified the Classroom Guidelines; it also has driven a wedge into the meaning and reliability of the guidelines themselves. The court bolstered the guidelines by using them to test the lawfulness of Kinko's copying, but the court also refused to apply the outright prohibition of "anthologies" set forth in the standards. Add to these developments the common university tendency to misapply the guidelines as "maximum" standards, and the result is widespread reliance on a model policy that has only dubious legal validity and questionable effects on actual behavior. Not only should universities avoid these guidelines, but Congress must initiate their official review and evisceration. The original congressional endorsement of these standards will remain until Congress takes it away.

Congressional action at this stage need not culminate in statutory revision. Instead, Congress should sponsor a series of meetings among diverse interest groups to review the guidelines, to propose amendments or revisions, and to clarify the nature of copyright and its effects on higher education and the dissemination of knowledge. Congress could ask the Copyright Office to sponsor the meetings, or it could appoint a specialized commission, such as the CONTU commission that advised Congress on issues from computer software to interlibrary lending. Congress should support future guidelines only after more openly soliciting comments specifically about the measures. Any final endorsement must come with stronger expressions about the limited role of the guidelines and the need to consider alternatives under the law. The original admonition that the Classroom Guidelines were "minimum" standards was inadequate; that language was lost at NYU and other universities. Each word from Congress is therefore vital. Amidst the vagueness of copyright law, all parties grope for each clue of congressional intent. Each word on the bleak terrain of fair use can also be misinterpreted and taken out of context or taken away. Congress must state its position more clearly and leave no room for the artistry of any narrow interests.

THE ROLE OF PROFESSIONAL ASSOCIATIONS

In the development of future guidelines, Congress will always look to professional and trade associations for their expertise, perspectives, and support. These associations will no doubt be called upon again to give advice and to negotiate new understandings of the law. They will continue to delineate compromises among interest groups and to spare Congress from revising the statutes themselves. Professional associations are also in a better position than their individual members to take a meaningful initiative in shaping the copyright environment. Innovative policy-making at the University of Wisconsin had some external influence, but the Wisconsin standards had much greater influence after the American Library Association adopted and promoted them. The professional association was far more effective than the individual institution.

Academic associations should increase their involvement in proceedings before Congress and in negotiations with other interest groups. Higher education was not well represented in negotiations that led to the Classroom Guidelines. These associations should also participate more fully in litigation affecting their interests. When a litigant asks the court to apply the Classroom Guidelines in a fair use case, for example, associations should be prepared to submit amicus briefs arguing their perspective on the issues, as a host of library organizations have done in the appeal of the *Texaco* decision. Associations must acknowledge that NYU's adoption of the Classroom Guidelines was not an isolated event but an occurrence affecting nearly all universities. More recently, the court's use of the Classroom Guidelines in the *Kinko's* case will expand their deep and lasting consequences for all educators, as universities and private copy shops seek to avoid potential liabilities. To improve their effectiveness, academic groups must continue cooperating with one another in advancing interpretations and creatively filling voids in the evolution of fair use.

THE FUTURE POTENTIAL

Building on these lessons, the next major set of guidelines shaping the copyright environment will most certainly come from a consortium of professional associations representing diverse views. The timing of any action will also be crucial. The Classroom Guidelines gained momentum in part simply because they were the first available model policy. The guidelines with earliest prominence can have the greatest influence. Any new guidelines must offer practical understandings of fair use, and they must receive "official" approval before any competition gains ground. Taking the initiative is therefore a vital element in shaping copyright standards.

The copyright issues ready for fresh development surround uses of computer software, works stored in electronic form, and multimedia applications. Universities generally have been unable to give fair use a meaningful application to software, and no model policy has gained widespread acceptance. Indeed, a 1992 study from the U.S. Office of Technology Assessment includes a recommendation that Congress or the Copyright Office begin the process of developing guidelines on lawful uses of software and works stored in electronic form, including the use of unpublished works, rights granted under Section 117, the ability of users to pursue reverse engineering, and library and research uses of electronic databases.[56] The entire report, however, offers little insight on proper procedures for establishing effective guidelines. It gives an overview of legal issues and suggests that diverse interest groups participate in shaping the standards, but nowhere does the report probe past experiences with the Classroom Guidelines and other "model policies." It only implies the hope that any new guidelines will gain uniform acceptance and have the desired consequences.

If educators want to prevent recurrence of potentially confining measures of fair use, and if they seek to influence future rights to software, they should work with their professional associations to formulate reasonable positions that preserve fair use and that respect the rights of creators. These associations should share perspectives with one another and ideally reach an agreed position.[57] They should then expand the process into negotiations with representatives of contrary positions. Any clash of ideals should not become a battle among enemies; universities and copyright proprietors need to comprehend and support the balance of interests that copyright embodies. The most effective guidelines will emerge from cooperation, not confrontation. The procedure should also include early contacts with—and guidance from—the Copyright Office and appropriate congressional committees. The most important result of the negotiations would be congressional approval of the guidelines. Only then can the guidelines have a maximum force on copyright development. As long as Congress has not initiated this process, educators must seize the opportunity.

Educators must also lessen their insistence on "answers" to all copyright questions. Their demand for specifics led to the meticulous and ultimately unrealistic Classroom Guidelines. Sometimes the questions are better left unanswered, or perhaps the best answers might be only general principles of law and practice. The ALA Model Policy, for example, allows "selective and sparing" copying for classroom distribution. That vagueness begs further questions, but it liberates the university from exacting and inflexible parameters. Precise answers are only a short-run solution. They do not respond to unpredictable future needs, and they do not preserve the fluidity of fair use that Congress intended.

Everyone participating in copyright policy-making must also recognize that no policy will last forever. Copyright is a dynamic force that will evolve with new technologies, new uses of materials, new demands, and new court rulings. Any model policy that emerges from negotiations should be scheduled for periodic reviews, much like the five-year studies originally mandated by Section 108 of the Copyright Act. As detailed in chapter three of this book, the Classroom Guidelines and the ALA Model Policy are now badly in need of a current review, but no such review is in the offing. Periodic reviews can also foster a renewed articulation of the spirit of copyright law and the relationship of fair use to the academic mission and to the encouragement of creativity. That improved perspective may not, in and of itself, answer daily questions, but it may engender a more realistic and beneficial position on the legal issues. It could also improve relations between the academe and copyright proprietors. All parties to the copyright controversy must respect both sides of the legal balance. The duality of copyright is not an inherent conflict; the two sides can instead complement one another. A clearer and more balanced view of fair use thus implies a clearer and more balanced comprehension of owners' rights. Such a cooperative spirit can lead to greater financial and ethical support for creators of copyrighted works; it can also better promote the university's mission of teaching, research, and community service.

Notes

CHAPTER ONE

1. U.S. Congress, Office of Technology Assessment, *Intellectual Property Rights in an Age of Electronics and Information* (Washington, DC: GPO, 1986), 33.

2. William A. Kaplin, *The Law of Higher Education: A Comprehensive Guide to Legal Implications of Administrative Decision Making,* 2d ed. (San Francisco: Jossey-Bass Publishers, 1985), 495.

3. Zechariah Chafee, "Reflections on the Law of Copyright: I," *Columbia Law Review* 45 (July 1945): 503.

4. Michael I. Pitman, "Why Copyright?" *Scholarly Publishing* 13 (January 1982): 124; Meredith A. Butler, "Publishers, Technological Change, and Copyright: Maintaining the Balance," *Drexel Library Quarterly* 20 (Summer 1984): 36, 39; and Note [David G. Golden], "Toward a Unified Theory of Copyright Infringement for an Advanced Technological Era," *Harvard Law Review* 96 (December 1982): 454.

5. Addison-Wesley Publishing v. New York University, 1983 Copyright Law Decisions ¶ 25,544 (S.D.N.Y. 1983). Further details on this case and the settlement appear in chapter three.

6. Details about the development and content of these guidelines appear in chapter two.

7. Copyright Act of 1976, 17 U.S.C. §§102 and 106 (1988).

8. Copyright Act of 1976, 17 U.S.C. §§107, 108, and 110 (1988).

9. See, for example, Irving Louis Horowitz and Mary E. Curtis, "Fair Use versus Fair Return: Copyright Legislation and Its Consequences," *Journal of the American Society for Information Science* 35 (March 1984): 73.

10. U.S. Const. art. I, § 8.

11. See, for example, Stephen Breyer, "The Uneasy Case for Copyright: A Study of Copyright in Books, Photocopies, and Computer Programs," *Harvard Law Review* 84 (December 1970): 284–323. *See also* Barry W. Tyerman, "The Economic Rationale for Copyright Protection for Published Books: A Reply to Professor Breyer," *UCLA Law Review* 18 (June 1971): 1100–1125; Stephen Breyer, "Copyright: A Rejoinder," *UCLA Law Review* 20 (October 1972): 75–83.

12. Gail Paul Sorenson, "Impact of the Copyright Law on College Teaching," *Journal of College and University Law* 12 (Spring 1986): 518 and 537.

13. L. Ray Patterson and Stanley W. Lindberg, *The Nature of Copyright: A Law of Users' Rights* (Athens, GA: The University of Georgia Press, 1991). Since completing the collection of policies for this study, the University of Georgia issued an elaborate policy based on the Patterson and Lindberg book. For more details, see chapter eight of this book.

14. Memorandum to Members of AAP's Professional and Scholarly Publishing Division from Barbara Meredith, 28 July 1992.

15. American Geophysical Union v. Texaco Inc., 802 F. Supp. 1, 13 n.13 (S.D.N.Y. 1992).

16. Copyright Act of 1976, Pub. L. 94–553, 90 Stat. 2541 (1976).

17. See generally, Lewis I. Flacks, "Living in the Gap of Ambiguity: An Attorney's Advice to Librarians on the Copyright Law," *American Libraries* 8 (September 1977): 252–57.

18. "Despite its importance, the answer to the problem of how to achieve a proper balance between the rights of copyright owners and the rights of users has escaped a rational solution, apparently because the issue has not been carefully analyzed" (Patterson and Lindberg, *The Nature of Copyright,* 156).

19. "[H]owever much importance one attaches to teaching and research, an academic institution is not justified in damaging the legally recognized interests of people who have not consented to assume such risks." See Derek Bok, *Beyond the Ivory Tower: Social Responsibilities of the Modern University* (Cambridge, MA: Harvard University Press, 1982), 300.

20. 758 F. Supp. 1522, 1526 (S.D.N.Y. 1991).

21. Ironically, Kinko's itself ultimately resolved its differences with the publishers by paying damages and attorneys' fees and by agreeing to seek permission when copying more than one page of any copyrighted work in an anthology. Thus, Kinko's adopted neither the guidelines nor the prohibition on all anthologies. Basic Books, Inc. v. Kinko's Graphics Corp., 21 U.S.P.Q. 2d 1639 (S.D.N.Y. 1991).

22. Lyman A. Glenny and Thomas K. Dalglish, "Higher Education and the Law," in *The University as an Organization,* pp. 173–202, edited by James A. Perkins (New York: McGraw Hill Book Company, 1973), 195.

23. One study of corporate software copyright policies defines them as "policies and guidelines designed to prohibit software copying by employees" ("Student Symposium: A Survey of Software Copying Policy in Corporate America," *Journal of Law and Technology* 2 [Winter 1987]: 39 n.2). A related study adopted a more open definition: "a formal set of rules and guidelines governing the use of software within a corporation" (Robert Greene Sterne and Edward J. Kessler, "An Overview of Software Copying Policies in Corporate America," *Journal of Law and Technology* 1 [Spring 1986]: 157). For language from university policies themselves about their purposes, see chapter four.

24. For example, the Boston University policy states in its introduction: "Boston University may be liable for actions taken by its faculty and staff in the course of their duties; it is therefore important that its policies on copyrights be followed" (see "BOSTON–1981" in Appendix A). For an example of an article on policies

as a means of avoiding liability, see Michael Gemignani, "A College's Liability for Unauthorized Copying of Microcomputer Software by Students," *Journal of Law and Education* 15 (Fall 1986): 433.

25. John Diebold, *Managing Information: The Challenge and the Opportunity* (New York: AMACOM, 1985), 19, 40–42, and 48.

26. Robert M. Rosenzweig, *The Research Universities and Their Patrons* (Berkeley: University of California Press, 1982), 1.

27. Weinstein v. University of Illinois, 811 F. 2d 1091, 1094 (7th Cir. 1987); Melville B. Nimmer and David Nimmer, *Nimmer on Copyright* (New York: Matthew Bender), ¶ 5.03[B][1][b]. Some commentators have argued that the 1976 Copyright Act requires a signed agreement if the faculty member is to retain ownership of writings created within the scope of employment. William A. Rome, "Scholarly Writings in the University Setting: Changes in the Works and on the Books," in *Copyright Law Symposium*, vol. 35 (New York: Columbia University Press, 1989), 41–68; Cory H. Van Arsdale, "Computer Programs and Other Faculty Writings Under the Work-for-Hire Doctrine: Who Owns the Intellectual's Property?" *Santa Clara Computer and High-Technology Law Journal* 1 (January 1985): 141–67. These analyses may change, however, with the Supreme Court's ruling in Community for Creative Non-Violence v. Reid, 409 U.S. 730 (1989).

28. Philip S. Bousquet, "Externally Sponsored Faculty Research Under the 'Work for Hire' Doctrine: Who's the Boss?" *Syracuse Law Review* 39 (1988): 1351–80.

29. Ivars Peterson, "Bits of Ownership," *Science News*, 21 September 1985, pp. 188–90.

30. See generally, Phyllis S. Lachs, "University Patent Policy," *Journal of College and University Law* 10 (Winter 1983–84): 263–64. For a content analysis of university policies governing ownership of copyrights, see Pat K. Chew, "Faculty-Generated Inventions: Who Owns the Golden Egg?" *Wisconsin Law Review* 1992 (1992): 259–314.

31. Copyright Act of 1976, 17 U.S.C. § 108 (1988), *as amended by* Copyright Amendments Act of 1992, Pub. L. 102–307, § 301, 106 Stat. 264, 272 (1992).

32. Copyright Act of 1976, 17 U.S.C. § 110 (1988).

33. The lawsuit against UCLA was dismissed on the ground that a suit against a state agency could not proceed in federal court under the Eleventh Amendment to the U.S. Constitution. BV Engineering v. University of California, Los Angeles, 858 F. 2d 1394 (9th Cir. 1988), *cert. denied,* 489 U.S. 1090 (1989). Congress has since amended the law to allow such lawsuits to continue. Copyright Act of 1976, 17 U.S.C. § 511 (1988), *as amended by* Copyright Remedy Clarification Act, Pub. L. 101–553, 104 Stat. 2749 (1990). For an article about the Oregon case, see David L. Wilson, "U. of Oregon Pays $130,000 to Settle Software-Copying Suit," *Chronicle of Higher Education,* 4 September 1991, pp. A27 and A30.

34. "The more general or diffuse the goals, the more difficult it is to design a structure to pursue them." See W. Richard Scott, *Organizations: Rational, Natural, and Open Systems,* 2d ed. (Englewood Cliffs, NJ: Prentice-Hall, Inc., 1987), 32.

35. Michael D. Cohen and James G. March, "Decisions, Presidents, and Status," in *Ambiguity and Choice in Organizations,* 2d ed., pp. 174–205, edited by

James G. March and John P. Olson (Oslo, Norway: Universitetsforlaget, 1979), 175.

36. The "environment" is "a set of elements and their relevant properties, which elements are not part of the system, but a change in any of which can cause or produce a change in the state of the system" (Russell L. Ackoff and Fred E. Emery, *On Purposeful Systems* [Seaside, CA: Intersystems Publications, 1972], 19).

37. Kenneth E. Knight and Reuben R. McDaniel, Jr., *Organizations: An Information Systems Perspective* (Belmont, CA: Wadsworth Publishing Company, Inc., 1979), 53.

38. Scott, *Organizations*, 79–80.

39. Robert L. Swinth, *Organizational Systems for Management: Designing, Planning, and Implementation* (Columbus, OH: Grid, Inc., 1974), 42–43.

40. "Integrity involves . . . an insistence that all of the university's activities advance its capabilities to pursue each of its missions. . . . " See James A. Perkins, *The University in Transition* (Princeton, NJ: Princeton University Press, 1966), 49.

41. "The university is not an orderly structure that yields to authoritarian management as does the military division or the corporation. The university's function is to serve the private processes of faculty and students, on the one hand, and the large public interests of society on the other" (Perkins, *The University in Transition*, 50).

42. Scott, *Organizations*, 268; Swinth, *Organizational Systems*, 18.

43. Richard M. Cyert and James G. March, *A Behavioral Theory of the Firm* (Englewood Cliffs, NJ: Prentice-Hall, Inc., 1963), 27.

44. Ibid., 26.

45. Faculty in particular are often accused of being factional and specialized. "Consequently, the faculty's administrative stance contains elements of senatorial courtesy—maximum permissiveness with respect to individual faculty desires, combined with maximum protection if anyone would interfere with this permissiveness. Such a posture is exactly right for the protection of the classroom, but it is quite inadequate for educational or institutional management" (Perkins, *The University in Transition*, 55).

46. Gunnar Boalt and Herman Lantz, *Universities and Research: Observations on the United States and Sweden* (New York: Wiley Interscience Division, John Wiley & Sons, Inc., 1970), 25.

47. Administrators are generally aware of the "need for sophisticated legal advice in adjusting an institution's policies and procedures to reduce exposure to legal problems." See Lanora F. Welzenbach, ed., *College and University Business Administration*, 4th ed. (Washington, DC: National Association of College and University Business Officers, 1982), 110.

48. Paul L. Dressel, "Mission, Organization, and Leadership," *Journal of Higher Education* 58 (January–February 1987): 101–2.

49. Cyert and March, *A Behavioral Theory of the Firm*, 13.

50. Glenny and Dalglish, "Higher Education and the Law," 196.

51. James Grier Miller, *Living Systems* (New York: McGraw-Hill Book Co., 1978), 686.

52. Irwin T. Sanders, "The University as a Community," in *The University as an Organization*, edited by James A. Perkins (New York: McGraw Hill Book Company, 1973), 67–69.

53. Although faculty members were among the defendants named in the infringement action against New York University, they were clearly not the primary target of the plaintiffs. David Izakowitz, "Fair Use of the Guidelines for Classroom Copying? An Examination of the *Addison-Wesley* Settlement," *Rutgers Computer and Technology Law Journal* 11 (1985): 111–40.

54. Sanders, "The University as a Community," 60–63.

55. Richard M. Dougherty, "Libraries and Computing Centers: A Blueprint for Collaboration," *College and Research Libraries* 48 (July 1987): 294.

56. Ingmar Lundberg, "Photocopying at Scientific Libraries and the Copyright Legislation: Present Situation and Future Perspectives," *Copyright Bulletin* 13, no. 2 (1979): 23.

57. Verner W. Clapp, "The Copyright Dilemma: A Librarian's View," *Library Quarterly* 38 (October 1968): 352.

58. Irving Louis Horowitz, *Communicating Ideas* (New York: Oxford University Press, 1986), 59 and 61.

59. Michael Les Benedict, "Historians and the Continuing Controversy over Fair Use of Unpublished Manuscript Materials," *American Historical Review* 91 (October 1986): 870–71.

60. Roderick K. Daane, "The Role of University Counsel," *Journal of College and University Law* 12 (Winter 1985): 399; Cheryl Fields, "Academics' Increased Reliance on Legal Advice Documented by College Attorney's Association," *Chronicle of Higher Education*, 17 July 1985, pp. 15–16.

61. John E. Corbally, Jr., "University Counsel—Scope and Mission," *Journal of College and University Law* 2 (Fall 1974): 4.

62. Robert W. Harris, "Memorandum: Introductory Guide to Academic Risks of Copyright Infringement," *Journal of College and University Law* 7 (1980–81): 329 (reprints a copyright policy developed for the University of New Mexico; it is no longer in effect and is not included among policies analyzed in this study).

63. See "HAWAII–1988" in Appendix A.

64. See "NY/ALB–1987" in Appendix A.

65. "The greater the participation of organizational managers in trade and professional associations, the more likely the organization will be, or will become, like other organizations in its field." See Paul J. DiMaggio and Walter W. Powell, "The Iron Cage Revisited: Institutional Isomorphism and Collective Rationality in Organizational Fields," *American Sociological Review* 48 (April 1983): 155.

66. The ALA and AAP policies are described more fully in chapters three and five.

67. James A. Perkins, "Organization and Functions of the University," in *The University as an Organization*, pp. 3–14, edited by James A. Perkins (New York: McGraw Hill Book Company, 1973), 4–10.

68. E. D. Duryea, "Evolution of University Organization," in *The University as an Organization*, pp. 15–37, edited by James A. Perkins (New York: McGraw Hill Book Company, 1973), 26–35.

69. Perkins, *The University in Transition*, 54; Duryea, "Evolution of University Organization," 35–37.

70. Duryea, "Evolution of University Organizations," 36–37.

71. *The Control of the Campus: A Report on the Governance of Higher Education* (Washington, DC: The Carnegie Foundation for the Advancement of Teaching, 1982), 7.

72. Some commentators have argued that fair use privileges are essentially linked to the fulfillment of academic freedom. Eric D. Brandfonbrener, "Fair Use and University Photocopying: *Addison-Wesley Publishing Co. v. New York University*," in *Copyright Law Symposium*, vol. 36 (New York: Columbia University Press, 1990), 41.

CHAPTER TWO

1. William W. Fisher III, "Reconstructing the Fair Use Doctrine, *Harvard Law Review* 101 (June 1988): 1794.

2. Jessica D. Litman, "Copyright, Compromise, and Legislative History," *Cornell Law Review* 72 (July 1987): 861.

3. Copyright Act of 1976, 17 U.S.C. § 106 (1988).

4. U.S. Const. art. I, § 8 ("The Congress shall have Power . . . To promote the Progress of Science and useful Arts, by securing for limited Times to Authors and Inventors the exclusive Right to their respective Writings and Discoveries. . . . ").

5. An Act for the Encouragement of Learning, ch. 15, 1 Stat. 124 (1790). The federal copyright law was revised several times between 1790 and 1909. The 1909 act remained until the 1976 act took effect.

6. Copyright Act of 1976, 17 U.S.C. § 302 (1988).

7. Copyright Act of 1976, 17 U.S.C. § 102 (1988).

8. Feist Publications, Inc. v. Rural Telephone Service Company, Inc., 111 S.Ct. 1282 (1991).

9. Sound Recording Amendment of 1971, 85 Stat. 391 (1971).

10. Melville B. Nimmer, "The Subject Matter of Copyright Under the Act of 1976," *UCLA Law Review* 24 (June–August 1977): 975–96; Melville B. Nimmer, "Inroads on Copyright Protection," *Harvard Law Review* 64 (May 1951): 1125–41.

11. Harper & Row, Publishers, Inc. v. Nation Enterprises, 471 U.S. 539, 545 (1985) ("copyright is intended to increase and not to impede the harvest of knowledge").

12. Sony Corporation of America v. Universal City Studios, Inc., 464 U.S. 417, 429 (1984).

13. Ibid.

14. Iowa State University Research Foundation, Inc. v. American Broadcasting Companies, Inc., 463 F. Supp. 902, 904–5 (S.D.N.Y. 1978), *aff'd*, 621 F. 2d 57 (2d Cir. 1980). *See also* Iowa State University Research Foundation, Inc. v. American Broadcasting Companies, Inc., 475 F. Supp. 78 (S.D.N.Y. 1979).

15. Iowa State University Research Foundation, Inc. v. American Broadcasting Companies, Inc., 621 F. 2d 57, 60–61 (2d Cir. 1980).

16. Weinstein v. University of Illinois, 811 F. 2d 1091, 1093–95 (7th Cir. 1987).

17. Debra E. Blum, "Yeshiva Professor Wins Copyright Lawsuit," *Chronicle of Higher Education,* 5 April 1989, p. A14.

18. William A. Rome, "Scholarly Writings in the University Setting: Changes in the Works and on the Books" in *Copyright Law Symposium,* vol. 35 (New York: Columbia University Press, 1989), 41–68; Lisa Gerrard, "When a University Faculty Member Develops Academic Software, Who Should Share in the Profits?" *Chronicle of Higher Education,* 22 July 1987, p. 64; Ivars Peterson, "Bits of Ownership: Growing Computer Software Sales Are Forcing Universities to Rethink Their Copyright and Patent Policies," *Science News,* 21 September 1985, pp. 188–90; Cory H. Van Arsdale, "Computer Programs and Other Faculty Writings Under the Work-for-Hire Doctrine: Who Owns the Intellectual's Property?" *Santa Clara Computer and High-Technology Law Journal* 1 (January 1985): 141–67.

19. Rosemont Enterprises, Inc. v. Random House, Inc., 366 F. 2d 303, 307 (2d Cir. 1966), *cert. denied,* 385 U.S. 1009 (1967); Meeropol v. Nizer, 560 F. 2d 1061, 1068 (2d Cir. 1977), *cert. denied,* 434 U.S. 1013 (1978). *See also* H. C. Wainwright & Co. v. Wall Street Transcript Corp., 418 F. Supp. 620 (S.D.N.Y. 1976). For an example of the awkwardness of obtaining permissions from copyright owners, see James W. Tankard, Jr., "Getting Permissions for Class Readings Is a Tangled Web," *Chronicle of Higher Education,* 13 December 1989, pp. B2–B3.

20. Harper & Row, Publishers, Inc. v. Nation Enterprises, 471 U.S. 539, 549 (1985); Dowling v. U.S., 473 U.S. 207, 216 (1985).

21. Maxtone-Graham v. Burtchaell, 803 F. 2d 1253, 1265 (2d Cir. 1986) (allowed quoting for criticism and comment, even for commercial purposes and with some errors); H. C. Wainwright & Co. v. Wall Street Transcript Corp., 418 F. Supp. 620, 625 (S.D.N.Y. 1976); Thompson v. Gernsback, 94 F. Supp. 453, 454 (S.D.N.Y. 1950); Henry Holt & Co. v. Liggett & Myers Tobacco Co., 23 F. Supp. 302, 304 (E.D. Pa. 1938).

22. Harper & Row, Publishers, Inc. v. Nation Enterprises, 471 U.S. 539, 549–50 (1985); Rubin v. Boston Magazine Co., 645 F. 2d 80, 83 (1st Cir. 1981); Time Inc. v. Bernard Geis Associates, 293 F. Supp. 130, 144 (S.D.N.Y. 1968); Holdredge v. Knight Publishing Corp., 214 F. Supp. 921, 924 (S.D. Cal. 1963). Fair use in American law was first established in Folsom v. Marsh, 9 Fed. Cas. 343 (C.C.D. Mass. 1841) (No. 4901), in which the court evaluated several factors, but largely relied on whether the use "may interfere, in some measure, with the very meritorious labors" of authors.

23. Copyright Act of 1976, 17 U.S.C. § 107 (1988), *as amended by* Judicial Improvements Act of 1990, Pub. L. 101–650, §607, 104 Stat. 5089, 5132 (1990), and Pub. L. 102–492, 106 Stat. 3145 (1992).

24. Meeropol v. Nizer, 560 F. 2d 1061, 1068 (2d Cir. 1977), *cert. denied,* 434 U.S. 1013 (1978) ("The line which must be drawn between fair use and copyright

infringement depends on an examination of the fact in each case. It cannot be determined by resort to any arbitrary rules or fixed criteria.").

25. Haberman v. Hustler Magazine, Inc., 626 F. Supp. 201, 210–11 (D. Mass. 1986) (the issue was not monetary gain, but exploitation without payment of royalties); Rosemont Enterprises, Inc. v. Random House, Inc., 366 F. 2d 303, 309 (2d Cir. 1966), *cert. denied,* 385 U.S. 1009 (1967) (distinguished uses in advertising from use in writing a biography); Pacific and Southern Company, Inc. v. Duncan, 572 F. Supp. 1186, 1194 (N.D. Ga. 1983), *aff'd,* 744 F. 2d 1490 (11th Cir. 1984), *cert. denied,* 471 U.S. 1004 (1985) (a "clipping service" of videotaped news broadcasts had a commercial purpose); Addison-Wesley Publishing Company v. Brown, 223 F. Supp. 219, 228 (E.D.N.Y. 1963) (a book of problem solutions to accompany a physics textbook was an infringement).

26. Rosemont Enterprises, Inc. v. Random House, Inc., 366 F. 2d 303, 309 (2d Cir. 1966), *cert. denied,* 385 U.S. 1009 (1967) (a profit motive is irrelevant to determining whether a use offers some public benefit); Bourne Co. v. Speeks, 670 F. Supp. 777, 779–80 (E.D. Tenn. 1987). *But see* Meeropol v. Nizer, 560 F. 2d 1061, 1069 (2d Cir. 1977), *cert. denied,* 434 U.S. 1013 (1978) (criticizing the broad language of the *Rosemont* decision); New York Times Co. v. Roxbury Data Interface, Inc., 434 F. Supp. 217, 221 (D. N.J. 1977) (defendants' profit motive does not preclude fair use).

27. Marcus v. Rowley, 695 F. 2d 1171, 1175 (9th Cir. 1983).

28. Rosemont Enterprises, Inc. v. Random House, Inc., 366 F. 2d 303, 307 (2d Cir. 1966), *cert. denied,* 385 U.S. 1009 (1967). *But see* Craft v. Kobler, 667 F. Supp. 120, 130 (S.D.N.Y. 1987) (use of song lyrics and extensive book excerpts in biography is infringement); Toksvig v. Bruce Publishing Co., 181 F. 2d 664, 667 (7th Cir. 1950) (use of copyrighted translations of materials in writing a biography is an infringement).

29. Meeropol v. Nizer, 560 F. 2d 1061, 1068 (2d Cir. 1977), *cert. denied,* 434 U.S. 1013 (1978); Time Inc. v. Bernard Geis Associates, 293 F. Supp. 130, 144 (S.D.N.Y. 1968); Karll v. Curtis Publishing Co., 39 F. Supp. 836, 837 (E.D. Wisc. 1941).

30. Wihtol v. Crow, 309 F. 2d 777, 781 (8th Cir. 1962).

31. Rohauer v. Killiam Shows, Inc., 379 F. Supp. 723, 733 (S.D.N.Y. 1974), *rev'd on other grounds,* 551 F. 2d 484 (2d Cir. 1977), *cert. denied,* 431 U.S. 949 (1977).

32. Sinkler v. Goldsmith, 623 F. Supp. 727, 732 (D. Ariz. 1985).

33. Harper & Row, Publishers, Inc. v. Nation Enterprises, 471 U.S. 539, 549, 566 (1985); Meeropol v. Nizer, 560 F. 2d 1061, 1070 (2d Cir. 1977), *cert. denied,* 434 U.S. 1013 (1978) ("A key issue in fair use is whether the defendant's work tends to diminish or prejudice the potential sale of plaintiff's work."). The court nevertheless held that a "minimal" market effect will not preclude fair use. 560 F. 2d at 1069–70. *See also* Haberman v. Hustler Magazine, Inc., 626 F. Supp. 201, 212 (D. Mass. 1986).

34. According to a Copyright Office report: "As a general premise, we believe that photocopying should not be permitted where it would compete with the publisher's market." U.S. Congress, House Committee on the Judiciary, *Copyright*

Law Revision: Report of the Register of Copyrights, 87th Cong., 1st Sess., 1961, p. 26 (hereafter cited as *Report of the Register,* 1961).

35. Although quantity is a persuasive factor. See, for example, Harper & Row, Publishers, Inc. v. Nation Enterprises, 471 U.S. 539, 566 (1985).

36. *But see* Gardner v. Nizer, 391 F. Supp. 940, 943–44 (S.D.N.Y. 1975), *modified on other grounds,* 396 F. Supp. 63 (S.D.N.Y. 1975) (reliance on three passages from plaintiff's book did not constitute infringement).

37. Trebonik v. Grossman Music Corp., 305 F. Supp. 339, 346 (N.D. Ohio 1969).

38. Holdredge v. Knight Publishing Corp., 214 F. Supp. 921, 924 (S.D. Cal. 1963).

39. Broderbund Software, Inc. v. Unison World, Inc., 648 F. Supp. 1127, 1136–37 (N.D. Cal. 1986).

40. Rubin v. Boston Magazine Co., 645 F. 2d 80, 84–85 (1st Cir. 1981).

41. Sony Corporation of America v. Universal City Studios, Inc., 464 U.S. 417, 455 n.40 (1984).

42. Alan Latman, "Fair Use of Copyrighted Works," in *Copyright Law Revision: Studies Prepared for the Subcommittee on Patents, Trademarks, and Copyrights,* Study 14, 86th Cong., 2d Sess., 1960, pp. 39–43.

43. Irving Louis Horowitz and Mary E. Curtis, "Fair Use versus Fair Return: Copyright Legislation and Its Consequences," *Journal of the American Society for Information Science* 35 (March 1984): 69–73. Curtis is associated with the publisher John Wiley & Sons, Inc. Horowitz is a sociology professor at Rutgers University and publisher of Transactions Publications, a journal publishing enterprise based at Rutgers but operated on "private entrepreneurial terms." He has claimed to share the concerns of private publishers. U.S. Copyright Office, *Report of the Register of Copyrights: Library Reproduction of Copyrighted Works (17 U.S.C. 108)* (Washington, DC: Library of Congress, 1983), Appendix VI, pp. 159–60 (hereafter cited as *Report of the Register,* 1983).

44. Copyright Act of 1976, 17 U.S.C. § 108 (1988), *as amended by* Copyright Amendments Act of 1992, Pub. L. 102–307, § 301, 106 Stat. 264, 272 (1992).

45. The Copyright Office has completed two five-year reports since passage of the 1976 act. *See* U.S. Copyright Office, *Report of the Register of Copyrights: Library Reproduction of Copyrighted Works (17 U.S.C. 108)* (Washington, DC: Library of Congress, 1988) (hereafter cited as *Report of the Register,* 1988); *Report of the Register,* 1983. In 1992, Congress repealed the obligation for any further reports. See note 189 below.

46. Copyright Act of 1976, 17 U.S.C. § 108(a) (1988).

47. Ibid.

48. Ibid., § 108(b).

49. Ibid., § 108(c).

50. Ibid., §§ 108(d) and (e).

51. Ibid., § 108(f)(1).

52. Warnings of Copyright for Use by Certain Libraries and Archives, 37 C.F.R. § 201.14 (1991) (pursuant to Copyright Act of 1976, 17 U.S.C. §§ 108(d)(2) and (e)(2) (1988)). Regulations do not give official language for the

notice to be placed on unsupervised copying machines pursuant to Section 108(f)(1). The American Library Association recommends the following: "The copyright law of the United States (Title 17 U.S. Code) governs the making of photocopies or other reproductions of copyrighted material. The person using this equipment is liable for any infringement" ("Language Suggested for the Notices Required by the Copyright Revision Act of 1976," American Library Association, Reference and Adult Services Division, Interlibrary Loan Committee, September 1977).

53. Copyright Act of 1976, 17 U.S.C. § 108(h) (1988).

54. Ibid., § 108(g).

55. Ibid., § 109.

56. Ibid., § 108(g)(2).

57. Photocopying for interlibrary lending and the use of the "CONTU Guidelines" are examined more fully in chapter six.

58. Copyright Act of 1976, 17 U.S.C. §§ 110(1) and (2) (1988).

59. Ibid., § 117.

60. Ibid., § 111.

61. Under various legal theories, officers and directors of entities may be liable for the actions of employees. Liability may also be imposed on a "contributory infringer" who is "in a position to control the use of copyrighted works by others and had authorized the use without permission from the copyright owner." Sony Corporation of America v. Universal City Studios, Inc., 464 U.S. 417, 437 (1984).

62. Copyright Act of 1976, 17 U.S.C. § 504(a)(1) (1988).

63. Ibid., §§ 502 and 503.

64. Ibid., § 504(c)(1).

65. Ibid., § 504(c)(2).

66. 18 U.S.C. §§ 2318 and 2319 (1988), as amended by Pub. L. 102–561, § 1, 106 Stat. 4233 (1992).

67. Copyright Act of 1976, 17 U.S.C. § 504(c)(2) (1988).

68. Ibid.

69. U.S. Congress, House Committee on the Judiciary, Copyright Law Revision: H. Rept. 94–1476 on S. 22, 94th Cong., 2d Sess., 1976, p. 163 (hereafter cited as House Report 94–1476, 1976).

70. For a general discussion of the problem and the cases, see U.S. Copyright Office, Copyright Liability of States and the Eleventh Amendment: A Report of the Register of Copyrights (Washington, DC: Library of Congress, 1988).

71. U.S. Const. amend. XI. The leading case on the general scope and applicability of the Eleventh Amendment is Atascadero State Hospital v. Scanlon, 473 U.S. 234 (1985).

72. 28 U.S.C. § 1338(a) (1988).

73. 858 F. 2d 1394 (9th Cir. 1988), cert. denied, 489 U.S. 1090 (1989). Another case that received less attention involved the limited situation of a state university using copyrighted photographs in a promotional brochure. Richard Anderson Photography v. Brown, 852 F. 2d 114 (4th Cir. 1988), cert. denied, 489 U.S. 1033 (1989).

74. Copyright Act of 1976, 17 U.S.C. § 511 (1988), *as amended by* Copyright Remedy Clarification Act, Pub. L. 101–553, 104 Stat. 2749 (1990). See generally, Robert A. Burgoyne, "The Copyright Remedy Clarification Act of 1990: State Educational Institutions Now Face Significant Monetary Exposure for Copyright Infringement," *Journal of College and University Law* 18 (Winter 1992): 367–79.

75. Even during the brief period of immunity for the university itself, suits were still possible for injunctions, and actions were allowable directly against the individuals involved.

76. Sony Corporation of America v. Universal City Studios, Inc., 464 U.S. 417, 454–55 (1984).

77. See note 12 of chapter three. For a discussion of off-air video recordings and fair use, see chapter five.

78. Copyright Act of 1976, 17 U.S.C. § 110 (1988).

79. Ibid., § 117. See chapter seven.

80. G. Gervaise Davis III, "Fair Use of Software and Databases: A U.S. Report," *Canadian Computer Law Reporter* 4 (July 1987): 145–50; Daniel T. Brooks, "Copyright and the Educational Uses of Computer Software," *EDUCOM Bulletin* 20 (Summer 1985): 6–13; Daniel T. Brooks, "As New Technology Booms, What Is 'Fair Use' of Educational Software?" *NASSP Bulletin* 68 (February 1984): 66–74.

81. U.S. Congress, Senate Committee on the Judiciary, *Copyright Law Revision: Hearings before the Subcommittee on Patents, Trademarks, and Copyrights,* Part 2, 90th Cong., 1st Sess., 1967, p. 554 (testimony of James G. Miller) (hereafter cited as *1967 Senate Hearings*). Limits on the copyrightability of some databases are possible since the Supreme Court ruled that standard telephone book white pages lack sufficient originality for copyright protection. See note 8 above.

82. Thomas S. Warrick, "Large Databases, Small Computers and Fast Modems . . . An Attorney Looks at the Legal Ramifications of Downloading," *Online* 8 (July 1984): 60.

83. Rowland C. W. Brown, "OCLC, Copyright, and Access to Information: Some Thoughts," *Journal of Academic Librarianship* 11 (September 1985): 197–98.

84. Brown, "OCLC, Copyright," 197–98; Richard L. Brown, "Copyright and Computer Databases: The Case of the Bibliographic Utility," *Rutgers Computer and Technology Law Journal* 11 (1985): 36–48; Frank P. Grisham, "Copyright Is Wrong," *Journal of Academic Librarianship* 11 (September 1985): 199–200; David F. Bishop, "OCLC Copyright: A Threat to Sharing," *Journal of Academic Librarianship* 11 (September 1985): 202–3.

85. Richard M. Dougherty, "A 'Factory' for Scholarly Journals," *Chronicle of Higher Education,* 17 June 1992, pp. B1–B3; Scott Bennett and Nina Matheson, "Scholarly Articles: Valuable Commodities for Universities," *Chronicle of Higher Education,* 27 May 1992, pp. B1–B3; Jerry D. Campbell, "The Challenge of Managing Journal Collections," *Library Acquisitions: Practice and Theory* 14 (1990): 127–30. One institution has proposed a policy statement whereby faculty will retain the copyright to their journal articles. Triangle Research Libraries Network,

"University Policy Regarding Faculty Publication in Scholarly Journals," *Newsletter on Serials Pricing Issues,* 7 September 1992.

86. Barbara Ringer, "The Unfinished Business of Copyright Revision," *UCLA Law Review* 24 (June–August 1977): 976.

87. "The Gentlemen's Agreement and the Problem of Copyright," *Journal of Documentary Reproduction* 2 (March 1939): 29–36.

88. R. R. Bowker, "The National Library as the Central Factor of Library Development in the Nation," *Library Journal* 37 (January 1912): 5. Most commentators agree that practical limits make manual transcriptions of text a right of "fair use." See *Report of the Register,* 1961, p. 25. A spokesman for a journal publisher contended, however, that a student's manual transcription of an article would be a "technical infringement." U.S. Congress, Senate Committee on the Judiciary, *Copyright Law Revision: Hearings Before the Subcommittee on Patents, Trademarks, and Copyrights,* Part 3, 93d Cong., 1st Sess., 1973, pp. 152–53 (hereafter cited as *1973 Senate Hearings*).

89. See, for example, *Report of the Librarian of Congress for the Fiscal Year Ending June 30, 1936* (Washington, DC: GPO, 1936), 40.

90. Latman, "Fair Use," 10–11.

91. Various proposals for significant copyright reform arose in Congress from the 1920s through the 1940s, but without passage. Ibid., 18–24; Borge Varmer, "Photoduplication of Copyrighted Material by Libraries," in *Copyright Law Revision: Studies Prepared for the Subcommittee on Patents, Trademarks, and Copyrights,* Study 15, 86th Cong., 2d Sess., 1960, pp. 54–56. The American Library Association also issued a "Reproduction of Materials Code" in 1941. Ibid., 52–53. For a more detailed examination of various copying standards, see Henry P. Tseng, *New Copyright U.S.A.: A Guide for Teachers and Librarians* (Columbus, OH: AMCO International, Inc., 1979), 212–24.

92. U.S. Senate, *Copyright Law Revision: Studies Prepared for the Subcommittee on Patents, Trademarks, and Copyrights of the Committee on the Judiciary,* 86th Cong., 1st Sess., 1960–61.

93. Not everyone favored a statutory fair use, including many leading copyright experts. Latman, "Fair Use," 39–43.

94. For example, *Report of the Register,* 1961, p. 25 (recommended that fair use be in the statute, but without elaboration). The substantive language of fair use in the 1965 bill was merely "the fair use of a copyrighted work is not an infringement of copyright." U.S. Congress, House Committee on the Judiciary, *Copyright Law Revision, Part 6: Supplementary Report of the Register of Copyrights on the General Revision of the U.S. Copyright Law,* 89th Cong., 1st Sess., 1965, p. 192 (hereafter cited as *Report of the Register,* 1965).

95. The first draft of a bill with the four factors of fair use appeared in 1964. U.S. Congress, House Committee on the Judiciary, *Copyright Law Revision, Part 3: Preliminary Draft for Revised U.S. Copyright Law and Discussions and Comments on the Draft,* 1964, p. 6 (hereafter cited as *1964 House Discussions*).

96. U.S. Congress, House Committee on the Judiciary, *Copyright Law Revision, Part 5: 1964 Revision Bill with Discussions and Comments,* 89th Cong., 1st Sess., 1965, p. 5 (hereafter cited as *1965 House Discussions*).

97. U.S. Congress, House Committee on the Judiciary, *Copyright Law Revision: H. Rept. 2237 on H.R. 4347*, 89th Cong., 2d Sess., 1966, p. 60 (hereafter cited as *House Report 2237*, 1966). Educator groups in 1965 stated that their first priority was to assure that making copies would be allowed under fair use. U.S. Congress, Senate Committee on the Judiciary, *Copyright Law Revision: Hearings before the Subcommittee on Patents, Trademarks, and Copyrights*, 89th Cong., 1st Sess., 1965, p. 85 (hereafter cited as *1965 Senate Hearings*).

98. *Report of the Register*, 1961, p. 24.

99. U.S. Congress, House Committee on the Judiciary, *Copyright Law Revision: Hearings before Subcommittee No. 3*, Part 1, 89th Cong., 1st Sess., 1965, p. 39 (remarks of the Deputy Register of Copyrights) (hereafter cited as *1965 House Hearings*); Ibid., 1755 (remarks of the counsel for the Authors League of America); Varmer, "Photoduplication," 75 (comments of Melville B. Nimmer).

100. The "Joint Committee on Fair Use in Photocopying" was formed in 1957 to represent the interests of the American Library Association, the Association of Research Libraries, the American Association of Law Libraries, and the Special Libraries Association. U.S. Congress, House Committee on the Judiciary, *Copyright Law Revision, Part 2: Discussion and Comments on Report of the Register of Copyrights*, 88th Cong., 1st Sess., 1963, pp. 33–34.

101. Ibid., 35 (remarks of Horace S. Manges of the American Book Publishers Council).

102. *1964 House Discussions*, p. 164.

103. *1967 Senate Hearings*, Part 1, pp. 143–44.

104. Ibid. ("This will write into law for the first time that fair use of a copyrighted work includes copying to some degree.")

105. *House Report 94–1476*, 1976, pp. 5 and 66.

106. Ibid., 66–70.

107. *House Report 2237*, 1966, p. 61.

108. *House Report 94–1476*, 1976, p. 66.

109. Sony Corporation of America v. Universal City Studios, Inc., 464 U.S. 417, 451 (1984).

110. *House Report 2237*, 1966, p. 64; U.S. Congress, House Committee on the Judiciary, *Copyright Law Revision: H. Rept. 83 on H.R. 2512*, 90th Cong., 1st Sess., 1967, p. 35 (hereafter cited as *House Report 83*, 1967).

111. *House Report 2237*, 1966, p. 60. *See also* Harper & Row, Publishers, Inc. v. Nation Enterprises, 471 U.S. 539, 554 (1985). One commentator has concluded that fair use under the 1976 act allows activity that previously would have been infringement (Litman, "Copyright, Compromise," 885).

112. U.S. Congress, Senate Committee on the Judiciary, *Copyright Law Revision: S. Rept. 93–983 on S. 1361*, 93d Cong., 2d Sess., 1974, p. 115 (hereafter cited as *Senate Report 93–983*, 1974).

113. Pacific and Southern Co. v. Duncan, 744 F. 2d 1490, 1495 n.7 (11th Cir. 1984), *cert. denied*, 471 U.S. 1004 (1985) (the House Committee "may have overstated its intention to leave the doctrine of fair use unchanged").

114. Eric D. Brandfonbrener, "Fair Use and University Photocopying:

Addison-Wesley Publishing Co. v. New York University," in *Copyright Law Symposium,* vol. 36 (New York: Columbia University Press, 1990), 48–49.

115. At least one commentator has concluded that congressional reliance on negotiations among interest groups resulted in a law strongly favoring copyright proprietors (Litman, "Copyright, Compromise," 903).

116. *House Report 2237,* 1966, p. 61.

117. *House Report 94–1476,* 1976, p. 66.

118. *House Report 2237,* 1966, p. 61; *1965 Senate Hearings,* pp. 91 and 120.

119. *1965 House Discussions,* pp. 97 and 108 (twenty-five members). *See also 1965 Senate Hearings,* pp. 82–83 (thirty-five members, mostly representing primary and secondary education, but some members from higher education).

120. *1965 House Discussions,* p. 97.

121. See, for example, *1965 Senate Hearings,* pp. 85–91; *Report of the Register,* 1965, p. 27.

122. *House Report 2237,* 1966, pp. 62–64. According to one commentator, Congress "encouraged, cajoled, bullied, and threatened the parties through continuing negotiations" (Litman, "Copyright, Compromise," 871).

123. *House Report 2237,* 1966, p. 60.

124. *Report of the Register,* 1961, p. 24.

125. *House Report 2237,* 1966, pp. 62–64.

126. *1965 Senate Hearings,* p. 90.

127. *1965 House Hearings,* Part 1, pp. 86–87. Author groups were particularly concerned about the effect of photocopied "anthologies" on the potential market for poems and short stories. Carol A. Risher, Director of Copyright and New Technology, Association of American Publishers, telephone interview with author, 22 May 1989 (hereafter cited as Risher Interview).

128. U.S. Congress, Senate Committee on the Judiciary, *Copyright Law Revision: H. Rept. 91–519 on S. 597,* 90th Cong., 2d Sess., 1969, p. 8 (hereafter cited as *Senate Report 91–519,* 1969).

129. *1967 Senate Hearings,* Part 1, p. 152.

130. One commentator argued that publishers favored a flexible fair use, because it would allow judicial interpretations that might eventually close gaps in the law (Litman, "Copyright, Compromise," 887).

131. *1967 Senate Hearings,* Part 1, p. 145. *See also* Thomas Boggs Richards, "The Value of the Copyright Clause in Construction of the Copyright Law," *Hastings Constitutional Law Quarterly* 2 (Winter 1975): 225. According to one participant in negotiations leading to the Classroom Guidelines, teachers expressed most concern about providing for the "teachable moment" (Risher Interview).

132. *1973 Senate Hearings,* Part 3, p. 570. *See also* Litman, "Copyright, Compromise," 887.

133. Varmer, "Photoduplication," p. 75 (includes comments of Melville Nimmer).

134. *House Report 94–1476,* 1976, pp. 68–70. The final preparation of these guidelines began in September 1975 at the behest of Representative Robert Kastenmeier. *Report of the Register,* 1983, p. 52.

135. *Report of the Register,* 1983, Appendix VI, part 1, pp. 65–66 (comments

of Robert Wedgeworth, Executive Director of the American Library Association); Ibid., Appendix III, p. 77 (comments of Professor Neill Megaw of the English Department of the University of Texas).

136. *House Report 94–1476,* 1976, p. 68.

137. Ibid., 72. Although the Ad Hoc Committee represented several higher-education associations, most members and most testimony it offered before Congress tended to dwell on the needs of primary and secondary education. See *1965 Senate Hearings,* pp. 88–89. For commentary on the problems of the Classroom Guidelines for higher education, see Julius J. Marke, "United States Copyright Revision and Its Legislative History," *International Journal of Law Libraries* 5 (March 1977): 146.

138. The letters are reprinted in Tseng, *New Copyright U.S.A.,* 402–6.

139. *House Report 94–1476,* 1976, p. 72.

140. See, for example, Michael H. Cardozo, "To Copy or Not to Copy for Teaching and Scholarship: What Shall I Tell My Client?" *Journal of College and University Law* 4 (Winter 1976–77): 59–81; D. Bruce Robinson, "Copyright Legislation—Guidelines for Libraries, Educators, and Students," *Contemporary Education* 48 (Summer 1977): 228–29.

141. *House Report 94–1476,* 1976, pp. 70–71. The Music Guidelines are examined in chapter five.

142. U.S. Congress, House Committee on the Judiciary, *Piracy and Counterfeiting Amendments Act of 1982: H. Rept. 97–495,* 97th Cong., 2d Sess., 1982, pp. 8–9. *See also Congressional Record,* 97th Cong., 1st Sess., vol. 127, part 18, pp. 24,048–49. The Off-Air Guidelines are examined in chapter five.

143. Some librarians have opposed all forms of literary property protection. *Report of the Register,* 1983, p. 5.

144. Copyright Act of 1976, 17 U.S.C. §§ 407 and 408 (1988). See generally, Kenneth D. Crews, "Legal Deposit in Four Countries: Laws and Library Services," *Law Library Journal* 80 (Fall 1988): 551–76.

145. A. R. Spofford, "Copyright in Its Relations to Libraries and Literature," *American Library Journal* 1 (November 1876): 84.

146. *Annual Report of the Board of Regents of the Smithsonian Institution for the year 1871* (Washington, DC: GPO, 1873), 23 ("one source of the increase of the library is the copyright system").

147. Alexander Welsh, *From Copyright to Copperfield: The Identity of Dickens* (Cambridge, MA: Harvard University Press, 1987), 29–42.

148. Isabel Ely Lord, "Some Notes on the Principles and Practice of Bookbuying for Libraries," *Library Journal* 32 (February 1907): 57–58.

149. Copyright Act of 1976, 17 U.S.C. § 601 (1988).

150. Varmer, "Photoduplication," p. 49.

151. *1964 House Discussions,* pp. 6–7.

152. *1965 House Discussions,* p. 66.

153. *Report of the Register,* 1965, p. 26.

154. *1965 Senate Hearings,* p. 51; *1965 House Hearings,* Part 3, pp. 1555–57.

155. *1965 House Hearings,* Part 3, p. 1927.

156. Ibid., Part 1, pp. 448–49.

157. *1967 Senate Hearings,* Part 1, pp. 6–7; *House Report 2237,* 1966, p. 5.

158. *1967 Senate Hearings,* Part 2, p. 618.

159. *1967 Senate Hearings,* Part 2, pp. 617–18 ("Our committee strongly urges that the facts of life concerning single copying be recognized in this bill").

160. Ibid., Part 3, pp. 974–76 and 980–83.

161. U.S. Congress, Senate Committee on the Judiciary, *Patents, Trademarks, and Copyrights: S. Rept. 91–1219 on S. 543,* 91st Cong., 2d Sess., 1970, pp. 5–6; *Senate Report 91–519,* 1969, p. 9.

162. The Williams & Wilkins Company v. U.S., No. 73–68 (Ct. Cl., 16 February 1972), 2 and 15–24, *rev'd,* 487 F. 2d 1345 (Ct. Cl. 1973), *aff'd per curiam by an equally divided court,* 420 U.S. 376 (1974). Portions of the commissioner's opinion are reprinted at The Williams & Wilkins Company v. U.S., 487 F. 2d 1345, 1372–86 (Ct. Cl. 1973) (appendix to dissent from the appellate ruling).

163. *1973 Senate Hearings,* pp. 92–93 (statement of Philip B. Brown, counsel for ARL). *See also Report of the Register,* 1983, pp. 27 and 30.

164. *1973 Senate Hearings,* pp. 138–40 (comments on behalf of the Association of American University Presses).

165. Ibid., 158 and 169.

166. Ibid., 94.

167. *Report of the Register,* 1983, p. 45.

168. The Williams & Wilkins Company v. U.S., 487 F. 2d 1345, 1362 (Ct. Cl. 1973), *aff'd per curiam by an equally divided court,* 420 U.S. 376 (1974).

169. Ibid., 1354.

170. Ibid., 1356–59.

171. The Williams & Wilkins Company v. U.S., 420 U.S. 376 (1974).

172. The Williams & Wilkins Company v. U.S., 487 F. 2d 1345, 1348–49 (Ct. Cl. 1973), *aff'd per curiam by an equally divided court,* 420 U.S. 376 (1974).

173. U.S. Congress, Senate Committee on the Judiciary, *Copyright Law Revision: S. Rept. 94–473 on S. 22,* 94th Cong., 1st Sess., 1975, p. 71 (hereafter cited as *Senate Report 94–473,* 1975).

174. Copyright Act of 1976, 17 U.S.C. § 108(g)(2) (1988). Interlibrary lending is examined more fully in chapter six.

175. United States, National Commission on New Technological Uses of Copyrighted Works, *Final Report* (Washington, DC: Library of Congress, 1979), 54–55. For the formation of CONTU, see Pub. L. 93–573, 88 Stat. 1873, 1873–75 (1974); *Senate Report 93–983,* 1974, p. 123; *Senate Report 94–473,* 1975, p. 71.

176. CONTU, *Final Report,* 54–55. A Senate report seems to uphold this principle for interpreting "systematic copying." In listing three examples of prohibited activity, all involve a clear intent not to purchase a journal in lieu of obtaining photocopies of it. *Senate Report 93–983,* 1974, p. 122.

177. *Report of the Register,* 1983, Appendix VI, part 1, p. 53.

178. CONTU, *Final Report,* 55.

179. Ibid., 54.

180. U.S. Congress, House Committee of Conference, *Copyright Law Revision: H. Conf. Rept. 94–1733 on S. 22*, 94th Cong., 2d Sess., 1976, p. 71.

181. The CONTU Guidelines inevitably have been criticized for setting limits on library services, but most analyses have concluded that they are acceptable. *Report of the Register*, 1983, p. 144; Ibid., Appendix II, part 1, p. 8. See also those studies listed in note 60 of chapter six.

182. Litman, "Copyright, Compromise," 885.

183. For example, in 1964 the leading copyright authority, Melville B. Nimmer, wanted to limit library copying to four pages of any work without making the search of the market. *1964 House Discussions*, p. 400.

184. *House Report 83*, 1967, p. 37; *Senate Report 93–983*, 1974, p. 122.

185. U.S. Congress, House Committee on the Judiciary, *Copyright Law Revision: Hearings Before the Subcommittee on Courts, Civil Liberties, and the Administration of Justice*, Part 3, 94th Cong., 1st Sess., 1975, p. 2058.

186. *Report of the Register*, 1983, pp. 68–75. As will be examined in chapter six, the notice requirement may not be a significant issue following the U.S. entry into the Berne Convention.

187. Warnings of Copyright for Use by Certain Libraries and Archives, 37 C.F.R. § 201.14 (1991) (pursuant to Copyright Act of 1976, 17 U.S.C. §§ 108(d)(2) and (e)(2) (1988)).

188. *Report of the Register*, 1988.

189. Copyright Amendments Act of 1992, Pub. L. 102–307, § 301, 106 Stat. 264, 272 (1992).

CHAPTER THREE

1. Eric D. Brandfonbrener, "Fair Use and University Photocopying: *Addison-Wesley Publishing Co. v. New York University*," in *Copyright Law Symposium*, vol. 36 (New York: Columbia University Press, 1990), 81.

2. Sheldon Elliot Steinbach, "Have Professors Forgotten the Copyright Law on Photocopies?" *Chronicle of Higher Education*, 22 June 1988, p. A40.

3. Harper & Row, Publishers, Inc. v. Nation Enterprises, 471 U.S. 539, 569 (1985).

4. Ibid., 566–69.

5. Ibid., 567–68.

6. Ibid., 553–55.

7. Michael Les Benedict, "Historians and the Continuing Controversy over Fair Use of Unpublished Manuscript Materials," *American Historical Review* 91 (October 1986): 870–71.

8. Salinger v. Random House, Inc., 811 F. 2d 90, 98 (2d Cir.), *cert. denied*, 484 U.S. 890 (1987).

9. Wright v. Warner Books, Inc., 953 F. 2d 731, 736–40 (2d Cir. 1991); New Era Publications International, ApS v. Henry Holt and Company, Inc., 873 F. 2d 576, 583 (2d Cir. 1989), *cert. denied*, 493 U.S. 1094 (1990).

10. David A. Kaplan, "The End of History?: A Copyright Controversy Leads to Self-Censorship," *Newsweek*, 25 December 1989, p. 80; Ellen K. Coughlin, "After 'Salinger': Few Feel Sting of Ruling on Use of Papers," *Chronicle of Higher*

Education, 15 November 1989, pp. A4 and A6. *See also* Kenneth D. Crews, "Unpublished Manuscripts and the Right of Fair Use: Copyright Law and the Strategic Management of Information Resources," *Rare Books and Manuscripts Librarianship* 5 (1990): 61–70. In late 1992 Congress amended Section 107 to assure that fair use would apply to unpublished works, but the amendment does not explicitly overturn the court decisions nor prevent a narrower construction of fair use law. See note 23 of chapter two and accompanying text.

11. Sony Corporation of America v. Universal City Studios, Inc., 464 U.S. 417, 454–55 (1984).

12. Encyclopaedia Britannica Educational Corp. v. Crooks, 558 F. Supp. 1247, 1250–51 and 1254–55 (W.D.N.Y. 1983); Encyclopaedia Britannica Educational Corp. v. Crooks, 542 F. Supp. 1156, 1184–88 (W.D.N.Y. 1982).

13. U.S. Copyright Office, *Report of the Register of Copyrights: Library Reproduction of Copyrighted Works (17 U.S.C. 108)* (Washington, DC: Library of Congress, 1983), Appendix IV, part 2, pp. 184 and 318–19 (hereafter cited as *Report of the Register,* 1983). *See also* "Copyright Controversy," *College and Research Libraries News* 42 (September 1981): 286–88.

14. William A. Kaplin, *The Law of Higher Education: A Comprehensive Guide to Legal Implications of Administrative Decision Making,* 2d ed. (San Francisco, CA: Jossey-Bass Publishers, 1985), 15–16. *See also* Perry v. Sindermann, 408 U.S. 593, 602 (1972).

15. Harper & Row, Publishers, Inc. v. Tyco Copy Service, Inc., Copyright Law Decisions ¶ 25,230 (D.Conn. 1981); Basic Books, Inc. v. The Gnomon Corp., Copyright Law Decisions ¶ 25,145 (D. Conn. 1980).

16. David Izakowitz, "Fair Use of the Guidelines for Classroom Copying? An Examination of the *Addison-Wesley* Settlement," *Rutgers Computer and Technology Law Journal* 11 (1985): 112.

17. U.S. Copyright Office, *Report of the Register of Copyrights: Library Reproduction of Copyrighted Works (17 U.S.C. 108)* (Washington, DC: Library of Congress, 1988), Appendix II, p. 129 ("there was a great deal of concern about the invasion of the autonomy of the governance system of New York University, that the placing of the general counsel in the line of determination of penalties for faculty members was contrary to what most governance programs would allow in a university system"). Nevertheless, the AAP's copyright officer believes that relying on the legal counsel does not alter the guidelines or their status as "minimum" standards. Carol A. Risher, Director of Copyright and New Technology, Association of American Publishers, telephone interview with author, 22 May 1989.

18. The NYU policy states that individual faculty are to make their own evaluations of fair use in order to "minimize intrusiveness and over-centralization." The language appears generous, but it really means that faculty must individually conclude whether their actions are within the guidelines; they still bear all the risks of mistaken judgments.

19. Howard Fields, "AAP to Sue 'Large Eastern University,'" *Publishers Weekly,* 17 December 1982, p. 16.

20. Edwin McDowell, "Nine Publishers Sue N.Y.U., Charging Copyright Violation," *New York Times,* 15 December 1982, p. C34.

21. Townsend Hoopes, President of the Association of American Publishers, Inc., form letter to college and university administrators, 10 June 1983. *See also* ACRL Copyright Committee, "Copyright: An ACRL Resolution," *College and Research Libraries News* 45 (May 1984): 237–38.

22. Stacy E. Palmer, "Publishers Plan to Sue University over Copyrights," *Chronicle of Higher Education,* 8 December 1982, p. 1.

23. For examples of university copyright policies, some of which are based on the AAP guidelines, see Kenneth D. Crews, *University Copyright Policies,* SPEC Kit No. 138 (Washington, DC: Association of Research Libraries, 1987); Nancy Kranich, *Copyright Policies in ARL Libraries,* SPEC Kit No. 102 (Washington, DC: Association of Research Libraries, 1984).

24. Association of American Law Schools, *Directory of Law Teachers, 1977* (Washington, DC: AALS, 1977), 770.

25. Nancy Marshall, Director of Libraries at the College of William and Mary, telephone interview with author, 12 January 1989 (hereafter cited as Marshall Interview).

26. *Directory of Law Teachers, 1977,* p. 770.

27. U.S. Congress, Senate Committee on the Judiciary, *Copyright Law Revision: Hearings Before the Subcommittee on Patents, Trademarks, and Copyrights,* Part 3, 90th Cong., 1st Sess., 1967, pp. 910–11.

28. U.S. Congress, Senate Committee on the Judiciary, *Copyright Law Revision: Hearings Before the Subcommittee on Patents, Trademarks, and Copyrights,* Part 3, 93d Cong., 1st Sess., 1973, Part 3, p. 203.

29. Ibid., 204.

30. Stuart G. Gullickson, Acting Vice Chancellor for Legal Affairs, University of Wisconsin-Madison, telephone interview with author, 9 February 1989 (hereafter cited as Gullickson Interview). In 1982, Stedman wrote to the Copyright Office that the current law was "tolerable" but not satisfactory. *Report of the Register,* 1983, Appendix VII, p. 271.

31. U.S. Congress, House Committee on the Judiciary, *Copyright Law Revision: H. Rept. 94–1476 on S. 22,* 94th Cong., 2d Sess., 1976, p. 72 (hereafter cited as *House Report 94–1476,* 1976).

32. Gullickson Interview.

33. Ibid.

34. Association of American Law Schools, *The AALS Directory of Law Teachers, 1988–89* (St. Paul, MN: West Publishing Co., 1988), 384.

35. Gullickson Interview.

36. Ibid.

37. Copyright Act of 1976, 17 U.S.C. §§ 302–304 (duration of copyright) and 401 (notice requirement for published works) (1988).

38. Copyright Act of 1976, 17 U.S.C. § 105 (1988).

39. See the policy labeled "WISC–1983" in Appendix A.

40. Marshall Interview.

41. U.S. Congress, House Committee on the Judiciary, *Copyright Law Revision: Hearings Before the Subcommittee on Courts, Civil Liberties, and the Administration of Justice,* Part 1, 94th Cong., 1st Sess., 1975, pp. 215–16.

42. Marshall Interview.

43. *Report of the Register,* 1983, Appendix VII, pp. 267–68.

44. Marshall Interview; Mary Hutchings Reed, law firm of Sidley & Austin, telephone interview with author, 19 December 1988. American Library Association, *Model Policy Concerning College and University Photocopying for Classroom, Research and Library Reserve Use* (Washington, DC: ALA, 1982) (hereafter cited as *ALA Model Policy*).

45. "Guidelines for Fair Use of Copyrighted Materials," *Business Officer,* November 1983, pp. 14–21.

46. Kranich, *Copyright Policies in ARL Libraries,* 2.

47. *American Association of Law Libraries Newsletter* 19 (April 1988): 203–7.

48. Mark Mills, director of the Legal Reference Service, National Association of College and University Attorneys, telephone interview with author, 22 December 1988.

49. Gail Snowden, Senior Legal Counsel, Administrative Legal Services, University of Wisconsin-Madison, telephone interview with author, 7 February 1989. The policy was most probably not protected by copyright, so requesting permission was a courtesy rather than a requirement.

50. *Report of the Register,* 1983, p. 51 ("The significance of these voluntary arrangements should not be minimized").

51. "Second Business Session, June 28, 1977," *Law Library Journal* 70 (November 1977): 456 (speech by Barbara Ringer).

52. The House report with the guidelines stated: "the agreement refers only to copying from books and periodicals, and it is not intended to apply to musical or audiovisual works" (*House Report 94–1476,* 1976, p. 67).

53. John B. Harer and C. Edward Huber, "Copyright Policies in Virginia Academic Library Reserve Rooms," *College and Research Libraries* 43 (May 1982): 233–35; John C. Stedman, "Academic Library Reserves, Photocopying, and the Copyright Law," *College and Research Libraries News* 39 (October 1978): 263–66. The Copyright Office supports the argument that reserve room copying is subject to fair use and is not under Section 108 of the 1976 act. *Report of the Register,* 1983, p. 109.

54. *ALA Model Policy,* 5.

55. Ibid., 2–5.

56. *Report of the Register,* 1983, Appendix VII, pp. 77–78.

57. Basic Books, Inc. v. Kinko's Graphics Corp., 758 F. Supp. 1522, 1526 (S.D.N.Y. 1991).

58. Ibid., 1537.

59. Ibid., 1532–33.

60. Ibid., 1531.

61. Ibid., 1533–34.

62. For an example of one analysis that reads the case narrowly and argues against many claims of fair use, see Eileen N. Wagner, "Beware the Custom-Made Anthology: Academic Photocopying and *Basic Books v. Kinko's Graphics,*" *Education Law Reporter* 68 (1991): 1–20.

63. 758 F. Supp. at 1536 n.11.

64. The NYU case was a settlement, not a decision, so the court did not actually apply the guidelines to the facts.

65. 695 F. 2d 1171, 1177 (9th Cir. 1983).

66. Ibid., 1173.

67. Ibid., 1175–78.

68. Ibid., 1178.

69. Kenneth D. Crews, "Federal Court's Ruling Against Photocopying Chain Will Not Destroy 'Fair Use,'" *Chronicle of Higher Education,* 17 April 1991, p. A48.

70. Other model copyright policies exist, but none so elaborate nor so influential as the Classroom Guidelines and the ALA Model Policy. Examples of other model policies include the "Resolution on Permissions" by the Association of American University Presses, discussed in J. Jeffery Auer, "The Rules of Copyright for Students, Writers, and Teachers," *Communication Education* 30 (July 1981): 251–53.

CHAPTER FOUR

1. Robert D. Gratz and Philip J. Salem, *Organizational Communication and Higher Education,* AAHE-ERIC/Higher Education Research Report No. 10 (Washington, DC: American Association for Higher Education, 1981), 1.

2. PITT–1978.

3. Other studies of university copyright policies have offered many important insights, but those studies have been either less ambitious than this project or focused on narrower issues. Eric D. Brandfonbrener, "Fair Use and University Photocopying: *Addison-Wesley Publishing Co. v. New York University,*" in *Copyright Law Symposium,* vol. 36 (New York: Columbia University Press, 1990), 33–84 (examines policies from five universities); David B. Walch, "The Circulation of Microcomputer Software in Academic Libraries and Copyright Implications," *Journal of Academic Librarianship* 10 (November 1984): 262–66 (general concepts of software copyright at 211 academic libraries); Meredith A. Butler, "Copyright and Academic Library Photocopying," *College and Research Libraries News* 43 (April 1982): 123–25 (summarizes a survey of copyright standards at 140 academic libraries); Gary D. Byrd, "Copyright Compliance in Health Sciences Libraries: A Status Report Two Years after the Implementation of PL 94–553," *Bulletin of the Medical Library Association* 69 (April 1981): 224–30 (surveys 273 health science libraries).

4. "Association of American Universities," November 1986 [information flyer].

5. Two members, McGill University and the University of Toronto, are Canadian.

6. Association of Research Libraries, *Statement on Qualifications for Membership in the Association of Research Libraries* (Washington, DC: ARL, ca. 1985).

7. Since completing the data collection for this study, the membership of AAU and ARL changed slightly. ARL admitted the University of Illinois at Chicago

(Circle Campus) and Auburn University as new members; they are not within the population studied here. AAU admitted Rutgers University and the State University of New York at Buffalo as new members; both of them were already within the scope of this study through their participation in ARL.

8. ARL, *Statement on Qualifications.*

9. Listed in Appendix A.

10. Most of these policies are clearly identified by title, date, and issuer, but shorthand citations will more easily allow specific references throughout this study. For example, one of three policies received from the Massachusetts Institute of Technology is entitled "Memorandum to all Academic, Administrative, and Research Staff at MIT Concerning the Copyright Law of the United States" and is dated 11 March 1980. Shorthand references to that policy will be simply "MIT–1980." Appendix A lists all 183 policies with their abbreviated and full citations.

11. A study on another education issue offered this definition of "policy": "A statement concerning collective goals. Policy arguments consider the relative importance or desirability of particular social goals, and/or the relative efficiency and desirability of particular methods for achieving such goals" (Michael A. Rebell and Arthur R. Block, *Educational Policy Making and the Courts: An Empirical Study of Judicial Activism* [Chicago: The University of Chicago Press, 1982], 24).

12. Katherine F. Mawdsley, Assistant University Librarian, University of California, Davis, telephone interview with author, 19 December 1988. The two policies in question are CAL/DAVIS–1986a and CAL/DAVIS–1986b.

13. INDIANA–1983.

14. Only two policies were exclusively for other campus departments: BRANDEIS–1986 is for a computer facility, and VAND–1983d applies only to the business school. By directing the requests for policies to central university officers, this study may well have missed other specialized policies. Nevertheless, the policies analyzed here will reveal important trends and patterns among policies affecting large and diverse segments of the university communities.

15. TULANE–1985.

16. Neither the surveys for this study nor published literature reveal much evidence of university copyright policies before 1976. The surveys yielded only one pre–1976 policy: a March 1971 statement from Cornell University regarding reserve-room copying. It has not been included among the policies analyzed in this study on the assumption that the 1976 act necessitated a reevaluation of previous policies. For example, a study sponsored by the Copyright Office found that sixty-eight percent of academic libraries made some type of change in their reserve room services as a result of the 1976 act. U.S. Copyright Office, *Report of the Register of Copyrights: Library Reproduction of Copyrighted Works (17 U.S.C. 108)* (Washington, DC: Library of Congress, 1983), Appendix I, p. 1–5.

17. ILLINOIS–1983, JHU–1983, KANSAS–1983a, MICHIGAN–1983, NEBRASKA–1984, NOCAROLST–1983, NORTHWEST–1983, NOTREDM–1983, OKLA–1983, VATECH–1984, and WISC–1983. "Recent litigation" at that time could also have included a lawsuit against a school district in New York, charged with widespread reproductions of videotapes. But that suit was of narrower interest and received much less publicity. *See* Britannica Encyclopaedia Educational

Corporation v. Crooks, 558 F. Supp. 1247 (W.D.N.Y. 1983). Private industry has had similar reactions to litigation. A 1991 lawsuit against a law firm for photocopying an expensive newsletter apparently has motivated greater copyright policymaking. Lee R. Nemchek, "Copyright Compliance by Law Firms (17 U.S.C. § 108): An Ethical Dilemma for Librarians," *Law Library Journal* 83 (Fall 1991): 672 n.70.

18. Gordon Fretwell, Associate Library Director, University of Massachusetts at Amherst, telephone interview with author, 20 December 1988 (regarding MASS-1986); Roger Ditzel, Director of the Patent, Trademark and Copyright Office, University of California, telephone interview with author, 25 January 1989 (regarding CAL/BERK-1986a).

19. MIAMI-1986.

20. CORNELL-1984.

21. BROWN-1986.

22. Kathleen C. Farrell, Office of the General Counsel, Boston University, letter to author, 24 October 1986.

23. PITT-1978.

24. CAL/BERK-1986a.

25. Mary Stevens, University Counsel, Arizona State University, telephone interview with author, 8 December 1988.

26. Rosaline Hayes Crawford, Assistant to the General Counsel, Catholic University of America, letter to author, 16 December 1988.

27. Beryl Abrams, Legal Counsel, Columbia University, telephone interview with author, 12 December 1988. The interview took place before the lawsuit was filed against Kinko's Graphics Corporation involving "anthologies" of photocopied materials intended for use at Columbia University.

28. Lisa Ravella, Projects Manager, Office of the Provost, Carnegie Mellon University, telephone interview with author, 7 December 1988. Ms. Ravella attempts to answer most questions from William F. Patry, *The Fair Use Privilege in Copyright Law* (Washington, DC: Bureau of National Affairs, Inc., 1985).

29. Charles B. Osburn, Dean of the University Libraries, University of Alabama, letter to author, 11 December 1986.

30. Glenn L. Brudvig, Director of Information Resources, California Institute of Technology, letter to author, 15 December 1987.

31. Susan Coté, University Librarian, Case Western Reserve University, telephone interview with author, 14 December 1988; Margaret Anne Cannon, Assistant University Attorney, Case Western Reserve University, telephone interview with author, 9 January 1989.

32. Joe Zucca, Assistant to the Director of Libraries, Temple University, letter to author, 12 December 1988.

33. References to "CONTU" and other common standards in letters from respondents are inadequate; the possibility of confusion is too great. For example, NY/STONY-1979 summarizes the Classroom Guidelines in a formal policy statement, but mistakenly calls them the "CONTU guidelines." One respondent from Tulane University wrote in a letter that the university follows the ALA Model Policy, but the Faculty Handbook reveals that the university actually has adopted the Classroom Guidelines (see TULANE-1985).

34. Paul Willis, Library Director, University of Kentucky, telephone interview with author, 12 December 1988.

35. The sixteen universities without policies include all three universities located in the District of Columbia and five of the eighteen universities in the Southeast. With a few notable exceptions, most of the other thirteen Southeast universities do not have well-developed copyright policies. This pattern may be only a curiosity, or policy-making may be linked to factors that do vary by geography, such as university funding or staff size.

36. For example, at the University of Georgia, the legal counsel admitted that more pressing demands have kept his attention away from copyright policies. Alfred L. Evans, Jr., Senior Assistant Attorney General, State of Georgia, letter to author, 11 December 1986. For a discussion of a later University of Georgia policy, see chapter eight.

37. Susan Baughman, Library Director, Clark University, telephone interview with author, 13 December 1988.

38. Donna Rubens, Reference Librarian, University of Minnesota, telephone interview with author, 15 December 1988. The panel presentation that was especially influential to Ms. Rubens was "Copyright is Still with Us: Reviving Issues of the 1978 Copyright Law and Issues Posed by New Technologies," American Library Association Annual Conference, 11 July 1988, New Orleans, Louisiana. The policy in question is MINN-1988.

Chapter Five

1. U.S. Congress, House Committee on the Judiciary, *Copyright Law Revision: H. Rept. 94–1476 on S. 22*, 94th Cong., 2d Sess., 1976, p. 72 (hereafter cited as *House Report 94–1476*, 1976).

2. American Library Association, *Model Policy Concerning College and University Photocopying for Classroom, Research and Library Reserve Use* (Washington, DC: ALA, 1982), 5 (hereafter cited as *ALA Model Policy*).

3. Basic Books, Inc. v. Kinko's Graphics Corp., 758 F. Supp. 1522 (S.D.N.Y. 1991).

4. *ALA Model Policy.*

5. *House Report 94–1476*, 1976, p. 68. The Classroom Guidelines were published in this House report under the full title "Agreement on Guidelines for Classroom Copying in Not-For-Profit Educational Institutions."

6. Copyright Act of 1976, 17 U.S.C. §§ 108(d) and (e) (1988). Some commentators have argued that Sections 107 and 108 have no bearing on one another (see Section 108 (f) (4)), but that position is inconsistent with the legislative history.

7. Copyright Act of 1976, 17 U.S.C. § 107 (1988).

8. *House Report 94–1476*, 1976, p. 68.

9. Ibid., 68–70.

10. Basic Books, Inc. v. Kinko's Graphics Corp., 758 F. Supp. 1522, 1535–37 (S.D.N.Y. 1991).

11. TEXAS–1984a.

12. For example, CAL/BERK–1986a.

13. Donald Reidhaar, General Counsel, University of California, letter to Chancellors and Laboratory Directors, 27 May 1977.

14. COLO–1978 and COLO–1986.

15. One university defeating this trend is the University of Iowa, which adopted the Classroom Guidelines in 1977 but abandoned them in 1984 in favor of the ALA Model Policy. IOWA–1984.

16. See BROWN–1977, CHICAGO–1983, CORNELL–1977c, CORNELL–1984, PENN–1983, and SIU–1978. For example, BROWN–1977 mentions that a "great deal" of other copying may be allowed. SIU–1978 interprets "brevity" to mean ten pages of an article, and "spontaneity" to mean one month or less— standards somewhat broader than the original guidelines.

17. HARVARD–1986 and PRINCE–1981. At least one Harvard professor has described his university's policy as "distinctly unhelpful," because it lacks exact standards. William W. Fisher III, "Restructuring the Fair Use Doctrine," *Harvard Law Review* 101 (June 1988): 1694.

18. *House Report 94–1476,* 1976, p. 72. Criticism came from the American Association of University Professors and the Association of American Law Schools.

19. WISC–1983. The Wisconsin policy was developed in 1978, but the most recent version was issued in 1983, without changes in the substantive photocopy standards. Consistent with the treatment of all policies in this study, only the most recent policy version is included among the policies analyzed and listed in Appendix A. Hence, this text will often refer to the "1978" Wisconsin policy, but use the shorthand citation "WISC–1983."

20. Wayne State University adopted the original Wisconsin policy as its own in 1984 (WAYNEST–1984), and Washington University followed suit in 1988 (WASHU–1988).

21. BYU–1988, CAL/DAVIS–1986a, EMORY–1986, IOWA–1984, MARY-LAND–1985, MASS–1986, NEBRASKA–1984, NY/ALB–1982, NY/ALB–1987, NOCAROLST–1983, and RICE–1988.

22. *ALA Model Policy,* 4–5.

23. The ALA policy also reaffirms general principles of limiting copies to one per student, avoiding repeated uses of the same material, placing a notice on all copies, and not charging fees beyond actual costs.

24. DELAWARE–1987.

25. MICHIGAN–1983. This standard is considerably more lenient than the narrow reserve room policy (MICHIGAN–1979) that the university legal counsel reportedly mandated. See Jane Flener and Robert J. Starring, "A View from the University of Michigan," *Journal of Academic Librarianship* 5 (July 1979): 126–27.

26. WASHU–1988, WAYNEST–1984, and WISC–1983.

27. An irony in this analysis is that librarians write policies almost exclusively for library applications only (see table 4.3), and classroom copying is not necessarily a "library" issue. Such policies might apply to supervised copy centers lo-

cated in libraries, but they would have little effect on classroom copying performed elsewhere.

28. William L. Fillmore, Associate General Counsel, Brigham Young University, letter to author, 2 February 1989 (regarding BYU–1988); H. W. Trease, Office of the Vice President for Educational Development and Research, University of Iowa, telephone interview with author, 15 December 1988 (regarding IOWA–1984); and Joe W. Hightower, Office of Sponsored Research, Rice University, letter to author, 9 December 1988 (regarding RICE–1988).

29. Katherine F. Mawdsley, Assistant University Librarian, University of California, Davis, telephone interview with author, 19 December 1988 (regarding CAL/DAVIS–1986a); Joan I. Gotwals, University Library Director, Emory University, telephone interview with author, 21 December 1988 (regarding EMORY–1986); and Gordon Fretwell, Associate Library Director, University of Massachusetts at Amherst, telephone interview with author, 20 December 1988 (regarding MASS–1986). One "administrator" who adopted the ALA policy at her university was formerly Assistant Director of Libraries and since has become the Library Director. Meredith Butler, Assistant Vice President for Academic Planning and Development, State University of New York at Albany, letter to author, 27 December 1988 (regarding NY/ALB–1987).

30. Another pivotal year in the history of university policies was 1982, when the ALA Model Policy was published and became the only prominent alternative to the Classroom Guidelines. Yet the percentage data only for policies developed after 1982 differ little from the overall data on table 5.2.

31. Seventeen classroom copying policies were issued in 1978, the year that the 1976 act took effect. The NYU suit had more lingering consequences. Nine policies were issued in 1983 alone, while an actual peak of sixteen policies issued was reached in 1986. The 1986 data are skewed by the simultaneous issuance of policies at campuses throughout the University of California system. An interview with a University of California official confirmed that the new policy was a response to the NYU lawsuit. Roger Ditzel, Director of the Patent, Trademark and Copyright Office, University of California, telephone interview with author, 25 January 1989.

32. *House Report 94–1476*, 1976, pp. 70–71.

33. The trade associations were the Music Publishers' Association of the United States, Inc. and the National Music Publishers' Association, Inc. The professional associations were the Music Teachers National Association, the Music Educators National Conference, and the National Association of Schools of Music. The Ad Hoc Committee also participated in development of the Classroom Guidelines. *House Report 94–1476*, 1976, pp. 70–71.

34. *House Report 94–1476*, 1976, pp. 67 and 70.

35. Moreover, the trade associations that participated in developing the guidelines principally represented music publishers, rather than recording artists. Publishers may be able to grant rights to perform and record music, but not to use sound recordings themselves. Hence, one rule in the Music Guidelines closes with the warning that it extends only to the underlying music; users have no assurance from the Music Guidelines about the use of sound recordings.

36. Copyright Act of 1976, 17 U.S.C. § 106 (1988). However, the 1976 act applies fair use to all types of works—including music—and it secures limited performance rights for educational purposes. Copyright Act of 1976, 17 U.S.C. §§ 107 and 110 (1988).

37. *House Report 94–1476*, 1976, pp. 71–72.

38. *Congressional Record*, 97th Cong., 1st Sess., vol. 127, part 18, pp. 24,048–49.

39. Private firms included such television broadcasters as CBS, ABC, and the Public Broadcasting Service. Trade associations included the Association of American Publishers and the Motion Picture Association of America. Professional associations included the American Library Association and the National School Boards Association. Participants also included guilds and unions for actors, directors, and writers. Curiously absent from the list were leading representatives of higher education, such as the American Association of University Professors. Ibid., 24,049.

40. The Association of Media Producers, a "national trade association representing the producers and distributors of educational media materials," participated in developing the guidelines, but ultimately refused to endorse them. The Motion Picture Association took no position, but noted that seven of its members—all major film production companies—assented to the guidelines. Ibid. An officer of Walt Disney Productions wrote directly to Rep. Robert Kastenmeier uniformly opposing any guidelines that might promote use of video recordings without payment to copyright owners. Robert W. Miller, President of Walt Disney Productions, letter to Rep. Robert Kastenmeier, 13 October 1981.

41. The Off-Air Guidelines were discussed in one case, but the ruling neither relied on them nor rejected them. Encyclopaedia Britannica Educational Corporation v. Crooks, 558 F. Supp. 1247, 1250 (W.D.N.Y. 1983).

42. Only a 1987 statement from Washington State University modifies them significantly by deleting the "ten school day" limit on use of recordings; faculty are allowed to make their one use of the tape anytime during the forty-five day retention period (WASHST–1987). Northwestern University is alone in rejecting the off-air standards, opting for a more restrictive position. Northwestern prohibits all off-air recording without permission, other than for home use (NORTHWEST–1986).

43. See note 27 of chapter seven. The software provisions of this policy are examined in chapter seven.

44. HAWAII–1988, RICE–1988, and VAND–1986.

CHAPTER SIX

1. *Annual Report of the Board of Regents of the Smithsonian Institution for the year 1871* (Washington, DC: GPO, 1873), 23.

2. Verner W. Clapp, "The Copyright Dilemma: A Librarian's View," *Library Quarterly* 38 (October 1968): 352.

3. See, for example, Julie L. Nicklin, "University Librarians Promise to Fight High Journal Prices," *Chronicle of Higher Education*, 8 April 1992, pp. A33–A34;

David Ensign, "Copyright and the Use of Telefacsimile among Branch Library Facilities," *Law Library Journal* 83 (Summer 1991): 451–61; Robert L. Oakley, *Copyright and Preservation: A Serious Problem in Need of a Thoughtful Solution* (Washington, DC: The Commission on Preservation and Access, 1990).

4. Copyright Act of 1976, 17 U.S.C. § 108 (1988), *as amended by* Copyright Amendments Act of 1992, Pub. L. 102–307, § 301, 106 Stat. 264, 272 (1992).

5. Fritz Snyder, "Copyright and the Library Reserve Room," *Law Library Journal* 73 (Summer 1980): 702–14.

6. A report from the Copyright Office concludes that fair use, and not Section 108, should apply. U.S. Copyright Office, *Report of the Register of Copyrights: Library Reproduction of Copyrighted Works (17 U.S.C. 108)* (Washington, DC: Library of Congress, 1983), 109 (hereafter cited as *Report of the Register,* 1983).

7. John C. Stedman, "Academic Library Reserves: Photocopying and the Copyright Law," *AAUP Bulletin* 64 (September 1978): 142–49 [reprinted at *College and Research Libraries News* 39 (October 1978): 263–69]; John C. Stedman, "The New Copyright Law: Photocopying for Educational Use," *AAUP Bulletin* 63 (February 1977): 5–16.

8. Stedman, "Academic Library Reserves," 142–43.

9. For further remarks by Stedman on this issue, see *Report of the Register,* 1983, Appendix II, part 1, pp. 122–23.

10. Stedman, "Academic Library Reserves," 144.

11. Ibid., 145–48.

12. WISC–1983.

13. WISC–1978. Stedman participated in developing this reserve policy, but the principal developer was Nancy Marshall, then a librarian at the University of Wisconsin. The policy was approved by and issued in the name of the university's legal counsel office. Nancy Marshall, Director of Libraries, College of William and Mary, telephone interview with author, 12 January 1989.

14. Basic Books, Inc. v. Kinko's Graphics Corp., 758 F. Supp. 1522, 1533–34 (S.D.N.Y. 1991).

15. American Library Association, *Model Policy Concerning College and University Photocopying for Classroom, Research and Library Reserve Use* (Washington, DC: ALA, 1982), 6.

16. For example, the Copyright Office supports a prohibition on reuse of photocopies, because it implies an opportunity to have sought permission. *Report of the Register,* 1983, p. 110.

17. COLO–1978. Although the policy claims to follow Stedman's advice, in the end it also requires faculty members to certify that all copies comply with the Classroom Guidelines.

18. BROWN–1984, CINCIN–1983, EMORY–1986, HAWAII–1988, IOWA–1984, MARYLAND–1985, MASS–1986, MINN–1988, MISSOURI–1983, NEBRASKA–1984, NY/ALB–1982, NY/ALB–1987, NOCAROL–1984, NORTHWEST–1985, RICE–1988, VATECH–1983, and WAYNEST–1984. HAWAII–1988 is a conservative variation on the ALA Model Policy, but only after criticizing it as a "unilateral" statement of fair use. The seventeen do not include VIRGINIA–1987, which ultimately combines ALA standards with the Classroom Guidelines.

19. NOTREDM–1978 and NOTREDM–1983.

20. Anne Kearney, "Effects of the 1976 Copyright Law," *College and Research Libraries News* 49 (May 1988): 281.

21. Ibid.

22. The article on the Notre Dame survey mentions that from 1978 to 1983 the library followed the "ALA model policy" (ibid., 278–79). But the standards described in the article and in the 1978 policy received from the library (NOTREDM–1978) actually reflect the Classroom Guidelines. Moreover, the ALA Model Policy was not issued until 1982.

23. One policy seems to allow no copies at all, and so is left out of the categorization. A more recent policy from that same university, however, indicates that single copies are allowed. See NY/STONY–1978 and NY/STONY–1979.

24. In an informal survey, Nancy Marshall found that college and university libraries were issuing reserve policies that she regarded as narrow. *Report of the Register,* 1983, Appendix II, part 1, p. 8. *See also* Meredith Butler, "Copyright and Reserve Books—What Libraries Are Doing," *College and Research Libraries News* 39 (May 1978): 125–29 (concludes that New York libraries also apply "conservative" reserve policies).

25. A study sponsored by the Copyright Office found that the most common change in reserve room policies after passage of the 1976 act was a shift in responsibility for copyright compliance to the faculty. *Report of the Register,* 1983, Appendix I, p. 1–5.

26. Donna Rubens, Reference Librarian, University of Minnesota, telephone interview with author, 15 December 1988 (professing a need to "be as conservative as possible").

27. CAL/DAVIS–1985b.

28. Katherine F. Mawdsley, Assistant University Librarian, University of California, Davis, letter to author, 5 January 1987.

29. DARTMTH–1981.

30. At least one journal publisher offered libraries a license to make up to six reserve copies of its articles for a flat fee, provided that additional copies are paid for through the Copyright Clearance Center. The American Library Association responded that the publisher was overstating its rights. "ALA Responds to Publisher on Photocopying," *Wilson Library Bulletin* 58 (June 1984): 700–701.

31. Copyright Act of 1976, 17 U.S.C. § 108 (1988), *as amended by* Copyright Amendments Act of 1992, Pub. L. 102–307, § 301, 106 Stat. 264, 272 (1992).

32. Copyright Act of 1976, 17 U.S.C. § 108(g)(2) (1988).

33. Ibid.

34. Ibid., § 108(a).

35. Ibid., § 108(h). Sections 108(b) and (c) apply to all types of media.

36. Ibid., § 108(f)(1).

37. A study conducted in the early 1980s found that 85.9 percent of all photocopying machines in American libraries have a copyright notice. *Report of the Register,* 1983, Appendix I, p. 1–4.

38. See, for example, CAL/RIV–1987, MIT–1987, RICE–1988, ROCHEST–1986, STANFORD–1987, TEXASA&M–1987, and VAND–1986.

39. VIRGINIA–1987 clarifies that notices on unsupervised "reproducing equipment" should also be on microform readers as well.

40. Copyright Act of 1976, 17 U.S.C. §§ 108(c) and (e) (1988).

41. American Library Association, Resources and Technical Services Division, *Guidelines for Seeking or Making a Copy of an Entire Copyrighted Work for a Library, Archives, or User* (July 1982).

42. INDIANA–1983 and TEXAS–1988.

43. VATECH–1983. *Books in Print* is a multivolume catalog of books available for purchase from the publishers. It is revised annually and supplemented throughout the year.

44. U.S. Copyright Office, *Report of the Register of Copyrights: Library Reproduction of Copyrighted Works (17 U.S.C. 108)* (Washington, DC: Library of Congress, 1988), 27–28 (hereafter cited as *Report of the Register,* 1988) (noting that publishers have brought four lawsuits against private companies, but settled them out of court with the companies agreeing to pay fees to the Copyright Clearance Center).

45. Copyright Act of 1976, 17 U.S.C. § 108(a) (1988).

46. "Warning Notices for Copies and Machines," *American Libraries* 8 (November 1977): 530.

47. Copyright Act of 1976, 17 U.S.C. § 401 (1988). *See also* Donald F. Johnston, *Copyright Handbook,* 2d ed. (New York: R. R. Bowker Company, 1982), 168.

48. Copyright Act of 1976, 17 U.S.C. § 108(i) (1988).

49. See note 189 of chapter two.

50. *Report of the Register,* 1983, pp. 66–67 and 222.

51. *Report of the Register,* 1988, pp. 2 and 39–41 (at page 41: "These statements by the representatives of interested parties indicate a convergence of the sharply divergent views that these parties expressed during the first five-year review").

52. Copyright Act of 1976, 17 U.S.C. § 108(f)(3) (1988). In addition to the five University of California policies, see CAL/RIV–1987, MIT–1980, VIRGINIA–1987, WASH–1978, and WASHST–1978.

53. See generally, Cosette Kies, "The CBS-Vanderbilt Litigation: Taping the Evening News," in *Fair Use and Free Inquiry: Copyright Law and the New Media,* 2d ed., edited by John Shelton Lawrence and Bernard Timberg (Norwood, NJ: Ablex Publishing Corporation, 1989), 166–75; Cosette Kies, "Copyright Versus Free Access: CBS and Vanderbilt University Square Off," *Wilson Library Bulletin* 50 (November 1975): 242–46.

54. U.S. Congress, Senate Committee on the Judiciary, *Copyright Law Revision: S. Rept. 94–473 on S. 22,* 94th Cong., 2d Sess., 1976, p. 69.

55. See, for example, E. Van Tongeren, "The Effect of a Large-Scale Photocopying Service on Journal Sales," *Journal of Documentation* 32 (September 1976): 198 and 204.

56. See, for example, Maurice B. Line and D. N. Wood, "The Effect of a Large-Scale Photocopying Service on Journal Sales," *Journal of Documentation* 31 (December 1975): 238.

57. Graham P. Cornish, "The Conflict between Copyright and Document Supply: Real or Imagined?" *IFLA Journal* 16 (1990): 415.

58. See generally, *Report of the ARL Serials Prices Project* (Washington, DC: 1989).

59. For more details on CONTU and the creation of the guidelines, see chapter two.

60. John Steuben, "Interlibrary Loan of Photocopies of Articles Under the New Copyright Law," *Special Libraries* 70 (May–June 1979): 227–32; Suzanne H. Murray, "The New Copyright Law: Its Impact on Resource Sharing and Services of Health Sciences Libraries in New York State," *Bookmark* 38 (Summer 1979): 176–80; Johanna E. Tallman, "One Year's Experience with CONTU Guidelines for Interlibrary Loan Photocopies," *Journal of Academic Librarianship* 5 (May 1979): 71–74; Sandra R. Clevesy and Ingrid E. Inglis, "Predicting the Impact of the New Copyright Law on the Interlibrary Loan Transactions of a Hospital Library Consortium," *Bulletin of the Medical Library Association* 66 (July 1978): 339–42; Dale R. Middleton, "Predicting the Impact of Copyright Specifications on Interlibrary Borrowing," *Bulletin of the Medical Library Association* 65 (October 1977): 449–51; Patricia Dugan, "The Double Bind: The Environmental Impact of the 1976 Copyright Revision Law," *Journal of Academic Librarianship* 3 (July 1977): 146–48. By contrast, one informal survey of librarians disclosed some concern that the CONTU guidelines were too restrictive. *Report of the Register,* 1983, Appendix II, part 1, p. 8.

61. KENT–1982, MINN–1978, NOCAROLST–1977, NOCAROLST–1978, PENNST–1978, ROCHEST–1978, SIU–1978, VATECH–1983. Pennsylvania State University is the only institution still to reject explicitly the CONTU Guidelines, preferring instead to review interlibrary activity and to determine the need for new subscriptions on a less rigid measure.

62. See CAL/LA–1989, EMORY–1986, IOWAST–1979, MINN–1988, TEXASA&M–1987, WASHST–1978.

63. The King Research study of library copying found that 40.2 percent of academic libraries that engaged in interlibrary borrowing had refused to forward some requests to other libraries because of copyright limitations, and that 30.3 percent of academic libraries that received such requests had refused to fill them for copyright reasons. *Report of the Register,* 1983, Appendix I, p. 1–6.

64. One study revealed that when libraries reached the limits of photocopying they used many different techniques for serving patrons: subscribing to the journal requested, borrowing the original, obtaining copies through alternative sources, or seeking permission from the copyright owners for additional copies. Gary D. Byrd, "Copyright Compliance in Health Sciences Libraries: A Status Report Two Years after the Implementation of PL 94–553," *Bulletin of the Medical Library Association* 69 (April 1981): 224–30.

65. See, for example, INDIANA–1983, NY/BUF–1984, NOTREDM–1978, OKLA–1978, and OKLAST–1983.

66. *Report of the Register,* 1988, pp. 39–41.

CHAPTER SEVEN

1. U.S. Congress, House Committee on the Judiciary, *Copyright Law Revision: H. Rept. 94–1476 on S. 22*, 94th Cong., 2d Sess., 1976, p. 66 (hereafter cited as *House Report 94–1476*, 1976).

2. HAWAII–1988.

3. Judith Axler Turner, "Software Publishers in a College Market: Finding Their Way Through the Disarray," *Chronicle of Higher Education*, 21 October 1987, p. A19; Thomas J. DeLoughry, "Widespread Piracy by Students Frustrates Developers of Computer Software," *Chronicle of Higher Education*, 12 August 1987, pp. 1 and 31–32; Kenneth C. Green and Steven W. Gilbert, "Software Piracy: Its Cost and Consequences," *Change* 18 (January–February 1987): 46–49.

4. Particularly with respect to the specialized and technical issues of software use, a different research methodology might have yielded a different number of policies. Because the surveys requested copyright policies on all matters, some respondents may have overlooked or may not have known about software policies. Nevertheless, the relative lack of software policies suggests that the copyright issues either have not merited attention or are handled solely by officials outside the library and legal counsel offices. If in fact many other software policies exist, the inability of this study to reach them corroborates that copyright policy development is uncoordinated, with responsibilities scattered throughout each university. The surveys also requested copies of actual policies, rather than relying on claims about policies. An unrelated study conducted in 1986 surveyed 211 college and university officials with direct responsibility for computer matters and only inquired whether they had standards for copyright compliance. Without having to describe or reveal those standards, more than seventy percent of the respondents claimed to have "established procedures to discourage or impede illegal access to software" and sixty-five percent claimed "procedures to discourage or impede illegal copying." See Peat Marwick, *Microcomputer Use in Higher Education: Executive Summary of a Survey Conducted by EDUCOM and Peat Marwick* (New York: Peat Marwick, 1987), 7 and 12. A 1990 survey shows that many computer facilities claim to have "policies" on various matters, but nearly half of them are "undocumented." Ree Dawson, Bill Mitchell, and Lee Shope, "Managing Software Support in Higher Education," *EDUCOM Review* 25 (Spring 1990): 32. A 1991 survey revealed that fifty-two percent of all types of colleges and universities had "codes of conduct" for software use. See *The 1991 EDUCOM-USC Survey of Desktop Computing in Higher Education* (Los Angeles, CA: University of Southern California, 1991).

5. Daniel T. Brooks, "Copyright and the Educational Uses of Computer Software," *EDUCOM Bulletin* 20 (Summer 1985): 10–11; Daniel T. Brooks, "As New Technology Booms, What Is 'Fair Use' of Educational Software?" *NASSP Bulletin* 68 (February 1984): 70–74; G. Gervaise Davis III, "Fair Use of Software and Databases: A U.S. Report," *Canadian Computer Law Reporter* 4 (July 1987): 148–49. One article gives detailed guidance for software use in schools without even mentioning fair use. Lanny R. Gamble and Larry S. Anderson, "Nine Easy Steps

to Avoiding Software Copyright Infringement," *NASSP Bulletin* 73 (September 1989): 90–93.

6. Copyright Act of 1976, 17 U.S.C. § 117 (1988). The amendment was pursuant to the Computer Software Copyright Act of 1980, Pub. L. 96–517, 94 Stat. 3015, 3028–29 (1980).

7. Atari, Inc. v. JS&A Group, Inc., 597 F. Supp. 5, 9–10 (N.D.Ill. 1983).

8. *House Report 94–1476*, 1976, p. 116. As originally passed, Section 117 of the 1976 act stated merely that the new law would not change any rights of protection that copyright owners may previously have had with respect to "automatic systems capable of storing, processing, retrieving, or transferring information. . . . " Copyright Act of 1976, § 117, Pub. L. 94–553, 90 Stat. 2541, 2565 (1976).

9. National Commission on New Technological Uses of Copyrighted Works, *Final Report* (Washington, DC: Library of Congress, 1979), 12.

10. BOSTON–1981, BROWN–1986, CAL/LA–1989, DELAWARE–1987, HARVARD–1984, HAWAII–1988, INDIANA–1983, MASS–1986, MIT–1987, MINN–1988, NY/ALB–1987, RICE–1988, ROCHEST–1986, STANFORD–1987, UTAH–1985, VAND–1986, VIRGINIA–1987, and WASHST–1984.

11. BOSTON–1981, CAL/LA–1989, HAWAII–1988, INDIANA–1983, MASS–1986, NY/ALB–1987, ROCHEST–1986, and UTAH–1985.

12. For examples of other such policies, see Lee R. Nemchek, "Copyright Compliance by Law Firms (17 U.S.C. § 108): An Ethical Dilemma for Librarians," *Law Library Journal* 83 (Fall 1991): 676–78 (intended for law firms); Michael Gemignani, "A College's Liability for Unauthorized Copying of Microcomputer Software by Students," *Journal of Law and Education* 15 (Fall 1986): 433–34 (a short list of generally permissible and nonpermissible software uses); Michael Gemignani, "Copyright Law as It Applies to Computer Software," *College Mathematics Journal* 4 (September 1989): 337; Julie A. Mark, "Software Copying Policies: The Next Step in Piracy Prevention?" *Journal of Law and Technology* 2 (Winter 1987): 64–67 (intended for corporate users); International Council for Computers in Education, "1987 Statement on Software Copyright: An ICCE Policy Statement," *Computing Teacher* 14 (March 1987): 52–53 (intended for primary and secondary schools); Samuel Demas, "Microcomputer Software Collections," *Special Libraries* 76 (Winter 1985): 22 (regarding library circulation of software); *Software Use and the Law: A Guide for Individuals, Corporations, Institutions, and User Groups* (Washington, DC: Software Publishers Association, no date) (general principles with proposed school district and corporate policies). The AALL has proposed a comprehensive policy on academic uses of software that deserves wide attention. "Guidelines for the Use of Computer Software," *American Association of Law Libraries Newsletter* 21 (August 1989): 14–16; and 21 (September 1989): 59–60.

13. Washington, DC: EDUCOM; and Arlington, VA: Information Technology Association of America, 1992.

14. *EDUCOM's Directory of Members, Programs, and Projects: 1988–1989* (Washington, DC: EDUCOM, 1990), 3. Some readers would call "curious" an understatement. One analysis called the brochure's lack of emphasis on fair use

"troubling." It added: "This official-sounding document is thus incomplete—and dangerously one-sided in its emphasis. . . . " The analysis concluded that "EDU-COM and ADAPSO now seek through their brochure to negate fair use for computer software" (L. Ray Patterson and Stanley W. Lindberg, *The Nature of Copyright: A Law of Users' Rights* [Athens, GA: The University of Georgia Press, 1991]: 219–20).

15. EDUCOM has acted at times to help secure user rights. For example, when Congress revised the Copyright Act to restrict "rentals" of computer software, EDUCOM urged Congress to exclude nonprofit libraries and educational institutions from the restrictions. "The 'Software Rental Bill,'" *Software Initiative Newsletter* 3 (April–May 1989): 4–5. See note 33 below. EDUCOM has called for an extension of fair use to computers, but without elaboration. Steven W. Gilbert, "Information Technology, Intellectual Property, and Education," *EDUCOM Review* 25 (Spring 1990): 17. An EDUCOM spokesperson also testified before the Senate in 1967 to urge that the proposed copyright revision allow researchers to transcribe protected data into computers for analysis. See U.S. Congress, Senate Committee on the Judiciary, *Copyright Law Revision: Hearings Before the Subcommittee on Patents, Trademarks, and Copyrights,* Part 2, 90th Cong., 1st Sess., 1967, pp. 554–57 (testimony of James G. Miller).

16. *EDUCOM Directory,* pp. A1–A308.

17. Ibid., 5.

18. Originally known as the "Association of Data Processing Service Organizations," the acronym "ADAPSO" alone later became the association's formal name. ADAPSO issued its own brochure which similarly attacks "unauthorized copying": *Thou Shalt Not Dupe* (Arlington, VA: ADAPSO, 1984). That brochure is more oriented to businesses rather than universities.

19. Judith Axler Turner, "Technology Consortium Raps Software Piracy, Backs Intellectual Rights," *Chronicle of Higher Education,* 15 April 1987, p. 18.

20. "EDUCOM Code Adopted," *Software Initiative Newsletter* 2 (November–December 1988): 1.

21. Keith Patten, Office of General Counsel, Washington University, telephone interview with author, 19 December 1988.

22. NY/ALB–1987 and RICE–1988.

23. Steven W. Gilbert, "Report from EUIT," *EDUCOM Update* 1 (May–June 1992): 6; "Mathematics Association of America Endorses EDUCOM Code," *Software Initiative Newsletter* 3 (November–December 1989): 1 and 3; "EDUCOM Code Adopted," *Software Initiative Newsletter* 2 (November–December 1988): 1.

24. Carol Lennox, "*Using Software* Gets Results," *Software Initiative Newsletter* 2 (July–August 1988): 1.

25. EDUCOM Software Initiative, "Using Software Wisely and Well: Getting the Word Out," draft news release, 24 October 1987.

26. Ibid. *See also* "Syracuse University's Plan to Eliminate Illegal Software Copying," *Software Initiative Newsletter* 3 (April–May 1989): 1.

27. Mary Hutchings Reed and Debra Stanek, "Library and Classroom Use of Copyrighted Videotapes and Computer Software," *American Libraries* 17 (Febru-

ary 1986): supp., pp. A–D (hereafter cited as *1986 ALA Model Policy*). Reed was at that time an attorney with the Chicago law firm of Sidley & Austin. She also gave final approval to the ALA Model Policy on photocopying, detailed in chapter three.

28. RICE–1988 and VAND–1986.

29. HAWAII–1988 and STANFORD–1987.

30. BROWN–1986, HAWAII–1988, NOCAROLST–1987, and STANFORD–1987.

31. HAWAII–1988, NOCAROLST–1987, ROCHEST–1986, and STANFORD–1987.

32. David B. Walch, "The Circulation of Microcomputer Software in Academic Libraries and Copyright Implications," *Journal of Academic Librarianship* 10 (November 1984): 262–66.

33. Copyright Act of 1976, 17 U.S.C. § 109(b) (1988), *as amended by* Computer Software Rental Amendments Act of 1990, Pub. L. 101–650, 104 Stat. 5089 (1990).

34. STANFORD–1987.

35. HAWAII–1988. On a related issue, only the University of Rochester addresses reserve room use of software in libraries. The professor placing software on reserve must affirm whether copies comply with the law and whether the software may be lawfully copied by students for their own use. ROCHEST–1986.

36. CAL/RIV–1987, MIT–1987, and ROCHEST–1986. See also the two university policies that adopt the 1986 ALA Model Policy: RICE–1988 and VAND–1986.

37. At least one commentator claims that the notices on the purchase orders will be effective. Debra J. Stanek, "Videotapes, Computer Programs, and the Library," *Information Technology and Libraries* 5 (March 1986): 51.

38. BRANDEIS–1985, CAL/LA–1989, DELAWARE–1987, HARVARD–1984, MINN–1988, NOCAROLST–1987, ROCHEST–1986, STANFORD–1987, and WAYNEST–1986. See generally, David L. Wilson, "Some of the Best Things in Computing Are Free," *Chronicle of Higher Education,* 3 February 1993, pp. A19–A22. The U.S. Copyright Office recently began allowing registration of licenses and other documents related to public domain software and shareware. 37 C.F.R. § 201.26 (1992). *See also* Pub. L. 101–650, § 805, 104 Stat. 5089, 5136–37 (1990).

39. HAWAII–1988. License provisions that assert rights beyond privileges granted under copyright law may be unenforceable. Vault Corp. v. Quaid Software Ltd., 847 F. 2d 255, 269–70 (5th Cir. 1988).

40. ROCHEST–1986.

41. BRANDEIS–1985, BROWN–1986, GATECH–1986, HARVARD–1984, HAWAII–1988, JHU–1987, MINN–1988, NOCAROLST–1987, NY/STONY–1986, ROCHEST–1987, TENN–1985, VIRGINIA–1987, and WAYNEST–1986.

42. HARVARD–1984.

43. BRANDEIS–1985.

44. One of the software policies, TEXASA&M–1987, is not included in the categorization and analysis of policies. It states only: "A copyright notice is at-

tached to all software. In addition, a copyright notice is placed in each carrel housing a microcomputer." This policy says nothing about software duplications, and is therefore not comparable to the other university policies.

45. Category 1 policies: see note 41 above. Category 2 policies: BOSTON–1981, CAL/LA–1989, DELAWARE–1987, INDIANA–1983, MASS–1986, NY/ALB–1987, UTAH–1985, and WASHST–1984. Category 3 policies: CAL/RIV–1987, MIT–1980, MIT–1987, RICE–1988, ROCHEST–1986, STANFORD–1987, and VAND–1986.

46. Moreover, the focus of these efforts is often on software duplication by students—a group with little influence on university policies. For example, an interview with an official at Georgia Institute of Technology revealed that suspicions about software copying by students motivated policy development, even though the policy applies to the entire university (GATECH–1986). Miriam Drake, Library Director, Georgia Institute of Technology, telephone interview with author, 21 December 1988. The policy at Harvard is aimed specifically at students (HAR-VARD–1984). By adopting strict policies to attack student concerns, universities are implicitly tightening standards for the entire campus.

47. See note 33 of chapter one.

CHAPTER EIGHT

1. Robert D. Bickel, "The Role of College or University Legal Counsel," *Journal of Law and Education* 3 (January 1974): 78.

2. Lyman A. Glenny and Thomas K. Dalglish, "Higher Education and the Law," in *The University as an Organization*, pp. 173–202, edited by James A. Perkins (New York: McGraw Hill Book Company, 1973), 195.

3. Denise K. Manger, "Publishers Sue Copyshop for Selling Anthologies Without Obtaining Copyright Permission," *Chronicle of Higher Education*, 11 March 1992, pp. A1 and A14. *See also Chronicle of Higher Education*, 22 April 1992, p. A15.

4. John W. Meyer and Brian Rowan, "Institutionalized Organizations: Formal Structure as Myth and Ceremony," *American Journal of Sociology* 83 (September 1977): 348. *See also* Lynne G. Zucker, "Where Do Institutional Patterns Come From? Organizations as Actors in Social Systems," in *Institutional Patterns and Organizations: Culture and Environment* (Cambridge, MA: Ballinger Publishing Company, 1988), 38. The specific role of the Classroom Guidelines in particular cases is detailed in earlier chapters of this book.

5. Meyer and Rowan, "Institutionalized Organizations," 349. *See also* Paul J. DiMaggio and Walter W. Powell, "The Iron Cage Revisited: Institutional Isomorphism and Collective Rationality in Organizational Fields," *American Sociological Review* 48 (April 1983): 155.

6. Meyer and Rowan, "Institutionalized Organizations," 347; DiMaggio and Powell, "The Iron Cage," 147; Algo D. Henderson and Jean Glidden Henderson, *Higher Education in America* (San Francisco, CA: Jossey-Bass Publishers, 1975), 202–3. Some policy developers rely on standard procedures simply because they perceive an obligation or expectation to follow accepted rules. See James G. March

and Johan P. Olsen, "Organizational Choice under Ambiguity," in *Ambiguity and Choice in Organizations*, 2d ed., pp. 10–23, edited by James G. March and Johan P. Olsen (Oslo, Norway: Universitetsforlaget, 1979), 15.

7. Meyer and Rowan, "Institutionalized Organizations," 348 and 350; DiMaggio and Powell, "The Iron Cage," 149.

8. Meyer and Rowan, "Institutionalized Organizations," 357–58.

9. The official at the University of Wisconsin who led development of the policy suggested this possible scenario. Stuart G. Gullickson, Emeritus Habush-Bascom Professor of Law, University of Wisconsin-Madison, telephone interview with author, 26 July 1991.

10. "The University of Georgia Copyright Handbook" (Winter 1990) and "The University of Georgia Guidelines for the Use of Copyrighted Material" (Winter 1990).

11. L. Ray Patterson and Stanley W. Lindberg, *The Nature of Copyright: A Law of Users' Rights* (Athens, GA: The University of Georgia Press, 1991). Their work is also discussed in chapter one.

12. American Geophysical Union v. Texaco Inc., 802 F. Supp. 1 (S.D.N.Y. 1992); Basic Books, Inc. v. Kinko's Graphics Corp., 758 F. Supp. 1522 (S.D.N.Y. 1991).

13. DiMaggio and Powell, "The Iron Cage," 154.

14. Irving Louis Horowitz, *Communicating Ideas* (New York: Oxford University Press, 1986), 59 and 61; Michael Les Benedict, "Historians and the Continuing Controversy over Fair Use of Unpublished Manuscript Materials," *American Historical Review* 91 (October 1986): 870–71.

15. Carol A. Risher, Director of Copyright and New Technology, Association of American Publishers, telephone interview with author, 22 May 1989. By contrast, Charles Lieb, an attorney for the AAP, stated in 1981 that he had been successful in convincing one university legal counsel to change the university's policy on classroom copying, but not on library copying. "Apparently, the librarians present more of a problem than classroom instructors," he concluded. U.S. Copyright Office, *Report of the Register of Copyrights: Library Reproduction of Copyrighted Works (17 U.S.C. 108)* (Washington, DC: Library of Congress, 1983), Appendix VI, part 1, pp. 318–19 (hereafter cited as *Report of the Register*, 1983).

16. In contrast to the immunity available to libraries for copying conducted on unsupervised machines where warning notices are posted. Copyright Act of 1976, 17 U.S.C. § 108(f)(1) (1988).

17. See, for example, Association of American Publishers, Inc. and Authors League of America, Inc., *Photocopying by Academic, Public And Nonprofit Research Libraries* (May 1978).

18. Attorneys for the Association of American Publishers have analyzed and criticized the ALA Model Policy, but publishers have not made any formal or legal challenges against it. See *Report of the Register*, 1983, Appendix VII, pp. 77–82.

19. Bickel, "The Role of College or University Legal Counsel," 78.

20. John A. Beach, "The Management and Governance of Academic Institutions," *Journal of College and University Law* 12 (Winter 1985): 338 (governance ultimately depends on individuals).

21. Paul L. Dressel, "Mission, Organization, and Leadership," *Journal of Higher Education* 58 (January–February 1987): 102.

22. Robert G. Cope, *Management Aids and Procedures for Strategic Planning: Staff Report* (Boulder, CO: National Center for Higher Education Management Systems, 1980), 18–26 [ED272064].

23. Douglas J. Collier, *The Concept of Strategic Decisionmaking* (Boulder, CO: National Center for Higher Education Management Systems, 1981), 5–6 [ED272068].

24. Cope, *Management Aids*, 18.

25. Collier, *The Concept of Strategic Decisionmaking*, 5–6.

26. James A. Perkins, *The University in Transition* (Princeton, NJ: Princeton University Press, 1966), 54; E. D. Duryea, "Evolution of University Organization," in *The University as an Organization*, edited by James A. Perkins (New York: McGraw Hill Book Company, 1973), 35–37.

27. Leonard G. Boonin, "The University, Scientific Research, and the Ownership of Knowledge," in *Owning Scientific and Technical Information: Value and Ethical Issues*, edited by Vivian Weil and John W. Snapper (New Brunswick, NJ: Rutgers University Press, 1989), 260–61.

28. These cases are examined more fully in chapters one, three, and five.

29. Meeropol v. Nizer, 417 F. Supp. 1201, 1210 (S.D.N.Y. 1976), *aff'd*, 560 F. 2d 1061 (2d Cir.), *cert. denied*, 434 U.S. 1013 (1978) ("the alleged standard rule in the publishing industry . . . that use of more than 300 words of a copyrighted work does not qualify as a fair use, even if such a rule exists, is not dispositive of the fair use question. Fair use is a legal question to be determined by the court not by alleged industry practice"). Similar language appears in CORNELL–1977c.

30. Perry v. Sindermann, 408 U.S. 593, 602 (1972).

31. Patterson and Lindberg, *The Nature of Copyright*, 11.

32. Richard M. Cyert and James G. March, *A Behavioral Theory of the Firm* (Englewood Cliffs, NJ: Prentice-Hall, Inc., 1963), 119.

33. Ibid.; James Grier Miller, *Living Systems* (New York: McGraw-Hill Book Co., 1978), 655.

34. Cyert and March, *A Behavioral Theory of the Firm*, 119.

35. David P. White and Virginia Riordan, "Copyright Clearance Center," in *The Bowker Annual of Library and Book Trade Information*, 27th ed. (New York: R. R. Bowker Company, 1982), 72.

36. Debra E. Blum, "Use of Photocopied Anthologies for Courses Snarled by Delays and Costs of Copyright-Permission Process," *Chronicle of Higher Education*, 11 September 1991, p. A19.

37. Louis Freedberg, "Court Ruling Raises Cost of College 'Reader,'" *San Francisco Chronicle*, 28 August 1991, p. A14.

38. Blum, "Use of Photocopied Anthologies," p. A19.

39. Jane C. Ginsburg, "Reproduction of Protected Works for University Research or Teaching," *Journal of the Copyright Society of the USA* 39 (Spring 1992): 210. The university program parallels creation of similar blanket licenses—the "Annual Authorizations Service"—for private companies. A crucial difference,

however, is that educational institutions enjoy a much greater right of fair use than do for-profit companies. See Louise Levy Schaper and Alicja T. Kawecki, "Towards Compliance: How One Global Corporation Complies with Copyright Law," *Online* 15 (March 1991): 15–21.

40. As of this writing, the CCC has declined to make its "Final Report" on the University Pilot Program available to outside researchers because it includes data about the participants that the CCC would like to keep confidential. A revised version of the report may be available in the near future.

41. For one copy shop's difficult experiences with the CCC, see Raymond Tackett, "Copyright Law Needs to Include 'Fair Use' for Course Materials," *Chronicle of Higher Education,* 12 February 1992, pp. B3–B4.

42. Few publishers from some fields of study—such as law—participate in the CCC. Lee R. Nemchek, "Copyright Compliance by Law Firms (17 U.S.C. § 108): An Ethical Dilemma for Librarians," *Law Library Journal* 83 (Fall 1991): 664.

43. Robert L. Oakley, *Copyright and Preservation: A Serious Problem in Need of a Thoughtful Solution* (Washington, DC: The Commission on Preservation and Access, 1990), 45–47.

44. Joseph S. Alen, "Collective Licensing as a Practical Solution," *Bookmark* 50 (Winter 1992): 118–20.

45. Ginsburg, "Reproduction of Protected Works," 210–11; Calvin Reid, "Permissions Requests Grow as Copy Shops Complain of Bottlenecks," *Publishers Weekly,* 6 September 1991, p. 12.

46. Ginsburg, "Reproduction of Protected Works," 211. *See also Chronicle of Higher Education,* 22 April 1992, p. A23.

47. American Geophysical Union v. Texaco Inc., 802 F. Supp. 1, 18–19 and 24–26 (S.D.N.Y. 1992).

48. Ginsburg, "Reproduction of Protected Works," 212–13.

49. John R. Garrett, "Text to Screen Revisited: Copyright in the Electronic Age," *Online* 15 (March 1991): 24.

50. U.S. Congress, Office of Technology Assessment, *Finding a Balance: Computer Software, Intellectual Property and the Challenge of Technological Change* (Washington, DC: GPO, 1992), 177.

51. Michael W. Miller, "Professors Customize Textbooks, Blurring Roles of Publisher, Seller and Copy Shop," *Wall Street Journal,* 16 August 1990, pp. B1 and B3.

52. Garrett, "Text to Screen Revisited," 24.

53. Ann Okerson, "With Feathers: Effects of Copyright and Ownership on Scholarly Publishing," *College and Research Libraries* 52 (September 1991): 434–35.

54. David L. Wilson, "Critics of Copyright Law Seek New Ways to Prevent Unauthorized Use of Computerized Information," *Chronicle of Higher Education,* 6 May 1992, pp. A23–A24.

55. Ginsburg, "Reproduction of Protected Works," 184–91. See, generally, *Collective Administration of Copyright and Neighboring Rights* (Geneva: World Intellectual Property Organization, 1990). Compare this aspect of the Berne Con-

vention with the court's analysis of the CCC in the *Texaco* case, discussed earlier in this chapter.

56. U.S. Congress, *Finding a Balance,* 31 and 35.

57. Meyer and Rowan, "Institutionalized Organizations," 348; DiMaggio and Powell, "The Iron Cage," 155.

Appendix A

Policies Obtained from the Universities

Part One:
Universities Responding that They Had no Written Policy

University of Alabama
Arizona State University
California Institute of Technology
Carnegie Mellon University
Case Western Reserve University
Catholic University of America
Clark University
Columbia University
Duke University
University of Georgia
Georgetown University
Howard University
University of Kentucky
Louisiana State University
Ohio State University
Temple University

Part Two:
Written Policies Received

University of Arizona
ARIZONA-1986   "Handbook for Appointed Personnel," Section 2.11.02, revised 1 July 1986.

Boston University
BOSTON-1981   "The Copyright Law: A Summary for Use by Boston University and Its Staff," Office of Publications Production, 1981.

Brandeis University
BRANDEIS-1985   "Software Copyright Policy," Office of Educational Comput-
                 ing, ca. 1985.

Brigham Young University
BYU-1988   "Photocopying Policy," Office of the General Counsel, 1
                 June 1988.

Brown University
BROWN-1986   "Software Vendor Policy," Computer Center, 1986.
BROWN-1984   "Library Policy & Information Manual," Section X, April
                 1984.
BROWN-1977   "Application of the Copyright Revision Act of 1976," Mem-
                 orandum from Provost to Faculty, 23 May 1977.

University of California, Berkeley
CAL/BERK-1986a   "Policy and Guidelines for the Reproduction of Copyrighted
                 Materials for Teaching and Research," issued by Provost, 31
                 July 1986. [Version of policy issued by the university sys-
                 tem president on 29 April 1986.]
CAL/BERK-1986b   "Policy and Procedures of The General Library (Berkeley)
                 on Reserve Operations Involving Photocopied Materials,"
                 June 1986.
CAL/BERK-1985   "University of California Policy for Off-Air Recording of
                 Broadcast Programming for Educational Purposes," Office
                 of the President, September 1985. [Version of policy issued
                 by the university system president on 24 September 1985.]

University of California, Davis
CAL/DAVIS-1986a "Copyright and the Classroom: A practical guide to Copy-
                 rights and Copywrongs," Office of the Vice Chancellor for
                 Academic Affairs, June 1986.
CAL/DAVIS-1986b "University of California Policy on the Reproduction of
                 Copyrighted Materials for Teaching and Research," April
                 1986. [Version of policy issued by the university system
                 president on 29 April 1986.]
CAL/DAVIS-1985a "University of California Policy for Off-Air Recording of
                 Broadcast Programming for Educational Purposes," Office
                 of the President, September 1985. [Version of policy issued
                 by the university system president on 24 September 1985.]
CAL/DAVIS-1985b "Revised Policy on Reserve Materials and Copyright,"
                 Memorandum with attachments from the Acting University
                 Librarian to Faculty, 10 May 1985.

University of California, Irvine
CAL/IRV-1986   "University of California Policy on the Reproduction of
                 Copyrighted Materials for Teaching and Research," April

1986. [Version of policy issued by the university system president on 29 April 1986.]

CAL/IRV-1985   "University of California Policy for Off-Air Recording of Broadcast Programming for Educational Purposes," Office of the President, September 1985. [Version of policy issued by the university system president on 24 September 1985.]

University of California, Los Angeles

CAL/LA-1989   "UCLA Library Copyright Policy," June 1989.

CAL/LA-1986   "Reproduction of Copyrighted Materials for Teaching and Research," 1 July 1986. [Version of policy issued by the university system president on 29 April 1986.]

CAL/LA-1985   "University of California Policy for Off-Air Recording of Broadcast Programming for Educational Purposes," Office of the President, September 1985. [Version of policy issued by the university system president on 24 September 1985.]

University of California, Riverside

CAL/RIV-1987   General Administration memorandum no. 16, University Library, 30 September 1987.

CAL/RIV-1986   "University of California Policy on the Reproduction of Copyrighted Materials for Teaching and Research," Office of the Executive Vice Chancellor, 27 May 1986. [Version of policy issued by the university system president on 29 April 1986.]

CAL/RIV-1985   "University of California Policy for Off-Air Recording of Broadcast Programming for Educational Purposes," Office of the President, September 1985. [Version of policy issued by the university system president on 24 September 1985.]

University of California, San Diego

CAL/SD-1986   "University of California Policy on the Reproduction of Copyrighted Materials for Teaching and Research," April 1986. [Version of policy issued by the university system president on 29 April 1986.]

CAL/SD-1985   "University of California Policy for Off-Air Recording of Broadcast Programming for Educational Purposes," Office of the President, September 1985. [Version of policy issued by the university system president on 24 September 1985.]

University of California, Santa Barbara

CAL/SB-1986   "University of California Policy on the Reproduction of Copyrighted Materials for Teaching and Research," April 1986. [Version of policy issued by the university system president on 29 April 1986.]

CAL/SB-1985   "University of California Policy for Off-Air Recording of Broadcast Programming for Educational Purposes," Office

of the President, September 1985. [Version of policy issued by the university system president on 24 September
1985.]

University of Chicago
CHICAGO-1983   "Limitations on Copying of Written Material Under Copy-
                right Act," Office of Legal Counsel, January 1983.
CHICAGO-1978   "Policies for Library Copying," Library Manual, January
                1978.

University of Cincinnati
CINCIN-1984   "Copyright Compliance Guidelines: Inter Library Loan and
                Duplication Services," University Libraries, 14 June 1984.
CINCIN-1983a   "Copyright Compliance Guidelines: Reserves," University
                Libraries, 12 July 1983.
CINCIN-1983b   "Copyright Compliance Guidelines: How to Obtain Copy-
                right Permission," University Libraries, 15 June 1983.

University of Colorado
COLO-1986   "Copyright," General Procedures Manual, 1986.
COLO-1982a   Untitled [Regarding Interlibrary Loan Compliance], Decem-
                ber 1982.
COLO-1982b   "A Scholar's Guide to the Law of Copyright," Graduate
                School, Office of University Counsel, and Publications Ser-
                vice, March 1982.
COLO-1978   "Copyright Law Information," Memorandum from Director
                of Libraries to Library Faculty, 20 January 1978 (with "Re-
                vised Reserve Guidelines," 26 July 1978).
COLO-1977   "Activities to Comply with the Copyright Law," in "just
                b'TWX us: An interlibrary loan service newsletter," Decem-
                ber 1977.

Colorado State University
COLOST-1986a   "Reserve Lists for Fall Semester—1986," Memorandum
                from Acting Circulation Librarian and Reserve Desk Super-
                visor to Faculty, 13 August 1986.
COLOST-1986b   "Federal Copyright Law," Memorandum from Special As-
                sistant for Legal Affairs to Assistant to the Library Director,
                30 July 1986.
COLOST-1978   "CSUL Copyright Policy," University Libraries, ca. 1978.

University of Connecticut
CONN-1987   Untitled [Regarding Reserve Room Procedures], Memoran-
                dum from Reserve Operations Supervisor to Faculty, 1987.

Cornell University
CORNELL-1984   "Photocopying for Classroom and Research Use," Faculty
                Handbook, University Counsel, 1984.

CORNELL-1977a   "Staff Guidelines for Photocopying," Cornell University Libraries, December 1977.

CORNELL-1977b   "The Library and the Copy Machine," Memorandum from University Libraries to Faculty, December 1977.

CORNELL-1977c   "Copyrights/Photocopying/Recent Law Revisions," issued by Dean of the Faculty to all University Faculty, 14 December 1977.

Dartmouth College

DARTMTH-1981   "Photocopy Permissions Manual," 1981.

University of Delaware

DELAWARE-1987   "Compliance with U.S. Copyright Law," Memorandum from Provost to the University Community, 4 May 1987.

Emory University

EMORY-1986   "Policy on the Reproduction of Written Works by the Libraries of Emory University," Copyright Task Force, 23 May 1986.

University of Florida

FLORIDA-n.d.   "Interlibrary Loan Copyright Policy," University Libraries, no date.

Florida State University

FLORIDST-1985   "Guidelines for Reserve," 21 May 1985.

Georgia Institute of Technology

GATECH-1986   "Policy Regarding Software Piracy," Memorandum from Office of the President to All Faculty, Staff, and Students, 22 August 1986.

Harvard University

HARVARD-1986   "Multiple Copying and the Copyright Laws: A Guide for Harvard Faculty," Office of the General Counsel, September 1986.

HARVARD-1984   "Harvard College Rules and Regulations Concerning Computer Use: A Commentary," ca. 1984.

University of Hawaii

HAWAII-1988   "University Copying Guidelines," draft policy, Copying Guidelines Committee, 12 May 1988.

HAWAII-1979   "Copyright—Guidelines to the 1976 Act," Director of Contracts, December 1977, revised March 1979.

University of Houston

HOUSTON-1983   "Library Reserve Service," University Libraries, General Policy Manual, policy no. 21, 10 May 1982, revised 27 June 1983.

University of Illinois

ILLINOIS-1983   Untitled [Regarding Research and Classroom Copying],
                       Memorandum from Vice Chancellor for Academic Affairs
                       to Faculty, 11 April 1983.

ILLINOIS-1979a   "Library Photocopy Policy," Undergraduate Library Policy
                       and Procedures Manual, Area no. 345, Directive no. 1,
                       1979.

ILLINOIS-1979b   "Agreement on Guidelines for Classroom Copying in Not-
                       for-Profit Educational Institutions with Respect to Books
                       and Periodicals," Undergraduate Library Policy and Proce-
                       dures Manual, Area no. 345, Directive no. 2, 1979.

Indiana University

INDIANA-1983   "Copyright Information and Guidelines," University Librar-
                       ies, 15 August 1983.

University of Iowa

IOWA-1984   "University Guidelines on Copyright Law," Office of the
                       Vice President for Educational Development & Research,
                       28 September 1984.

Iowa State University

IOWAST-1986   "Copyright Law and the University Community," University
                       Library, revised June 1986.

IOWAST-1979   "Copying Book Material for the ISU Library Collection,"
                       University Library, 26 January 1977, revised 16 August
                       1979.

Johns Hopkins University

JHU-1987   "University Policy Regarding Unauthorized Use and Dupli-
                       cation of Computer Software," Office of the General Coun-
                       sel, October 1987.

JHU-1983   "University Copyright Guidelines," News Release, Office of
                       the General Counsel, ca. 1983.

JHU-1978   "New Copyright Law Implementation," Memorandum from
                       Provost to Council of Deans, ca. 1978.

University of Kansas

KANSAS-1983a   "Guidelines for Classroom Copying in Not-For-Profit Edu-
                       cational Institutions," Office of the General Counsel, 1983.

KANSAS-1983b   "Negotiating Committee Guidelines on 'Fair Use' of Video-
                       tapes for Educational Purposes," Office of the General
                       Counsel, January 1983.

Kent State University

KENT-1982   "Interlibrary Loan Request for Photo Copy of an Excerpt
                       from a Periodical or a Collected Work," May 1982.

KENT-1981   "Important Notes Concerning Reserve Books," Memorandum from Reserve Books Supervisor to Faculty, December 1981.

University of Maryland at College Park

MARYLAND-1985   "Guidelines Concerning Photocopying for Classroom, Research and Library Reserve Use," issued by Office of the Vice Chancellor for Academic Affairs, 29 May 1985.

University of Massachusetts at Amherst

MASS-1986   "Guidelines for Use of Copyrighted Materials," September 1986.

Massachusetts Institute of Technology

MIT-1987a   "Computer Software Copyright," Libraries, 4 December 1987.

MIT-1987b   "Videotapes and Copyright," Libraries, 4 December 1987.

MIT-1980   "Memorandum to all Academic, Administrative, and Research Staff at MIT Concerning the Copyright Law of the United States," from Associate Provost, 11 March 1980.

University of Miami

MIAMI-1986   "Copyright Laws," Business Affairs Policies and Procedures Manual, October 1984, revised August 1986.

University of Michigan

MICHIGAN-1983   "University Policy Concerning Photocopying Copyrighted Materials for Classroom Use," Internal Memorandum of the Office of General Counsel, 4 May 1983.

MICHIGAN-1979   "Reserve Service: Office Guidelines for Photocopying," University Library, 1979.

Michigan State University

MICHST-1980   "We May Copy," Library Copy Center, ca. 1980.

University of Minnesota

MINN-1988a   "Copyright Guidelines (Draft)," Library Copyright Task Force, 25 July 1988.

MINN-1988b   "Software Copyright Policy for the University Libraries" and "Questions You Might Have About Software Copyright Laws," June 1988.

MINN-1978   "Draft Report to President Magrath from the Working Group on Library Photocopy, Reserve, and Interlibrary Loan," 3 May 1978.

University of Missouri

MISSOURI-1983   "Copyright," University Libraries General Policy Manual, Policy no. 8, 31 May 1983.

University of Nebraska
NEBRASKA-1984 "Fair Use of Copyrighted Materials," Executive Vice President and Provost, 4 June 1984.
NEBRASKA-1978 "Photocopying Guidelines for Library Reserve Use," 1978.

University of New Mexico
NEWMEX-1978 "General Library Copyright Manual," 15 July 1978.

New York University
NYU-1983 "Statement of Policy On Photocopying Copyrighted Materials," Board of Trustees, 9 May 1983.

State University of New York at Albany
NY/ALB-1987 "Copyright Handbook," Assistant Vice President for Academic Planning and Development, September 1987.
NY/ALB-1982 "Policy Concerning University Photocopying for Classroom, Research and Library Reserve Use," University Libraries, Policy C:24, 29 October 1982.
NY/ALB-1981 "Sound Recordings Duplication," University Libraries, Policy C:22, July 1981.

State University of New York at Buffalo
NY/BUF-1984 "Copyright Fact Sheet," University Libraries, August 1984.
NY/BUF-1978a "University Libraries Loan Code: Reserve Collections," 1978.
NY/BUF-1978b "Compliance with the New Copyright Law," Memorandum from Library Director to Public Service Staff, 25 January 1978.
NY/BUF-1976 "Policy on Library Photocopy of Copyrighted Material," 17 November 1976.

State University of New York at Stony Brook
NY/STONY-1986 "Compliance with Copyright Laws," Memorandum from Administrator for Claims, Records and Risk Management to "All Staff, Faculty, Students and Others who use Software Acquired by the SUSB from Outside Sources," 8 August 1986.
NY/STONY-1979 "Reserve Photocopy Procedures" and "Guidelines for Obtaining Copies of Copyright Materials for Reserve Use," ca. 1979.
NY/STONY-1978 "Compliance with Copyright Law at the University Center," issued by the Acting President, 15 May 1978.

University of North Carolina
NOCAROL-1984 "Reserve Reading Services," Academic Affairs Library, August 1984.

North Carolina State University

NOCAROLST-1987	"Unauthorized Copying or Use of Computer Software," Memorandum from Legal Counsel to Deans, Directors, and Department Heads, 26 August 1987.
NOCAROLST-1983	"Guidelines for Photocopying," Memorandum from Legal Counsel to School Deans, 10 August 1983.
NOCAROLST-1982	"Policies Pertaining to the Use of Copyrighted Video Recordings," Library, August 1982.
NOCAROLST-1979	"Copyright Compliance Policies for Sound Recordings and Audiovisual Works," Library, September 1979.
NOCAROLST-1978	"Copyright Compliance Policies," Library, 14 September 1978.
NOCAROLST-1977	"Changes in Service Policies Pertaining to the New Copyright Law," Library Photocopy Service, 8 December 1977.

Northwestern University

NORTHWEST-1986	"Application and Policy for Use of Video in the Forum Room," University Library Media Facility, 15 August 1986; "Media Facility," University Library, 5 September 1986.
NORTHWEST-1985	"Policy for Use of the Reserve Book Room," 16 July 1985; "Policy and Procedures for Repetitive Use of Multiple Photocopies on Reserve—Internal Guidelines," 1 September 1983; "Policy and Procedures for Photocopied Materials on Reserve—Internal Guidelines," 13 July 1978, revised 1 September 1983; "Policy for Photocopied Materials on Reserve," Library Reserve Book Room, 13 July 1978.
NORTHWEST-1983	"Report on Northwestern University Library Copyright Policies and Concerns," 31 January 1983.
NORTHWEST-n.d.	"Dubbing Requests," Music Library Listening Center, no date.

University of Notre Dame

NOTREDM-1988	"Everything You Always Wanted to Know about Educational Media," Educational Media, revised edition 1983, further revised Fall 1988.
NOTREDM-1983	"Policy Change: Copyright, Reserve and the University Libraries," in "Notre Dame Report," 9 September 1983; "Copyright, Reserve and the University Libraries," University Libraries, Library Policies and Procedures, LPP:83:09, 20 June 1983 (with "Copyright: Things to Remember in Addition to Guidelines Listed in the Procedures Manual," Memorandum to accompany the foregoing policies, no date).
NOTREDM-1978	"New Copyright Law, 1 January 1978," in "Notre Dame Report," 7 April 1978.

University of Oklahoma

OKLA-1983   "Photocopying of Copyrighted Materials," Memorandum
                 from Chief Legal Counsel to Deans, 31 May 1983.

OKLA-1981   "To Ensure Compliance with the Copyright Law (Title 17,
                 United States Code), the University Libraries' Copy Shop
                 Has Adopted the Following Policies," Memorandum to
                 Copy Shop Patrons, ca. 1981.

OKLA-1978   "Policies Adopted by the Interlibrary Loan Office to Ensure
                 Compliance with the Copyright Law (Title 17, United States
                 Code)," University Libraries, 1978.

Oklahoma State University

OKLAST-1983   "Copyright Guidelines for Photocopying," University Li-
                 brary, Fall 1983.

University of Oregon

OREGON-1977   "OSSHE Policies re Copyright," Memorandum from Chair-
                 man of the Oregon State System of Higher Education Li-
                 brary Council to Systems Library Directors, 19 December
                 1977.

University of Pennsylvania

PENN-1986   Assistant Director of Libraries, letter to author, 17 Decem-
                 ber 1986.

PENN-1983   "Photocopying for Educational Uses," Office of the General
                 Counsel, 19 August 1983.

Pennsylvania State University

PENNST-1983   "Guidelines and Procedures for Off-Air Taping of Television
                 Programs," Audio-Visual Services, 6 January 1983; "Proce-
                 dures Statement: Copyright Procedures," Division of Learn-
                 ing and Telecommunications Services, no date.

PENNST-1982   "University Copyright Handbook," University Patent Coun-
                 sel, Office of the Vice President for Research and Graduate
                 Studies, November 1982.

PENNST-1978   "Interim Statement for Librarians Concerning the Handling
                 of Photocopying under the New Copyright Law (Title 17,
                 United States Code)," University Libraries, 14 March 1978.

University of Pittsburgh

PITT-1978   "University Photocopy Policy and Reserve Book Room Pho-
                 tocopy Policy," Memorandum from Provost to Deans, Di-
                 rectors, and Department Chairpersons, Standard Library
                 Administrative Procedure no. 6, 17 January 1978 (with
                 "University Photocopying Policy to Comply with Copyright
                 Law").

Princeton University

PRINCE-1986   "Guidelines Concerning Educational Uses of Videotapes,"
               Office of the General Counsel and Secretary, 1 May 1986.
PRINCE-1981   "Copyright Implications for Classroom Use," Memorandum
               from Office of the General Counsel and Secretary to Prince-
               ton University Press, 2 November 1981.

Purdue University

PURDUE-1977   "Principles and Procedures Regarding Duplication of Copy-
               righted Materials Used for Teaching and Research," Execu-
               tive Memorandum no. B-53, Office of the President, 1 No-
               vember 1977.

Rice University

RICE-1988   "Rice University's Policy, Procedures, and Guidelines for
               Instructional, Research, and Library Use of Copyrighted
               Material," Attachment C to "Intellectual Property Policy,"
               Memorandum no. 303-88, 28 July 1988.

University of Rochester

ROCHEST-1987   "Software Copying and Use Policy," November 1987.
ROCHEST-1986   "Copyright and Software—A Background Summary" and
               "Software and Copyright—Recommendations to Staff,"
               University Library, 1986.
ROCHEST-1984a "Reserve tapes for Music History 270," 4 December 1984.
ROCHEST-1984b "Sibley Music Library Guidelines for Placement of Copied
               Materials on Reserve," 1 December 1984.
ROCHEST-1983   "River Campus Libraries Photocopy Service Policy" and
               "River Campus Libraries Photocopy Service Policies and
               Procedures—Staff Guidelines," July 1983.
ROCHEST-1980   Untitled [Regarding Photocopying], Memorandum from le-
               gal counsel to Eastman School of Music, 22 May 1980.
ROCHEST-1978a "Copyright Information for Library Staff and Faculty,"
               1978.
ROCHEST-1978b "Guidelines for the Copying by the Rush Rhees Interlibrary
               Loan Section (ILL) of Monographs Published in the Last 75
               Years," 27 March 1978.
ROCHEST-1978c "Copyright Law," Memorandum from Associate Treasurer-
               Administration to Deans, Directors, and Department Chair-
               men, 9 January 1978.
ROCHEST-1978d Untitled [Regarding Photocopying, Interlibrary Loan, and
               Reserve Collection], Medical Center Library, 1 January
               1978.
ROCHEST-n.d.   "New Procedures for Copying Articles from Certain SML
               Journals for Use in the Reserve Collections," Memorandum

from Sibley Music Library to Eastman School of Music
Faculty, no date.

Rutgers University

RUTGERS-1984   "Photocopying for Reserve/Copyright," Memorandum from
Assistant University Librarian for Public Services to Library
Directors, 6 April 1984 (with "Reserve Copying Proce-
dures," 4 January 1983).

University of South Carolina

SOCAROL-1981a   "The Copyright Law and the Reserve Book Room Procedures," University Libraries Director, 26 May 1981 (with
"The Copyright Law and the Reserve Book Room Procedures," no date); "Placing Multiple Copies on Reserve,"
Memorandum from Legal Affairs and Legislation, 21 May
1981.

SOCAROL-1981b   Correspondence, Legal Affairs and Legislation to Assistant
Director of Libraries for Operations, 28 April 1981.

SOCAROL-1978   "Provisions of the New Copyright Law Relevant to Copying," Memorandum from Legal Affairs and Legislation to
Deans, Department Heads, and Librarians, 13 February
1978.

University of Southern California

SOCAL-1984   "Statement on Photocopying of Copyrighted Materials," Office of the General Counsel, 2 April 1984 (Appendix B of
"Copyright Manual," revised March 1985).

Southern Illinois University

SIU-1978   "Circulation Photocopy Policy," "Reserve Room Photocopying," and "Interlibrary Loan Photocopy Policy," University
Library, ca. 1978.

Stanford University

STANFORD-1987   "Copying of Computer Software," Guide Memo 62, 1 September 1987; "Guidelines on Software Copying Issued," in
"Campus Report," 18 March 1987.

STANFORD-1978   "Library Copyright Guidelines for Stanford University," 30
December 1977, revised November 1978.

Syracuse University

SYRACUSE-1978   "Copyright Law 1976," University Libraries, 14 March
1978.

University of Tennessee

TENN-1985   "Copying Software," Memorandum from the Chancellor to
Deans, Directors, and Department Heads, 28 January 1985.

University of Texas

TEXAS-1988	"Copying Books for Acquisition Purposes," Memorandum from Assistant Librarian for Public Service Programs to Bibliographers, 27 October 1988.
TEXAS-1986	"Audio Visual Reserves," Fine Arts Library, December 1986; "Reserve Policy of Audio Visual Materials," Audio Visual Library, Undergraduate Library, no date.
TEXAS-1985	"Reserve Requests for Summer Semester 1985," Memorandum from the General Libraries to Faculty, 2 April 1985; "Reserve Policies," University Libraries, Policies and Guidelines no. 15, 5 September 1974, revised 23 June 1982.
TEXAS-1984a	"The University of Texas System's Photocopying Policy and Settlement of an Unauthorized Copying Issue with the National Music Publishers Association (NMPA)," Memorandum from Vice President for Academic Affairs and Research to Deans, Departmental Chairpersons, Administrative Officials, and Project Directors, 15 August 1984.
TEXAS-1984b	"Policy Statement Regarding Photocopying Copyrighted Materials," Executive Vice Chancellors, 26 June 1984.
TEXAS-1978	"Copyright Law," Memorandum from Assistant Director of General Libraries for Public Services to Department Heads, Unit Heads, Branch Librarians, and Supervisors, 3 January 1978.

Texas A&M University

TEXASA&M-1987   Library Director, letter to author, 12 January 1987.

Tulane University

TULANE-1985   "Policy Statement on Photocopying of Copyrighted Materials for Classroom and Research Use," in "Faculty Handbook," Part III.K., July 1986, adopted by Faculty Senate, Spring 1985.

University of Utah

UTAH-1985	"Copyright Policy: Copying of Copyrighted Works," Policy and Procedures Manual no. 6-5, approved by the Institutional Council on 16 January 1978, editorially revised 27 September 1985.
UTAH-1984	"Copyright Policy: Performance or Display of Copyrighted Works," Policies and Procedures Manual no. 6-6, approved by the Institutional Council on 11 February 1980, editorially revised 8 November 1984.

Vanderbilt University

VAND-1986   "Copyrighted Videotapes and Computer Software," Memo-
                 randum from Associate Library Director to Division Direc-
                 tors/Heads of Special Units, 12 March 1986.

VAND-1983a   "Copyright Policies and Practices in the Divinity Library
                 and School," Memorandum from Divinity Library to Assist-
                 ant University Library Director, 10 November 1983.

VAND-1983b   "Music Library Copyright Policies," Memorandum from
                 Music Library to Assistant University Library Director, 9
                 November 1983.

VAND-1983c   "Copyright Policies, Medical Center Library," Memoran-
                 dum from Medical Center Library to Assistant University
                 Library Director, 4 November 1983; "Document Delivery
                 Service," October 1983.

VAND-1983d   "Use of Copyrighted Materials in the Classroom," Associate
                 Dean of the Business School to Faculty, 10 January 1983
                 (with two additional memoranda attached: "Permission to
                 Reproduce Copyrighted Material," 19 January 1983; "Use
                 of Copyrighted Materials in Class," 20 July 1983).

VAND-1978   "The New Copyright Law and the JUL," 6 February 1978.

VAND-1977   "Report of the Task Force," Memorandum from the Task
                 Force to the Library Director, 20 December 1977.

University of Virginia

VIRGINIA-1987   "Copying of Copyrighted Material," Financial and Adminis-
                 trative Policies Manual, Policies XV.F.1 through XV.F.9
                 and Procedure 15-6, issued by University Comptroller, 16
                 March 1987 (developed earlier and continuously revised and
                 reissued).

VIRGINIA-1983   "Reserve Policy Statement," University Library, 2 May
                 1983; "Reserve Request," University Library, December
                 1983.

Virginia Polytechnic Institute

VATECH-1985   "Copyright Guidelines, Policies, and Procedures," Univer-
                 sity Copyright Committee, 23 April 1985.

VATECH-1984   "Copyright at a Glance," internal guidelines drafted by User
                 Services Librarian, 29 August 1984.

VATECH-1983   "Copyright Procedures in the Library," Memorandum from
                 User Services Librarian to Legal Counsel, 7 February 1983;
                 "Changes in Copyright-based Policies," Memorandum from
                 User Services Librarian to LAC, 20 January 1983.

University of Washington

WASH-1979   "Reproduction of Copyrighted Materials," University Li-
                 braries, Operations Manual, vol. IV, section C, no. 2, 1 Oc-
                 tober 1979.

WASH-1978   "The Copyright Act of 1976: Guidelines for Educators," Office of the Attorney General, State of Washington, January 1978, revised December 1978. [Same as WASHST-1978.]

Washington State University

WASHST-1987   "IMS Off-Air Video Recording Policy for Classroom Use," Instructional Media Services, September 1987.

WASHST-1986   "Photocopy Rules under Copyright Law," University Library Copy Center, 5 October 1978, reissued 1 April 1986.

WASHST-1984   "Software Protected by Copyright," in "Bulletin/Calendar," issued by Associate Provost, 5 October 1984.

WASHST-1983   "Library Policy for Initial Operation under New Copyright Law, PL94-553," University Libraries Policy and Procedures Manual, Policy XXV-78, 1 January 1978, revised August 1983.

WASHST-1978   "The Copyright Act of 1976: Guidelines for Educators," Office of the Attorney General, State of Washington, January 1978, revised December 1978. [Same as WASH-1978.]

Washington University

WASHU-1988   "Guidelines for Reproducing Copyrighted Works for Use in Teaching and Research," Office of the General Counsel, January 1988.

WASHU-1978   "Copyright Information," University Libraries, January 1978.

Wayne State University

WAYNEST-1986   "Copying of Computer Software Programs," Executive Order 86-1, Policy-Making by the President, 11 February 1986.

WAYNEST-1984   "Guidelines for Photocopying for Teaching and Research," Office of the General Counsel, 1 February 1984.

University of Wisconsin

WISC-1983   "Guidelines for Photocopying for Teaching and Research," Office of Administrative Legal Services, 15 February 1978, revised April 1983 (with Memorandum from Office of Administrative Legal Services to Deans, Directors, and Department Chairpersons, 7 March 1983).

WISC-1978   "Reserve Operations," Chapter II-F, Office of Administrative Legal Services, 13 June 1978.

Yale University

YALE-1981   "Copying Procedures and Copyright Law," University Library Policy Manual, Policy B-4, 27 March 1978, revised 15 July 1981.

YALE-1978   "Copyright Compliance," Memorandum from University Librarian to Faculty and Academic Staff, 17 November 1978.

Appendix B

Model Copyright Policies

CLASSROOM GUIDELINES

Agreement on Guidelines for Classroom Copying in Not-For-Profit Educational Institutions

With Respect to Books and Periodicals

The purpose of the following guidelines is to state the minimum and not the maximum standards of educational fair use under Section 107 of H.R. 2223. The parties agree that the conditions determining the extent of permissible copying for educational purposes may change in the future; that certain types of copying permitted under these guidelines may not be permissible in the future; and conversely that in the future other types of copying not permitted under these guidelines may be permissible under revised guidelines.

Moreover, the following statement of guidelines is not intended to limit the types of copying permitted under the standards of fair use under judicial decision and which are stated in Section 107 of the Copyright Revision Bill. There may be instances in which copying which does not fall within the guidelines stated below may nonetheless be permitted under the criteria of fair use.

GUIDELINES

I. Single Copying for Teachers

A single copy may be made of any of the following by or for a teacher at his or her individual request for his or her scholarly research or use in teaching or preparation to teach a class:

A. A chapter from a book;

B. An article from a periodical or newspaper;

C. A short story, short essay or short poem, whether or not from a collective work;

D. A chart, graph, diagram, drawing, cartoon or picture from a book, periodical, or newspaper;

II. Multiple Copies for Classroom Use

Multiple copies (not to exceed in any event more than one copy per pupil in a course) may be made by or for the teacher giving the course for classroom use or discussion; *provided that:*

A. The copying meets the tests of brevity and spontaneity as defined below; *and,*

B. Meets the cumulative effect test as defined below; *and,*

C. Each copy includes a notice of copyright.

DEFINITIONS

Brevity

(*i*) Poetry: (a) A complete poem if less than 250 words and if printed on not more than two pages or, (b) from a longer poem, an excerpt of not more than 250 words.

(*ii*) Prose: (a) Either a complete article, story or essay of less than 2,500 words, or (b) an excerpt from any prose work of not more than 1,000 words or 10 percent of the work, whichever is less, but in any event a minimum of 500 words.

[Each of the numerical limits stated in "i" and "ii" above may be expanded to permit the completion of an unfinished line of a poem or of an unfinished prose paragraph.]

(*iii*) Illustration: One chart, graph, diagram, drawing, cartoon or picture per book or per periodical issue.

(*iv*) "Special" works: Certain works in poetry, prose or in "poetic prose" which often combine language with illustrations and which are intended sometimes for children and at other times for a more general audience fall short of 2,500 words in their entirety. Paragraph "ii" above notwithstanding such "special works" may not be reproduced in their entirety; however, an excerpt comprising not more than two of the published pages of such special work and containing not more than 10 percent of the words found in the text thereof, may be reproduced.

Spontaneity

(*i*) The copying is at the instance and inspiration of the individual teacher, and

(*ii*) The inspiration and decision to use the work and the moment of its use for maximum teaching effectiveness are so close in time that it would be unreasonable to expect a timely reply to a request for permission.

Cumulative Effect

(*i*) The copying of the material is for only one course in the school in which the copies are made.

(*ii*) Not more than one short poem, article, story, essay or two excerpts may be copied from the same author, nor more than three from the same collective work or periodical volume during one class term.

(*iii*) There shall not be more than nine instances of such multiple copying for one course during one class term.

[The limitations stated in "ii" and "iii" above shall not apply to current news periodicals and newspapers and current news sections of other periodicals.]

III. Prohibitions as to I and II Above

Notwithstanding any of the above, the following shall be prohibited:

(A) Copying shall not be used to create or to replace or substitute for anthologies, compilations or collective works. Such replacement or substitution may occur whether copies of various works or excerpts therefrom are accumulated or reproduced and used separately.

(B) There shall be no copying of or from works intended to be "consumable" in the course of study or of teaching. These include workbooks, exercises, standardized tests and test booklets and answer sheets and like consumable material.

(C) Copying shall not:

(a) substitute for the purchase of books, publishers' reprints or periodicals;

(b) be directed by higher authority;

(c) be repeated with respect to the same item by the same teacher from term to term.

(D) No charge shall be made to the student beyond the actual cost of the photocopying.

Agreed March 19, 1976.
Ad Hoc Committee on Copyright Law Revision:

By Sheldon Elliott Steinbach.
Author-Publisher Group:
Authors League of America:
By Irwin Karp, *Counsel.*
Association of American Publishers, Inc.:
By Alexander C. Hoffman,
Chairman, Copyright Committee.

ALA MODEL POLICY

**Model Policy Concerning College and University Photocopying for
Classroom, Research and Library Reserve Use**

This model policy, another in a series of copyright advisory documents
developed by the American Library Association (ALA), is intended for
the guidance and use of academic librarians, faculty, administrators, and
legal counsel in response to implementation of the rights and responsibilities provisions of Public Law 94–553, *General Revision of the Copyright
Law,* which took effect on January 1, 1978.

Prepared by ALA Legal Counsel Mary Hutchings of the law firm Sidley
& Austin, with advice and assistance from the Copyright Subcommittee
(ad hoc) of ALA's Legislation Committee, Association of College and
Research Libraries (ACRL) Copyright Committee, Association of Research Libraries (ARL) and other academic librarians and copyright attorneys, the model policy outlines "fair use" rights in the academic environment for classroom teaching, research activities and library services.
Please note that it does not address other library photocopying which may
be permitted under other sections of the Copyright Law, e.g., § 108 (Reproduction by Libraries and Archives).

Too often, members of the academic community have been reluctant or
hesitant to exercise their rights of fair use under the law for fear of courting
an infringement suit. It is important to understand that in U.S. law, copyright is a limited statutory monopoly and the public's *right* to use materials
must be protected. Safeguards have been written into the legislative history
accompanying the new copyright law protecting librarians, teachers, researchers and scholars and guaranteeing their rights of access to information as they carry out their responsibilities for educating or conducting

research. It is, therefore, important to heed the advice of a former U.S. Register of Copyrights:

"If you don't *use* fair use, you will *lose* it!"

American Library Association
Washington Office
March 1982
Second printing, July 1982

MODEL POLICY CONCERNING COLLEGE AND UNIVERSITY PHOTOCOPYING FOR CLASSROOM, RESEARCH AND LIBRARY RESERVE USE

Prepared by
The American Library Association
March 1982

I. THE COPYRIGHT ACT AND PHOTOCOPYING

From time to time, the faculty and staff of this University [College] may use photocopied materials to supplement research and teaching. In many cases, photocopying can facilitate the University's [College's] mission; that is, the development and transmission of information. However, the photocopying of copyrighted materials is a right granted under the copyright law's doctrine of "fair use" which must not be abused. This report will explain the University's [College's] policy concerning the photocopying of copyrighted materials by faculty and library staff. Please note that this policy does not address other library photocopying which may be permitted under other sections of the copyright law, e.g., 17 U.S.C. § 108.

Copyright is a constitutionally conceived property right which is designed to promote the progress of science and the useful arts by securing for an author the benefits of his or her original work of authorship for a limited time. U.S. Constitution, Art. I, Sec. 8. The Copyright statute, 17

U.S.C. § 101 *et seq.,* implements this policy by balancing the author's interest against the public interest in the dissemination of information affecting areas of universal concern, such as art, science, history and business. The grand design of this delicate balance is to foster the creation and dissemination of intellectual works for the general public.

The Copyright Act defines the rights of a copyright holder and how they may be enforced against an infringer. Included within the Copyright Act is the "fair use" doctrine which allows, under certain conditions, the copying of copyrighted material. While the act lists general factors under the heading of "fair use" it provides little in the way of specific directions for what constitutes fair use. The law states:

17 U.S.C. § 107. Limitations on exclusive rights: Fair use

Notwithstanding the provisions of section 106, the fair use of a copyrighted work, *including such use by reproduction in copies* or phonorecords or by any other means specified by that section, for purposes such as criticism, comment, news reporting, *teaching (including multiple copies for classroom use), scholarship, or research, is not an infringement of copyright.* In determining whether the use made of a work in any particular case is a fair use the factors to be considered shall include—

(1) the purpose and character of the use, including whether such use is of a commercial nature or is for nonprofit educational purposes;
(2) the nature of the copyrighted work;
(3) the amount and substantiality of the portion used in relation to the copyrighted work as a whole; and
(4) the effect of the use upon the potential market for or value of the copyrighted work. (Emphasis added.)

The purpose of this report is to provide you, the faculty and staff of this University [College], with an explanation of when the photocopying of copyrighted material in our opinion is permitted under the fair use doctrine. Where possible, common examples of research, classroom, and library reserve photocopying have been included to illustrate what we believe to be the reach and limits of fair use.

Please note that the copyright law applies to all forms of photocopying, whether it is undertaken at a commercial copying center, at the University's [College's] central or departmental copying facilities or at a self-service machine. While you are free to use the services of a commercial establishment, you should be prepared to provide documentation of permission from the publisher (if such permission is necessary under this policy), since many commercial copiers will require such proof.

We hope this report will give you an appreciation of the factors which weigh in favor of fair use and those factors which weigh against fair use, but faculty members must determine for themselves which works will be photocopied. This University [College] does not condone a policy of photocopying instead of purchasing copyrighted works where such photocopying would constitute an infringement under the copyright law, but it does encourage faculty members to exercise good judgment in serving the best interests of students in an efficient manner. This University [College] and its faculty and staff will make a conscientious effort to comply with these guidelines.

Instructions for securing permission to photocopy copyrighted works when such copying is beyond the limits of fair use appear at the end of this report. It is the policy of this University that the user (faculty, staff or librarian) secure such permission whenever it is legally necessary.

II. UNRESTRICTED PHOTOCOPYING

A. Uncopyrighted Published Works

Writings published before January 1, 1978 which have never been copyrighted may be photocopied without restriction. Copies of works protected by copyright must bear a copyright notice, which consists of the letter "c" in a circle, or the word "Copyright," or the abbreviation "Copr.," plus the year of first publication, plus the name of the copyright owner. 17 U.S.C. § 401. As to works published before January 1, 1978, in the case of a book, the notice must be placed on the title page or the reverse side of the title page. In the case of a periodical the notice must be placed either on the title page, the first page of text, or in the masthead. A pre-1978 failure to comply with the notice requirements resulted in the work being injected into the public domain, i.e., unprotected. Copyright notice requirements have been relaxed since 1978, so that the absence of notice on copies of a work published after January 1, 1978 does not necessarily mean the work is in the public domain. 17 U.S.C. § 405 (a) and (c). However, you will not be liable for damages for copyright infringement of works published after that date, if, after normal inspection, you photocopy a work on which you cannot find a copyright symbol and you have not received actual notice of the fact the work is copyrighted. 17 U.S.C. § 405(b). However, a copyright owner who found out about your photocopying would have the right to prevent further distribution of the copies if in fact the work were copyrighted and the copies are infringing. 17 U.S.C. § 405(b).

B. Published Works with Expired Copyrights

Writings with expired copyrights may be photocopied without restriction. All copyrights prior to 1906 have expired. 17 U.S.C. § 304(b).

Copyrights granted after 1906 may have been renewed; however the writing will probably not contain notice of the renewal. Therefore, it should be assumed all writings dated 1906 or later are covered by a valid copyright, unless information to the contrary is obtained from the owner or the U.S. Copyright Office (see Copyright Office Circular 15t).

Copyright Office Circular R22 explains how to investigate the copyright status of a work. One way is to use the *Catalog of Copyright Entries* published by the Copyright Office and available in [the University Library] many libraries. Alternatively you may request the Copyright Office to conduct a search of its registration and/or assignment records. The Office charges an hourly fee for this service. You will need to submit as much information as you have concerning the work in which you are interested, such as the title, author, approximate date of publication, the type of work or any available copyright data. The Copyright Office does caution that its searches are not conclusive; for instance, if a work obtained copyright less than twenty-eight years ago, it may be fully protected although there has been no registration or deposit.

C. Unpublished Works

Unpublished works, such as theses and dissertations, may be protected by copyright. If such a work was created before January 1, 1978, and has not been copyrighted or published without copyright notice, the work is protected under the new act for the life of the author plus fifty years, 17 U.S.C. § 303, but in no case earlier than December 31, 2002. If such a work is published on or before that date, the copyright will not expire before December 31, 2027. Works created after January 1, 1978, and not published enjoy copyright protection for the life of the author plus fifty years. 17 U.S.C. § 302.

D. U.S. Government Publications

All U.S. Government publications with the possible exception of some National Technical Information Service Publications less than five years old may be photocopied without restrictions, except to the extent they contain copyrighted materials from other sources. 17 U.S.C. § 105. U.S. Government publications are documents prepared by an official or employee of the government in an official capacity. 17 U.S.C. § 101. Government publications include the opinions of courts in legal cases, congressional reports on proposed bills, testimony offered at congressional hearings and the works of government employees in their official capacities. Works prepared by outside authors on contract to the government may or may not be protected by copyright, depending on the specifics of the contract. In the absence of copyright notice on such works, it would be reasonable to assume they are government works in the public domain. It should be noted that state government works may be protected by copyright. *See,* 17 U.S.C. § 105. However, the opinions of state courts are not protected.

III. PERMISSIBLE PHOTOCOPYING OF COPYRIGHTED WORKS

The Copyright Act allows anyone to photocopy copyrighted works without securing permission from the copyright owner when the photocopying amounts to a "fair use" of the material. 17 U.S.C. § 107. The guidelines in this report discuss the boundaries for fair use of photocopied material used in research or the classroom or in a library reserve operation. Fair use cannot always be expressed in numbers—either the number of pages copied or the number of copies distributed. Therefore, you should weigh the various factors listed in the act and judge whether the intended use of photocopied, copyrighted material is within the spirit of the fair use doctrine. Any serious questions concerning whether a particular photocopying constitutes fair use should be directed to University [College] counsel.

A. Research Uses

At the very least, instructors may make a single copy of any of the following for scholarly research or use in teaching or preparing to teach a class:

1. a chapter from a book;
2. an article from a periodical or newspaper;
3. a short story, short essay, or short poem, whether or not from a collective work;
4. a chart, diagram, graph, drawing, cartoon or picture from a book, periodical, or newspaper.

These examples reflect the most conservative guidelines for fair use. They do not represent inviolate ceilings for the amount of copyrighted material which can be photocopied within the boundaries of fair use. When exceeding these minimum levels, however, you again should consider the four factors listed in Section 107 of the Copyright Act to make sure that any additional photocopying is justified. The following demonstrate situations where increased levels of photocopying would continue to remain within the ambit of fair use:

1. the inability to obtain another copy of the work because it is not available from another library or source or cannot be obtained within your time constraints;

2. the intention to photocopy the material only once and not to distribute the material to others;

3. the ability to keep the amount of material photocopied within a reasonable proportion to the entire work (the larger the work, the greater amount of material which may be photocopied).

Most single-copy photocopying for your personal use in research—even when it involves a substantial portion of a work—may well constitute fair use.

B. Classroom Uses

Primary and secondary school educators have, with publishers, developed the following guidelines, which allow a teacher to distribute photocopied material to students in a class without the publisher's prior permission, under the following conditions:

1. the distribution of the same photocopied material does not occur every semester;

2. only one copy is distributed for each student which copy must become the student's property;

3. the material includes a copyright notice on the first page of the portion of material photocopied;

4. the students are not assessed any fee beyond the actual cost of the photocopying.

In addition, the educators agreed that the amount of material distributed should not exceed certain brevity standards. Under those guidelines, a prose work may be reproduced in its entirety if it is less than 2,500 words in length. If the work exceeds such length, the excerpt reproduced may not exceed 1,000 words, or ten percent of the work, whichever is less. In the case of poetry, 250 words is the maximum permitted.

These minimum standards normally would not be realistic in the university setting. Faculty members needing to exceed these limits for college education should not feel hampered by these guidelines, although they should attempt a "selective and sparing" use of photocopied, copyrighted material.

The photocopying practices of an instructor should not have a significant detrimental impact on the market for the copyrighted work. 17 U.S.C. § 107(4). To guard against this effect, you usually should restrict use of an item of photocopied material to one course and you should not repeatedly photocopy excerpts from one periodical or author without the permission of the copyright owner.

C. Library Reserve Uses

At the request of a faculty member, a library may photocopy and place on reserve excerpts from copyrighted works in its collection in accordance with guidelines similar to those governing formal classroom distribution for face-to-face teaching discussed above. This University [College] believes that these guidelines apply to the library reserve shelf to the extent it functions as an extension of classroom readings or reflects an individual student's right to photocopy for his personal scholastic use under the doctrine of fair use. In general, librarians may photocopy materials for reserve room use for the convenience of students both in preparing class assignments and in pursuing informal educational activities which higher education requires, such as advanced independent study and research.

If the request calls for only *one* copy to be placed on reserve, the library may photocopy an entire article, or an entire chapter from a book, or an entire poem. Requests for *multiple* copies on reserve should meet the following guidelines:

1. the amount of material should be reasonable in relation to the total amount of material assigned for one term of a course taking into account the nature of the course, its subject matter and level, 17 U.S.C. § 107(1) and (3);
2. the number of copies should be reasonable in light of the number of students enrolled, the difficulty and timing of assignments, and the number of other courses which may assign the same material, 17 U.S.C. § 107(1) and (3);
3. the material should contain a notice of copyright, *see,* 17 U.S.C. § 401;
4. the effect of photocopying the material should not be detrimental to the market for the work. (In general, the library should own at least one copy of the work.) 17 U.S.C. § 107(4).

For example, a professor may place on reserve as a supplement to the course textbook a reasonable number of copies of articles from academic journals or chapters from trade books. A reasonable number of copies will in most instances be less than six, but factors such as the length or difficulty of the assignment, the number of enrolled students and the length of time allowed for completion of the assignment may permit more in unusual circumstances.

In addition, a faculty member may also request that multiple copies of photocopied, copyrighted material be placed on the reserve shelf if there is insufficient time to obtain permission from the copyright owner. For example, a professor may place on reserve several photocopies of an entire article from a recent issue of *Time* magazine or the *New York Times* in lieu of distributing a copy to each member of the class. If you are in doubt as to whether a particular instance of photocopying is fair use in the reserve reading room, you should seek the publisher's permission. Most publishers will be cooperative and will waive any fee for such a use.

D. Uses of Photocopied Material Requiring Permission

1. *Repetitive copying:* The classroom or reserve use of photocopied materials in multiple courses or successive years will normally require advance permission from the owner of the copyright, 17 U.S.C. § 107(3).

2. *Copying for profit:* Faculty should not charge students more than the actual cost of photocopying the material, 17 U.S.C. § 107(1).

3. *Consumable works:* The duplication of works that are consumed in the classroom, such as standardized tests, exercises, and workbooks, normally requires permission from the copyright owner, 17 U.S.C. § 107(4).

4. *Creation of anthologies as basic text material for a course:* Creation of a collective work or anthology by photocopying a number of copyrighted articles and excerpts to be purchased and used together as the basic text for a course will in most instances require the permission of the copyright owners. Such photocopying is more likely to be considered as a substitute for purchase of a book and thus less likely to be deemed fair use, 17 U.S.C. § 107(4).

E. How to Obtain Permission

When a use of photocopied material requires that you request permission, you should communicate complete and accurate information to the copyright owner. The American Association of Publishers suggests that the following information be included in a permission request letter in order to expedite the process:

1. Title, author and/or editor, and edition of materials to be duplicated.

2. Exact material to be used, giving amount, page numbers, chapters and, if possible, a photocopy of the material.

3. Number of copies to be made.

4. Use to be made of duplicated materials.

5. Form of distribution (classroom, newsletter, etc.).

6. Whether or not the material is to be sold.

7. Type of reprint (ditto, photography, offset, typeset).

The request should be sent, together with a self-addressed return envelope, to the permissions department of the publisher in question. If the address of the publisher does not appear at the front of the material, it may be readily obtained in a publication entitled *The Literary Marketplace,* published by the R. R. Bowker Company and available in all libraries.

The process of granting permission requires time for the publisher to check the status of the copyright and to evaluate the nature of the request. It is advisable, therefore, to allow enough lead time to obtain permission before the materials are needed. In some instances, the publisher may assess a fee for the permission. It is not inappropriate to pass this fee on to the students who receive copies of the photocopied material.

The Copyright Clearance Center also has the right to grant permission and collect fees for photocopying rights for certain publications. Libraries may copy from any journal which is registered with the CCC and report the copying beyond fair use to CCC and pay the set fee. A list of publications for which the CCC handles fees and permissions is available from the CCC, [27 Congress Street, Salem, MA 01970].

Sample Letter to Copyright Owner (Publisher) Requesting Permission to Copy:

March 1, 1982

Material Permissions Department
Hypothetical Book Company
500 East Avenue
Chicago, Illinois 60601

Dear Sir or Madam:

I would like permission to copy the following for continued use in my classes in future semesters:

Title: *Learning is Good,* Second Edition
Copyright: Hypothetical Book Co., 1965, 1971
Author: Frank Jones
Material to be duplicated: Chapters 10, 11 and 14 (photocopy enclosed).
Number of copies: 500
Distribution: The material will be distributed to students in my classes and they will pay only the cost of the photocopying.
Type of reprint: Photocopy
Use: The chapter will be used as supplementary teaching materials.

I have enclosed a self-addressed envelope for your convenience in replying to this request.

Sincerely,

Faculty Member

F. Infringement

Courts and legal scholars alike have commented that the fair use provisions in the Copyright Act are among the most vague and difficult that can be found anywhere in the law. In amending the Copyright Act in 1976, Congress anticipated the problem this would pose for users of copyrighted materials who wished to stay under the umbrella of protection offered by fair use. For this reason, the Copyright Act contains specific provisions which grant additional rights to libraries and insulate employees of a nonprofit educational institution, library, or archives from statutory damages for infringement where the infringer believed or had reasonable ground to believe the photocopying was a fair use of the material. 17 U.S.C. § 504(c)(2).

Normally, an infringer is liable to the copyright owner for the actual losses sustained because of the photocopying and any additional profits of the infringer. 17 U.S.C. § 504(a)(1) and (b). Where the monetary losses are nominal, the copyright owner usually will claim statutory damages instead of the actual losses. 17 U.S.C. § 504(a)(2) and (c). The statutory damages may reach as high as [$20,000] (or up to [$100,000] if the infringement is willful). In addition to suing for money damages, a copyright owner can usually prevent future infringement through a court injunction. 17 U.S.C. § 502.

The Copyright Act specifically exempts from statutory damages any employee of a nonprofit educational institution, library, or archives, who "believed and had reasonable grounds for believing that his or her use of the copyrighted work was a fair use under Section 107." 17 U.S.C. § 504(c)(2). While the fair use provisions are admittedly ambiguous, any employee who attempts to stay within the guidelines contained in this report should have an adequate good faith defense in the case of an innocently committed infringement.

If the criteria contained in this report are followed, it is our view that no copyright infringement will occur and that there will be no adverse effect on the market for copyrighted works.

(Many educational institutions will provide their employees legal counsel without charge if an infringement suit is brought against the employee for photocopying performed in the course of employment. If so, this should be noted here.)

MUSIC GUIDELINES

Guidelines for Educational Uses of Music

The purpose of the following guidelines is to state the minimum and not the maximum standards of educational fair use under Section 107 of HR 2223. The parties agree that the conditions determining the extent of permissible copying for educational purposes may change in the future; that certain types of copying permitted under these guidelines may not be permissible in the future, and conversely that in the future other types of copying not permitted under these guidelines may be permissible under revised guidelines.

Moreover, the following statement of guidelines is not intended to limit the types of copying permitted under the standards of fair use under judicial decision and which are stated in Section 107 of the Copyright Revision Bill. There may be instances in which copying which does not fall within the guidelines stated below may nonetheless be permitted under the criteria of fair use.

A. PERMISSIBLE USES

1. Emergency copying to replace purchased copies which for any reason are not available for an imminent performance provided purchased replacement copies shall be substituted in due course.

2. (a) For academic purposes other than performance, multiple copies of excerpts of works may be made, provided that the excerpts do not comprise a part of the whole which would constitute a performable unit such as a section, movement or aria, but in no case more than ten percent of the whole work. The number of copies shall not exceed one copy per pupil.

(b) For academic purposes other than performance, a single copy of an entire performable unit (section, movement, aria, etc.) that is, (1) confirmed by the copyright proprietor to be out of print or (2) unavailable except in a larger work, may be made by or for a teacher solely for the purpose of his or her scholarly research or in preparation to teach a class.

3. Printed copies which have been purchased may be edited or simplified provided that the fundamental character of the work is not distorted or the lyrics, if any, altered or lyrics added if none exist.

4. A single copy of recordings of performances by students may be made for evaluation or rehearsal purposes and may be retained by the educational institution or individual teacher.

5. A single copy of a sound recording (such as a tape, disc, or cassette) of copyrighted music may be made from sound recordings owned by an educational institution or an individual teacher for the purpose of constructing aural exercises or examinations and may be retained by the educational institution or individual teacher. (This pertains only to the copyright of the music itself and not to any copyright which may exist in the sound recording.)

B. PROHIBITIONS

1. Copying to create or replace or substitute for anthologies, compilations or collective works.

2. Copying of or from works intended to be "consumable" in the course of study or of teaching such as workbooks, exercises, standardized tests and answer sheets and like material.

3. Copying for the purpose of performance, except as in A(1) above.

4. Copying for the purpose of substituting for the purchase of music, except as in A(1) and A(2) above.

5. Copying without inclusion of the copyright notice which appears on the printed copy.

OFF-AIR GUIDELINES

Federal Guidelines for Off-Air Recording of Broadcast Programming for Educational Purposes

In March of 1979, Congressman Robert Kastenmeier, Chairman of the House Subcommittee on Courts, Civil Liberties and Administration of Justice, appointed a Negotiating Committee consisting of representatives of education organizations, copyright proprietors, and creative guilds and unions. The following guidelines reflect the Negotiating Committee's consensus as to the application of "fair use" to the recording, retention and use of television broadcast programs for educational purposes. They specify periods of retention and use of such off-air recordings in classrooms and similar places devoted to instruction and for homebound instruction. The purpose of establishing these guidelines is to provide standards for both owners and users of copyrighted television programs.

1. The guidelines were developed to apply only to off-air recording by nonprofit educational institutions.

2. A broadcast program may be recorded off-air simultaneously with broadcast transmission (including simultaneous cable retransmission) and retained by a nonprofit educational institution for a period not to exceed the first forty-five (45) consecutive calendar days after date of recording. Upon conclusion of such retention period, all off-air recordings must be erased or destroyed immediately. "Broadcast programs" are television programs transmitted by television stations for reception by the general public without charge.

3. Off-air recordings may be used once by individual teachers in the course of relevant teaching activities, and repeated once only when instructional reinforcement is necessary, in classrooms and similar places devoted to instruction within a single building, cluster or campus, as well

as in the homes of students receiving formalized home instruction, during the first ten (10) consecutive school days in the forty-five (45) day calendar day retention period. "School days" are school session days—not counting weekends, holidays, vacations, examination periods, or other scheduled interruptions—within the forty-five (45) calendar day retention period.

4. Off-air recordings may be made only at the request of and used by individual teachers, and may not be regularly recorded in anticipation of requests. No broadcast program may be recorded off-air more than once at the request of the same teacher, regardless of the number of times the program may be broadcast.

5. A limited number of copies may be reproduced from each off-air recording to meet the legitimate needs of teachers under these guidelines. Each such additional copy shall be subject to all provisions governing the original recording.

6. After the first ten (10) consecutive school days, off-air recordings may be used up to the end of the forty-five (45) calendar day retention period only for teacher evaluation purposes, i.e., to determine whether or not to include the broadcast program in the teaching curriculum, and may not be used in the recording institution for student exhibition or any other non-evaluation purpose without authorization.

7. Off-air recordings need not be used in their entirety, but the recorded programs may not be altered from their original content. Off-air recordings may not be physically or electronically combined or merged to constitute teaching anthologies or compilations.

8. All copies of off-air recordings must include the copyright notice on the broadcast program as recorded.

9. Educational institutions are expected to establish appropriate control procedures to maintain the integrity of these guidelines.

MEMBERS OF THE NEGOTIATING TEAM

Eugene Aleinkoff, Agency for Instructional Television
Joseph Bellon, CBS
Ivan Bender, Association of Media Producers
James Bouras, Motion Picture Association of America
Eileen D. Cooke, American Library Association
Bernard Freitag, National Education Association
Howard Hitchens, Association for Educational Communications and Technology
Irwin Karp, Authors League of America
John McGuire, Screen Actors Guild

Frank Norwood, Joint Council on Educational Communications
Ernest Ricca, Directors Guild of America
Carol Risher, Association of American Publishers
James Popham, National Association of Broadcasters
Judith Bresler, ABC
Eric H. Smith, Public Broadcasting Service
Sheldon Steinbach, American Council on Education
August W. Steinhilber, National School Boards Association
Leonard Wasser, Writers Guild of America, East
Sanford Wolff, American Federation of Television and Radio Artists

EDUCOM BROCHURE (1992 EDITION)

Using Software: A Guide to the Ethical and Legal Use of Software for Members of the Academic Community

Software enables us to accomplish many different tasks with computers. Unfortunately, in order to get our work done quickly and conveniently, some people make and use unauthorized software copies. The purpose of this brochure is to provide a brief outline of what you legally can and cannot do with software. Hopefully it will help you better understand the implications and restrictions of the U.S. Copyright Law.

HERE ARE SOME RELEVANT FACTS:

UNAUTHORIZED copying of software is illegal. Copyright law protects software authors and publishers, just as patent law protects inventors.

UNAUTHORIZED copying of software by individuals can harm the entire academic community. If unauthorized copying proliferates on a campus, the institution may incur legal liability. Also, the institution may find it more difficult to negotiate agreements that would make software more widely and less expensively available to members of the academic community.

UNAUTHORIZED copying and use of software deprives publishers and developers of a fair return for their work, increases prices, reduces the level of future support and enhancements, and can inhibit the development of new software products.

RESPECT for the intellectual work of others has traditionally been essential to the mission of colleges and universities. As members of the academic community, we value the free exchange of ideas. Just as we do not tolerate plagiarism, we do not condone the unauthorized copying of software, including programs, applications, data bases and code.

THEREFORE, we offer the following statement of principle about intellectual property and the legal and ethical use of software.

THE EDUCOM CODE*

Software and Intellectual Rights

Respect for intellectual labor and creativity is vital to academic discourse and enterprise. This principle applies to works of all authors and publishers in all media. It encompasses respect for the right to acknowledgement, right to privacy, and right to determine the form, manner, and terms of publication and distribution.

Because electronic information is volatile and easily reproduced, respect for the work and personal expression of others is especially critical in computer environments. Violations of authorial integrity, including plagiarism, invasion of privacy, unauthorized access, and trade secret and copyright violations, may be grounds for sanctions against members of the academic community.

CLASSIFICATION OF SOFTWARE

In terms of copyright, there are four broad classifications of software:

- Commercial
- Shareware
- Freeware
- Public Domain

The restrictions and limitations regarding each classification are different.

Commercial

COMMERCIAL software represents the majority of software purchased from software publishers, commercial computer stores, etc. When you buy software, you are actually acquiring a license to use it, not own it. You acquire the license from the company that owns the copyright. The conditions and restrictions of the license agreement vary from program to program and should be read carefully. In general, commercial software licenses stipulate that (1) the software is covered by copyright, (2) although one archival copy of the software can be made, the backup copy cannot be used except when the original package fails or is destroyed, (3) modifications to the software are not allowed, (4) decompiling (i.e., re-

---

* EDUCOM's Educational Uses of Information Technology (EUIT) Program encourages the broadest possible adoption of this statement of principle. The EDUCOM Code is intended for adaptation and use by individuals, and educational institutions at all levels.

verse engineering) of the program code is not allowed without the permission of the copyright holder, and (5) development of new works built upon the package (derivative works) is not allowed without the permission of the copyright holder.

Shareware

SHAREWARE software is covered by copyright, as well. When you acquire software under a shareware arrangement, you are actually acquiring a license to use it, not own it. You acquire the license from the individual or company that owns the copyright. The conditions and restrictions of the license agreement vary from program to program and should be read carefully. The copyright holders for SHAREWARE allow purchasers to make and distribute copies of the software, but demand that if, after testing the software, you adopt it for use, you must pay for it. In general, shareware software licenses stipulate that (1) the software is covered by copyright, (2) although one archival copy of the software can be made, the backup copy cannot be used except when the original packages fails or is destroyed, (3) modifications to the software are not allowed, (4) decompiling (i.e., reverse engineering) of the program code is not allowed without the permission of the copyright holder, and (5) development of new works built upon the package (derivative works) is not allowed without the permission of the copyright holder. Selling software as SHAREWARE is a marketing decision, it does not change the legal requirements with respect to copyright. That means that you can make a single archival copy, but you are obliged to pay for all copies adopted for use.

Freeware

FREEWARE also is covered by copyright and subject to the conditions defined by the holder of the copyright. The conditions for FREEWARE are in direct opposition to normal copyright restrictions. In general, FREEWARE software licenses stipulate that (1) the software is covered by copyright, (2) copies of the software can be made for both archival and distribution purposes but that distribution cannot be for profit, (3) modifications to the software are allowed and encouraged, (4) decompiling (i.e., reverse engineering) of the program code is allowed without the explicit permission of the copyright holder, and (5) development of new works built upon the package (derivative works) is allowed and encouraged with the condition that derivative works must also be designated as FREEWARE. That means that you cannot take FREEWARE, modify or extend it, and then sell it as COMMERCIAL or SHAREWARE software.

Public Domain

PUBLIC DOMAIN software comes into being when the original copyright holder explicitly relinquishes all rights to the software. Since under current copyright law, all intellectual works (including software) are protected as soon as they are committed to a medium, for something to be PUBLIC DOMAIN it must be clearly marked as such. Before March 1, 1989, it was assumed that intellectual works were NOT covered by copyright unless the copyright symbol and declaration appeared on the work. With the U.S. adherence to the Berne Convention this presumption has been reversed. Now all works assume copyright protection unless the PUBLIC DOMAIN notification is stated. This means that for PUBLIC DOMAIN software (1) copyright rights have been relinquished, (2) software copies can be made for both archival and distribution purposes with no restrictions as to distribution, (3) modifications to the software are allowed, (4) decompiling (i.e., reverse engineering) of the program code is allowed, and (5) development of new works built upon the package (derivative works) is allowed without conditions on the distribution or use of the derivative work.

QUESTIONS YOU MAY HAVE ABOUT USING SOFTWARE

What do I need to know about software and the U.S. Copyright Act?

It's really very simple. The copyright law recognizes that all intellectual works (programs, data, pictures, articles, books, etc.) are automatically covered by copyright unless it is explicitly noted to the contrary. That means that the owner of a copyright holds the exclusive right to reproduce and distribute his or her work. For software this means it is illegal to copy or distribute software, or its documentation, without the permission of the copyright holder.

If you have a legal copy of software you are allowed to make a single archival copy of the software for backup purposes. However, the copy can only be used if the original software is destroyed or fails to work. When the original is given away, the backup copy must also be given with the original or destroyed.

If software is not copy-protected, do I have the right to copy it?

Lack of copy-protection does NOT constitute permission to copy software without authorization of the software copyright owner. "Non-copy-protected" software enables you to make a backup copy. In offering non-copy-protected software to you, the developer or publisher has demonstrated significant trust in your integrity.

May I copy software that is available through facilities on my campus, so that I can use it more conveniently in my own office or room?

Software acquired by colleges and universities is usually covered by licenses. The licenses should clearly state how and where the software may be legally used by members of the relevant campus communities (faculty, staff, and students). Such licenses cover software whether installed on stand-alone or networked systems, whether in private offices and rooms, or in public clusters and laboratories. Some institutional licenses permit copying for certain purposes. The license may limit copying, as well. Consult your campus authorities to be sure if you are unsure about the permissible use of a particular software product.

May I loan software?

The 1990 modification to the copyright law makes it illegal to "loan, lease or rent software" for purposes of direct or indirect commercial advantage without the specific permission of the copyright holder. Nonprofit educational institutions are exempted from the 1990 modification, so institutional software may be loaned.

Some licenses may even restrict the use of a copy to a specific machine, even if you own more than one system. In general, licenses usually do NOT allow the software to be installed or resident on more than a single machine, or to run the software simultaneously on two or more machines.

Isn't it legally "fair use" to copy software if the purpose in sharing it is purely educational?

Historically, the copyright law was modified to permit certain educational uses of copyrighted materials without the usual copyright restrictions. However, "fair use" of computer software is still a cloudy issue. The "fair use" amendments to the copyright law are intended to allow educational use of legally protected products, but it is limited (for paper-based products) to small portions of full works. For most software it is clearly illegal to make and distribute unauthorized, fully functional copies to class members for their individual use. Making copies of a small section of code from a program in order to illustrate a programming technique might not be a violation. The best alternative is to clear any such use with the copyright owner or consult the appropriate authorities at your institution.

ALTERNATIVES TO EXPLORE

Software can be expensive. You may think that you cannot afford to purchase certain programs that you need. Site-licensed and bulk-purchased software are legal alternatives that make multiple copies of software more affordable. Many educational institutions negotiate special prices for software used and purchased by faculty, staff and students. Consult your campus computing office for information. As with other software, site-licensed or bulk-purchased software is still covered by copyright, although the price per copy may be significantly lower than the normal commercial price. A usual condition of site-licensing or bulk-purchasing is that copying and distribution of the software is limited to a central office which must maintain inventories of who received it. When you leave the academic community by graduation, retirement, or resignation you may no longer be covered by the institutional agreement and may be required to return or destroy your copies of the software licensed to the institution.

Many colleges sell software through a campus store at "educational discounts." If you purchase software for yourself through such an outlet, the software is yours and need not be destroyed or surrendered when you leave the institution. It is, however, still covered by normal copyright protection and covered by the specific conditions of the licensing agreement.

A FINAL NOTE

Restrictions on the use of software are far from uniform. You should check carefully each piece of software and the accompanying documentation yourself. In general, you do not have the right to:

- Receive and use unauthorized copies of software, or
- Make unauthorized copies of software for others.

If you have questions not answered by this brochure about the proper use and distribution of a software product, seek help from your computing office, the software developer or publisher, or other appropriate authorities at your institution.

This brochure has been produced as a service to the academic community by the Educational Uses of Information Technology Program (EUIT) of EDUCOM and the Information Technology Association of America (ITAA). EDUCOM is a non-profit consortium of colleges and universities committed to the use and management of information technology in higher education. ITAA is an industry association providing issues management and advocacy, public affairs, business-to-business networking, education and other member services to companies which create and market products and services associated with computers, communications and data.

Although this brochure is copyrighted, you are authorized and encouraged to make and distribute copies of it, in whole or in part, providing the source is acknowledged. Additional copies of this brochure may be purchased by contacting one of the organizations listed below.

EDUCOM
1112 16th Street, NW
Suite 600
Washington, DC 20036
(202)872–4200

ITAA
1616 N. Fort Myer Drive
Suite 1300
Arlington, VA 22204
(703)284–5355

©January, 1992
EDUCOM and ITAA

1986 ALA MODEL POLICY

Library and Classroom Use of Copyrighted Videotapes and Computer Software

By Mary Hutchings Reed and Debra Stanek
Mary Hutchings Reed is a partner in the law firm of Sidley & Austin, Chicago, and counsel to the American Library Association. Debra Stanek will graduate in June from the University of Chicago Law School.

After receiving numerous queries regarding library use of copyrighted videotapes and computer programs, I asked ALA attorney Mary Hutchings Reed to prepare a paper that would address the issues that librarians had brought to my attention and offer some guidance. The result is the following which we've published as an insert* so that it can be removed and posted for ready access. A longer, more detailed article by Debra Stanek, "Videotapes, Computer Programs and the Library," will appear in the March 1986 issue of *Information Technology and Libraries*. These papers express the opinion of ALA's legal counsel; individuals and institutions deeply involved in copyright matters should consult their own attorneys. *Donna Kitta, Administrator, ALA Office of Copyright, Rights & Permissions*

I. VIDEOTAPES

The Copyright Revision Act of 1976 clearly protects audiovisual works such as films and videotapes. The rights of copyright include the rights of reproduction, adaptation, distribution, public performance and display. All

* This insert may be reprinted for distribution with credit to ALA, *American Libraries*, February 1986. Single copies are available from the ALA Office of Rights & Permissions with receipt of SASE; 25 or more copies available at 25¢ each.

of these rights are subject, however, to "fair use," depending on the purpose of the use, the nature of the work, the amount of the work used and the effect the use has on the market for the copyrighted work.

Libraries purchase a wide range of educational and entertainment videotapes for in-library use and for lending to patrons. Since ownership of a physical object is different from ownership of the copyright therein, guidelines are necessary to define what libraries can do with the videotapes they own without infringing the copyrights they don't. If a particular use would be an infringement, permission can always be sought from the copyright owner.

A. In-classroom Use

In-classroom performance of a copyrighted videotape is permissible under the following conditions:

1. The performance must be by instructors (including guest lecturers) or by pupils; and

2. the performance is in connection with face-to-face teaching activities; and

3. the entire audience is involved in the teaching activity; and

4. the entire audience is in the same room or same general area;

5. the teaching activities are conducted by a non-profit education institution; and

6. the performance takes place in a classroom or similar place devoted to instruction, such as a school library, gym, auditorium or workshop;

7. the videotape is lawfully made; the person responsible had no reason to believe that the videotape was unlawfully made.

B. In-library Use in Public Libraries

1. Most performances of a videotape in a public room as part of an entertainment or cultural program, whether a fee is charged or not, would be infringing and a performance license is required from the copyright owner.

2. To the extent a videotape is used in an educational program conducted in a library's public room, the performance will not be infringing if the requirements for classroom use are met (see I.A.).

3. Libraries which allow groups to use or rent their public meeting rooms should, as part of their rental agreement, require the group to warrant that it will secure all necessary performance licenses and indemnify the library for any failure on their part to do so.

4. If patrons are allowed to view videotapes on library-owned equipment, they should be limited to private performances, i.e., one person, or no more than one family, at a time.

5. User charges for private viewings should be nominal and directly related to the cost of maintenance of the videotape.

6. Even if a videotape is labelled "For Home Use Only," private viewing in the library should be considered to be authorized by the vendor's sale to the library with imputed knowledge of the library's intended use of the videotape.

7. Notices may be posted on videorecorders or players used in the library to educate and warn patrons about the existence of the copyright laws, such as: MANY VIDEOTAPED MATERIALS ARE PROTECTED BY COPYRIGHT. 17 U.S.C. § 101. UNAUTHORIZED COPYING MAY BE PROHIBITED BY LAW.

C. Loan of Videotapes

1. Videotapes labelled "For Home Use Only" may be loaned to patrons for their personal use. They should not knowingly be loaned to groups for public performances.

2. Copyright notice as it appears on the label of a videotape should not be obscured.

3. Nominal user fees may be charged.

4. If a patron inquires about a planned performance of a videotape, he or she should be informed that only private uses of it are lawful.

5. Videorecorders may be loaned to a patron without fear of liability even if the patron uses the recorder to infringe a copyright. However, it may be a good idea to post notices on equipment which may be used for copying (even if an additional machine would be required) to assist copyright owners in preventing unauthorized reproduction. (See I.B.7)

D. Duplication of Videotapes

1. Under limited circumstances libraries may dupe a videotape or a part thereof, but the rules of § 108 of the Copyright Revision Act of 1976 which librarians routinely utilize with respect to photocopying, apply to the reproduction.

II. COMPUTER SOFTWARE

A. Purchase Conditions Generally

Most computer software purports to be licensed rather than sold. Frequently the package containing the software is wrapped in clear plastic through which legends similar to the following appear:

> You should carefully read the following terms and conditions before opening this diskette package. Opening this diskette package indicates your

acceptance of these terms and conditions. If you do not agree with them you should promptly return the package unopened and your money will be refunded.

OR

Read this agreement carefully. Use of this product constitutes your acceptance of the terms and conditions of this agreement.

OR

This program is licensed on the condition that you agree to the terms and conditions of this license agreement. If you do not agree to them, return the package with the diskette still sealed and your purchase price will be refunded. Opening this diskette package indicates your acceptance of these terms and conditions.

While there is at present no caselaw concerning the validity of such agreements (which are unilaterally imposed by producers), in the absence of authority to the contrary, one should assume that such licenses are in fact binding contracts. Therefore by opening and using the software the library or classroom may become contractually bound by the terms of the agreement wholly apart from the rights granted the copyright owner under the copyright laws.

Following such legends are the terms and conditions of the license agreement. The terms vary greatly between software producers and sometimes between programs produced by the same producer. Many explicitly prohibit rental or lending; some limit the program to use on one identified computer or to one user's personal use.

B. Avoiding License Restrictions

Loans of software may violate the standard license terms imposed by the copyright owner. To avoid the inconsistencies between sale to a library and the standard license restriction, libraries should note on their purchase orders the intended use of software meant to circulate. Such a legend should read:

PURCHASE IS ORDERED FOR LIBRARY CIRCULATION
AND PATRON USE

Then, if the order is filled, the library is in a good position to argue that its terms, rather than the standard license restrictions, apply.

C. Loaning Software

1. Copyright notice placed on a software label should not be obscured.

2. License terms, if any, should be circulated with the software package.

3. An additional notice may be added by the library to assist copyright owners in preventing theft. It might read: SOFTWARE PROTECTED BY

COPYRIGHT. 17 U.S.C. § 101. UNAUTHORIZED COPYING IS PRO-
HIBITED BY LAW.

4. Libraries generally will not be liable for infringement committed by
borrowers.

D. Archival Copies

1. Libraries may lawfully make one archival copy of a copyrighted
program under the following conditions:

a) one copy is made;
b) the archival copy is stored;
c) if possession of the original ceases to be lawful, the archival copy
must be destroyed or transferred along with the original program;
d) copyright notice should appear on the copy.

2. The original may be kept for archival purposes and the "archival
copy" circulated. Only one copy—either the original or the archival—
may be used or circulated at any given time.

3. If the circulating copy is destroyed, another "archival" copy may be
made.

4. If the circulating copy is stolen, the copyright owner should be consulted before circulating or using the "archival" copy.

E. In-library and In-classroom Use

1. License restrictions, if any, should be observed.

2. If only one program is owned under license, ordinarily it may only
be used on one machine at a time.

3. Most licenses do not permit a single program to be loaded into a
computer which can be accessed by several different terminals or into several computers for simultaneous use.

4. If the machine is capable of being used by a patron to make a copy
of a program, a warning should be posted on the machine, such as: MANY
COMPUTER PROGRAMS ARE PROTECTED BY COPYRIGHT. 17
U.S.C. § 101. UNAUTHORIZED COPYING MAY BE PROHIBITED
BY LAW.

III. Examples

1. A high school English teacher wants to show a videotape of the film
"The Grapes of Wrath" to her class. The videotape has a label which says
"Home Use Only."

As long as the § 110(1) requirements for the classroom exception apply,
the class may watch the videotape.

2. Same situation as 1, but 4 classes are studying the book, may the videotape be shown in the school auditorium or gym?

Yes, as long as the auditorium and gym are actually used as classrooms for systematic instructional activities.

3. Several students miss the performance, may they watch the videotape at some other time in the school library?

Yes, if the library is actually used for systematic instructional activities the classroom exception applies. Most school libraries are probably used as such. If it is not, such a performance may be a fair use if the viewing is in a private place in the library.

4. May several students go to the public library and borrow the video-tape to watch it at home?

Yes, the library may lend the videotape for in-home viewing by a student and a small group of friends.

5. May the student go to the public library and watch the videotape in a private room?

This normally would not be permitted because more than one person would be watching the videotape. However such a use probably would be fair under § 107 because of its relationship to the classroom activities.

6. May an elementary school teacher show a videotape of the film "Star Wars" to his or her class on the last day of school?

Because a classroom is a place where a substantial number of persons outside of a family and friends are gathered, performances in them are public. Assuming that this performance is for entertainment rather than with systematic instruction, the classroom exception would not apply. It is unlikely that such a public performance would be a fair use.

7. A book discussion group meets in a classroom at the high school. May they watch a videotape of "The Grapes of Wrath"?

No, the discussion group is not made up of class members enrolled in a non-profit institution, nor is it engaged in instructional activities, there-fore the classroom exception would not apply. Any such performance would be an infringing public performance because it is a place where a group of persons larger than a family and its social acquaintances are gath-ered. Permission of the copyright owner should be sought.

8. Same as 7, but the group meets at a public library.

The performance may be infringing because the library is open to the public and the audience would be a group larger than a family and friends outside of a non-profit instructional program.

9. A patron asks if he can charge his friends admission to watch videotapes at his home.

The library's duty in this situation is merely to state that the videotape is subject to the copyright law. In fact, as long as the patron shows the videotape at home to family or social acquaintances the performance would not be a public one, and therefore not infringing even if they share the cost of the videotape rental.

10. A patron asks if he can charge admission to the general public and show the videotape at a public place.

The duty is the same as in the previous situation; however, the proposed use is an infringement of copyright.

11. A librarian learns that a patron is borrowing videotapes and using them for public performances.

Again, there is a duty to notify the patron that the material is subject to the copyright laws. There is room for a variety of approaches to this situation, but there is no legal reason to treat videotapes differently from any other copyrighted materials which are capable of performance. While there is no clear duty to refuse to lend, there is a point at which a library's continued lending with actual knowledge of infringement could possibly result in liability for contributory infringement.

12. A book about the Apple IIe computer contains a diskette with a program for the computer. May the software be loaned with the book?

If the software is not subject to a license agreement it may be freely loaned like any other copyrighted work. If it is licensed, the agreement may or may not prohibit lending. A careful reading of the license is in order. If the license appears to prohibit any ordinary library uses the software producer should be contacted, and the agreement amended in writing. If this is not possible, the library should be able to return the package for a refund, as the seller, by selling to a library, may be on notice of ordinary library uses.

13. A math teacher uses one diskette to load a computer program into several terminals for use by students.

This use would violate copyright laws as well as most license agreements. It violates § 117 of the Copyright Act, which authorizes the making of one copy if necessary in order to use the program, because it creates copies of the program in several terminals. Further, many license agreements prohibit use of the software on more than one terminal at a time, as well as prohibiting networking or any system which enables more than one person to use the software at a time.

14. A math teacher puts a copy of "Visicalc" on reserve in the school library. The disk bears no copyright notice. May the library circulate it?

The disk ought to bear the copyright notice, but whether it is the library's legal duty to require one or to affix it is unclear. Individual library reserve policies may govern this situation—it's probably a good idea to require that the appropriate notices be affixed prior to putting the copy on reserve. Further, the lack of copyright notices may put the library on notice that this is a copy rather than the original program. If the original is retained by the teacher as an archival copy (i.e., not used) there is no problem. If not, then the reserve copy is an unauthorized copy and its use would violate the copyright laws and most license agreements. While the library might not be legally liable in this situation it would be wise to establish a policy for placing materials on reserve which prevents this.

15. May the library make an archival copy of the "Visicalc" program on its reserve shelf?

Usually yes. Section 117 permits the owner of the software to make or authorize the making of one archival copy. If the teacher who put the program on reserve has not made one, she or he may permit the library to do so. Remember, most license agreements and the copyright laws permit the making of one archival copy.

16. Same as 15, except the reserve copy is damaged. May the library make another copy (assuming it has the archival copy) for circulation?

Yes, the purpose of an archival copy is for use as a back-up in case of damage or destruction. The library may then make another archival copy to store while circulating the other.

17. Same as 16, except the reserve copy is stolen.

Perhaps. It is not clear whether the purpose of a back-up copy includes replacement in the event of theft but arguably it does. However, § 108(c) permits reproduction of audiovisual works (which includes many computer programs) in the event of damage, loss, or theft only if a replacement may not be obtained at a fair price. Further, some license agreements require that archival copies be destroyed when possession (not ownership)

of the original ceases. Therefore a replacement copy may need to be purchased. A safe course is to consult the software vendor.

18. When the teacher retrieves his or her copy of the program may the
library retain the archival copy?

No. When possession of the original ceases, the archival copy must be
transferred with the original or destroyed. If it is returned with the original, the teacher would not be permitted to make additional copies—he or
she would have an original and the archival copy. Most license agreements
contain similar provisions.

19. A librarian learns that a patron is copying copyrighted software on
the library's public access computers.

There is a duty to notify the patron that the software is subject to the
copyright laws. The computers should have notices similar to those on
unsupervised photocopiers.

Appendix C

Surveys of Universities and the Travails of Obtaining
Their Policies

Chapter four of this book summarizes the surveys, correspondence, and interviews that enabled collection of the university copyright policies and background information essential for this study. This appendix provides additional details for the reader or researcher who is particularly interested in methodology and in the complications of obtaining information about university policies and their development. Gathering the data necessarily required a three-stage process involving several different techniques over a period of more than two years.

Some readers of this study will invariably find policies, perhaps from their own universities, that the methodology employed here did not reveal. Indeed, many more policies inevitably exist—especially policies outside the typical domain of library directors and central administrators—such as policies from some computer laboratories and video facilities. Missing policies, however, are not likely to change any results of this study. The absence of a particular university policy will in fact reaffirm one general point: that copyright policy-making is diffused and uncoordinated. The methodology reflects the difficulty of tracking down and retrieving the scattered policies. Perhaps for that reason, this study is the first broadly based analysis of diverse copyright standards from universities throughout the country.

Stage 1: The 1986 Survey

The analysis of university copyright policies began in 1986 as a component of a comprehensive examination of information resources at American research universities. With funding from the Council on Library Resources (CLR), the broader study was based at the University of California, Los Angeles, Graduate School of Library and Information Science. In October 1986, the CLR study supported a survey of ninety-three universities then belonging to the Association of Research Libraries (ARL). A letter went to two officials at each campus: the director of the research library and the university's legal counsel. Because of the university "system" structure at the University of California and the State University of New York, multiple campuses participate independently in ARL, but one "systemwide" legal counsel office serves all campuses. Therefore, the survey letter went to the library director at each campus, but only to the one legal counsel at central offices for these two "systems." Whenever possible, letters were addressed to individuals named in directories published by ARL and by the National Association of College and University Attorneys. The first survey letter, dated 8 October 1986, went to 178 university officials.

The selection of library directors and legal counsel was based on the assumption that they would necessarily be aware of copyright policies. Libraries are frequent users of copyrighted materials for academic needs, and they face frequent criticism as infringers of owners' rights. Libraries also have been well documented as developers or overseers of copyright policies that would be useful for this study.[1] Another assumption was that legal counsel offices would be aware of copyright policies and related legal issues affecting the campus and may be responsible for policy development. These two offices might also represent two different views of copyright: as users, libraries represent the need to facilitate information uses for the academic community; as attorneys with a duty to protect the institution, the legal counsel may seek to avoid infringement liability.

The original 178 letters, combined with a follow-up letter in December 1986, produced 154 responses, for a response rate of 86.5 percent. Useful responses came from ninety of the ninety-three universities.[2] Most responses came directly from the original addressees, while other addressees delegated the duty to colleagues within their own office or elsewhere at the university. Delegation by library directors was universally confined to other librarians, but legal counsel offices frequently asked officials from other campus offices to respond. Thus, policies analyzed in this study have arrived from administrators overseeing research, general administration, contracts and grants, and intellectual property of all types. In a few cases, respondents mentioned other university officials who might have additional insights on copyright issues; the total 154 responses included responses from nine such additional sources.

1. For example, before this study, at least one set of copyright policies developed or used by university libraries had been published. See Nancy Kranich, *Copyright Policies at ARL Libraries*, SPEC Kit No. 102 (Washington, DC: Association of Research Libraries, 1984).

2. Only Case Western Reserve University and Syracuse University failed to respond at all. Arizona State University responded only with respect to a policy for the ownership of copyrights, and not for the use of existing material.

Expanding the survey to embrace all members of the Association of American Universities (AAU) was a later addition. In November 1987 a similar survey letter went to the library director and legal counsel at each of the five United States universities belonging to AAU, but not participating in ARL: Brandeis University, California Institute of Technology, Carnegie Mellon University, Catholic University of America, and Clark University. These ten letters, and a follow-up letter in February 1988, produced five responses. Two of the five universities did not respond.[3] The combined ARL and AAU surveys yielded the following: 188 survey letters sent, producing 159 responses—a response rate of 84.6 percent.

Stage 2: Follow-up Survey

With the original survey having begun in October 1986, some copyright policies received early in the study may have been revised, superseded, or supplemented. In July 1988, a follow-up letter went to 146 of the respondents at ARL universities posing two questions: whether the university had issued any new or revised policies since the last correspondence, and whether the respondent may be contacted by telephone to discuss the university policies.[4] A reminder letter went to addressees who had not replied by 20 October 1988.

The letters were drafted in the form of a questionnaire, and 133 of the addressees (or 91.1 percent) completed and returned them. This 1988 survey went to respondents at ninety of the ninety-three ARL universities; it was limited to respondents who had earlier submitted a policy on the use of copyrighted materials or had indicated that the university had no such policy. Responses came from eighty-nine of the institutions (only Columbia University did not respond to this follow-up questionnaire). Nearly every respondent indicated that a telephone interview would be welcome, and many noted the name of an additional person who might share insights about a particular university copyright policy. Only eighteen of the responses (or 13.5 percent) provided a copy of a new or revised policy governing the use of copyrighted materials. The responses revealed that new or revised policies had been issued at only fifteen of the responding eighty-nine ARL universities during the preceding period of approximately two years.

3. Not responding were Carnegie Mellon and Catholic universities.
4. Because of the relatively late surveying of the five AAU universities, and because of the relatively poor response rate from them, the "follow-up" with them was handled as part of the interviews and other surveying techniques described in Stage 3. In sum, each AAU university was contacted in late 1988 with the objective, among others, of obtaining current policy data.

The strong response rate and the nearly unanimous participation by at least one person from each research university in both the 1986 and 1988 surveys allowed insight into the treatment of copyright issues at virtually the full population of research universities to be studied. Nevertheless, the two surveys left a few gaps.

Stage 3: Supplementary Data Collection

Three particular gaps in the data needed to be filled. First, several universities had not responded to the surveys at all or at least had not responded with respect to policies governing the use of materials. Some universities sent only their policies on the ownership of newly created works. Second, to conduct some planned analyses, relatively simple factual information was needed about some policies. Third, many of the policies merited extensive inquiry into their development and effects; interviews with campus officials might be the only means of disclosing those experiences. The means pursued for collecting these data proved to be diverse but productive.

No Response

Five universities effectively had given no response to the requests for their policies concerning the use of copyrighted works. Telephone interviews during December 1988 with at least one official at each of these five universities disclosed only one additional written policy: a photocopy policy at Syracuse University.[5] At most, other interviewees believed that common guidelines, such as the CONTU limits on photocopying for interlibrary lending, might be in force. A few interviewees explained that copyright questions are resolved on a case-by-case basis, rarely with any clearly established guidelines to ensure continuity.

Without a written policy, the remaining four universities are treated as having no university copyright policy. Like some other universities claiming to have "no policy," these institutions may follow routine guidelines or general notions of copyright compliance, but those standards are not reduced to writing.

Factual Data

Much of the general background in chapter one about university governance and policies is based on factual information that may not be drawn from the policy statements themselves. For example, the general literature suggests that librarians and faculty would develop relatively lenient copy-

5. SYRACUSE–1978.

right standards. Many policies include an attribution of authorship, or at least a mention of the university official or department issuing the policy. Sometimes an accompanying cover letter provided further details. But too often the policy arrived with little insight about its origins. To collect this factual information, twenty-nine letters, each with a standard set of questions and other inquiries focusing on the one policy at issue, went to survey respondents in November 1988. Combined with a follow-up letter in January 1989 and a few reminder telephone calls, the letters produced twenty-six responses, for a response rate of 89.6 percent.

INTERVIEWS

Many policies inspired inquiries beyond requests for factual information. Some policies were unique in their detail or scope of issues addressed. Others were clearly rooted in model policies, but evidenced no explanation for choosing that particular model. Some policies revealed changes in the university's position on copyright, and the forces behind those changes could be of interest. Telephone interviews with respondents and other interested parties provided important insight into policy development processes, the environmental forces shaping the policies, and the consequences of adopting a university copyright policy. Two groups of interviews were important for this research: interviews related to provocative policies or circumstances; and interviews with respondents claiming that their universities had no policy. These interviews were in addition to calls to officials at the five campuses not responding to the original requests for policies.

Nineteen survey respondents submitted policies that inspired inquiry beyond simple requests for factual information. In November 1988 letters went to those respondents informing them of their selection for interviews and outlining sample questions that might shape the interview. During December 1988 and January 1989 the author contacted each person by telephone and completed the interviews. In five cases, the original respondent referred the matter to a colleague who was more informed about the policy. At only one university had the original respondent departed with no forwarding address and no successor to handle copyright matters. Conversations with three other university officials failed to shed light on the particular policy in question. At four universities, the interview process expanded to include other officials in addition to the intended interviewee. In all, the original nineteen planned interviews expanded to twenty-four productive telephone interviews.

The selection of interviewees was based exclusively on their potential for disclosing useful data. The 1988 follow-up survey asked respondents whether they would be willing to participate in a telephone interview. While that question helped prepare for interviews, it did not affect whether anyone would or would not be called. Two of the nineteen selected interviewees originally did not want to be called; they nonetheless participated cordially. One preferred not to be bothered; the other simply had no information other than the policy itself.

A second group of interviews reached respondents who said that their universities had no policies governing uses of copyrighted materials. The original survey of the ninety-eight research universities produced 159 responses, and nine responses from seven different universities at that time indicated explicitly the total absence of a written copyright policy. That list does not include the universities that claimed to follow some general standards, but without developing a written policy statement. During December 1988, the researcher successfully engaged in a telephone interview with at least one official at six of the seven universities. These interviews had mixed effects: some disclosed that perfunctory guidelines were in fact followed; others revealed that general principles guided copyright decisions, without the benefit of a detailed policy. One written policy, dealing only with software copying, was confirmed at the University of Tennessee.[6]

Nearly every interviewee shared information without hesitation. One administrator emphasized that nothing he said should be quoted as "official university policy." One university attorney was disturbed that I had received from a librarian a copy of his internal memorandum on copyright problems; he also warned that his answers could be limited by the confidentiality of his attorney-client relationship. The interview nonetheless proceeded without noticeable restraint. A few interviewees were reluctant to be quoted, and this study reflects every effort to comply with such individual requests, while not hindering the objective of analyzing and sharing data about the development and function of university copyright policies. Otherwise the researcher made no representation or commitment at any time to any individual that any remarks, responses, or policy statements would be held in confidence or not disclosed.

These three stages of data collection produced a wealth of information, ranging from elaborate policy documents to unique observations about specific copyright policies. They also produced data from all ninety-eight research universities in the population. The data are current as of early

6. TENN–1985.

1989—before the *Kinko's* case renewed infringement fears on campus. The data are more than just the policy documents themselves; many letters and nearly all of the telephone interviews disclosed particulars about the history and effects of policies—data that would never likely be available by any other means.

Index